FAMILIES OF CHILDREN WITH SPECIAL NEEDS

Early Intervention Techniques
for the Practitioner

Allen A. Mori

University of Nevada, Las Vegas

AN ASPEN PUBLICATION®
Aspen Systems Corporation
Rockville, Maryland
London
1983

Library of Congress Cataloging in Publication Data

Mori, Allen A.
Families of children with special needs.

Bibliography: p. 235
Includes index.
1. Handicapped children—United States—
Family relationships. 2. Parenting—United
States. 3. Handicapped children—Education—
United States. I. Title.
HV888.5.M67   1983   362.8'2   83-2583
ISBN: 0-89443-934-0

Publisher: John Marozsan
Editorial Director: R. Curtis Whitesel
Executive Managing Editor: Margot Raphael
Editorial Services: Eileen Higgins
Printing and Manufacturing: Debbie Collins

Library of Congress Catalog Card Number: 83-2583
ISBN: 0-89443-934-0

Printed in the United States of America

1   2   3   4   5

To my parents, Carmella and Primo Mori,
who taught me the value of a loving family.

Table of Contents

Preface

Education, including special education, has been criticized for its extreme susceptibility to the "bandwagon effect." Someone somewhere declares, usually based either on flimsy "scientific" data or, better yet, strong philosophical beliefs, that one methodology is superior to all others.

I strongly believe that parent or family involvement is *not* just another fad, not just another bandwagon to be ridden while we all wait for some new proclamation. Parent or family involvement is the cornerstone of successful programs in early intervention for exceptional children. The impact of active parent involvement on the progress children make in intervention programs has been clearly documented. Yet, despite our knowledge of this fact and despite federal law mandating parent involvement, meaningful parental involvement remains an elusive goal.

If we are to achieve the optimal benefits for young exceptional childen in intervention programs, we must reexamine the whole concept of family involvement. Professionals must accept parents as partners in the intervention process. If family involvement is to be effective and meaningful, parents and professionals will need to learn to trust one another. Trust and respect are essential ingredients to a successful partnership.

Working effectively with parents and family members is a learned skill. Professionals must clearly understand the new roles they will play with parents as partners in the education of young exceptional children. Professionals must learn techniques to build trust, to share information effectively, to assess parental needs and abilities, and to accept parents as real experts on their own children.

This book was written for all professionals who work with families of exceptional young children. It is a source book, designed to provide practical information to professionals who must answer the difficult questions parents ask about their exceptional children. It is also a guide in that it provides information to assist professionals in establishing the parent-professional partnership necessary to meet the diverse and complex needs of young exceptional children. The book may also be useful to parents who want more information about their children and types of intervention programs.

Above all, this book is not the definitive work in the field. It is a beginning, a point of departure for all of us who are committed to increasing and enhancing the role of parents as partners in the education of young exceptional children.

Allen A. Mori, Ph.D.
March 1983

Acknowledgments

The preparation of a book is a "costly" venture. The "price" an author pays is substantial, as it involves many precious hours away from loved ones and family activities. Words alone cannot express my gratitude to my wife Barbara, whose undaunted love, support, and encouragement were the incentives that kept me on task during the most trying moments of this project. I also want to acknowledge my daughter Kirsten. So many times she sneaked into my den to ask, "How many chapters left now, Daddy?" I cannot recapture those lost times, but I can tell her, "Daddy's finished now, and I love you very much."

Families and Young Children

The first four chapters of this book are the foundation chapters for the further study of the needs of young special children and their families. In Chapter 1, the area of child development is explored, with specific reference to the impact of the family on child development. The important concept of attachment, or bonding, is presented and discussed in detail. The role of the father in child development is examined. Parenting styles and their influence on child behavior are explored. Other effects of families on areas such as intelligence and academic achievement are discussed.

Chapter 2 deals with the impact of a handicapped child on the family. Factors that influence parental feelings about their child's diagnosis are discussed, and the stages of parental reactions to the diagnosis are explored in detail. The extensive research on parental attitudes toward and interactions with young handicapped children is discussed. From the time the initial diagnosis is made to the events in the adult life of the handicapped person, families of young handicapped children encounter many critical incidents; these critical incidents are explored and discussed. Finally, the effects of a handicapped child on siblings are discussed.

Chapter 3 presents an in-depth exploration of the means by which professionals can build the parent-professional partnership. The role of physicians and other professionals in the service delivery system in the community; means of facilitating communication between professionals and families, and the use of the conference to foster a positive interaction are discussed. The final section of this chapter deals with the extended family and the attitudes of others toward young handicapped children.

Chapter 4 deals with the rights and responsibilities of families of young handicapped children. Included in this chapter are discussions of Public Law 94-142, the Education for All Handicapped Children Act; due process procedures for families; and the responsibilities of families to their handicapped children.

Families and Young Children

Chapter 1

The Impact of the Family on Child Development

The scientific study of child development has undergone a fundamental transformation over the course of the past several years. Scientists have become much more concerned with the role of the family as a socializing agent. As Garwood (1981) noted,

> Clearly there is a need to focus attention on the family, not only because it is such an important component of the care of children, a most valued resource, but also because the family is the context from which children emerge. Thus understanding the whole child can only be done by studying him or her in this real context. (p. ix)

Families have existed since the first semblance of civilization among human beings. Without families, the very essence of our culture would be threatened. Whether it is traditional (i.e., mother-father), single parent, extended, or foster, the family is the source of nurturing, the primary core of child care. Yet individuals do not magically acquire parenting skills when they become parents. They need information, skill training, and, often, support. The families of children who are exceptional have even greater needs.

The ability of the professional and parent to create a dynamic, nurturing home environment for the special child may make the difference between a future filled with promise and a future filled with uncertainty. If professionals accept the challenge by taking on new roles and expectations, by working creatively and cooperatively with families, and by establishing an atmosphere characterized by mutual trust and respect, these young children with diverse and complex needs will benefit enormously. As Berger (1981) noted, "Parent involvement has many dimensions. Though it is not a panacea for all the ills of society, it is one component that will help ameliorate these concerns" (p. 18).

THE FAMILY AS A SOCIALIZING AGENT

Adult members of the family not only attend to a child's basic needs by feeding, diapering, and comforting the child, but also serve as an important source of social interaction by talking to, cuddling, and playing with the child. The process of social interaction produces two especially critical byproducts: (1) attachment, a special emotional relationship between infants and caregivers, and (2) the promotion of cognitive and social development.

Infant Attachment

Attachment is a relationship between two individuals, such as mother and child, in which each feels strongly about the other and attempts to ensure the continuation of the relationship. Infants who are attached direct many of their behaviors—smiling, babbling, eye contact—toward the mother. They may also attempt to maintain physical contact with the mother by following her or clinging to her.

The concept of attachment is significant in both ethological (Ainsworth, 1973, 1979) and psychoanalytical (Erikson, 1963, 1968) theory. Ainsworth suggested two important ideas regarding attachment. First, it is important to distinguish between the underlying attachment system (i.e., the bond between mother and infant) and the overt attachment behaviors (i.e., crying or proximity-seeking behavior by the infant). Second, distinct and significant differences in the pattern of mother-child interactions have profound consequences for the type of attachment developed. Securely attached infants use their mothers as a base from which to explore the environment; these infants move away from their mothers freely (although they may occasionally look to make sure their mothers are still there) and respond positively to being picked up. Insecurely attached infants react ambivalently to physical contact and demonstrate ambivalent attachment behaviors.

Erikson (1963, 1968), representing the psychoanalytic view of attachment, believes the importance of attachment between infant and mother rests in the development of trust. When the mother performs her caregiving duties with warmth and affection, the child learns to trust her. This trust then becomes the basis for the later development of a positive self-image and trust in others.

Not only does the infant develop attachment to the mother, but also the mother develops a reciprocal attachment to the infant. When caring for her child, the mother holds, feeds, touches, kisses, and talks to the infant. The mother frequently experiences deep feelings of love and satisfaction and establishes a bond with the baby.

How important is attachment to child development? Securely attached infants engage more freely in exploratory activities that can serve as a basis for sensorimotor development. Hartup (1979) believes that the relationship between the mother and child forms the basis for this exploration:

> Specific competencies, such as language and role-taking skills, as well as self-esteem, may emanate from this system . . . [that serves as a] . . . basis for environmental exploration. Exploratory activity then brings the child into contact with many different social objects. . . . These associations also result in the direct acquisition of a constellation of unique attitudes and affects— each essential to social adaptation. (p. 949)

Socialization

The relationship between parents and children is complex. To comprehend the nature of the socializing effects of the family on the infant, it is necessary to examine the family constellation. Feiring and Lewis (1978) described the family as a constellation of subsystems defined in terms of generation, gender, and role. Members of the family interact within these subsystems according to attachments and division of labor. Relationships can be classified as dyadic (two person interactions), such as mother-father or mother-child, or polyadic (more than two person interactions), such as mother-father-child. The relationships between parents and child can be the source of satisfaction or dissatisfaction. They are also the basis for the socialization process by which the child acquires culturally appropriate behaviors and values.

Parents tend to train their children in social skills according to a personal hierarchy of importance. They may use a variety of methods, including modeling or imitation learning and the use of reward and punishment, which is a direct means of shaping behavior. Those who first studied the socialization process assumed a unidirectional influence, that is, parents conduct or orchestrate the socialization process by acting on the child. Child development specialists now realize that the socialization process is dynamic and that parents both influence and are influenced by their children. Johnson and Medinnus (1974) used the term *developmental interaction* to denote that children's changing developmental demands induce comparable changes in the caregiving responses of parents (Exhibit 1-1). Thus, parents are significantly affected by their children in their development as parents, just as they affect the development of their children.

Exhibit 1-1 Developmental Interaction in the Socialization Process

Parent Characteristics ⟷	Child Characteristics
Individual traits	Individual traits
Attitudes	Personality
Personality	Sex of individual
Sex of individual	Behavior
Behavior	Developmental stage

Autonomy

During the child's second year of life, a sense of self emerges. The child who is securely attached and who has sufficient motor skills begins to utilize these increased skills in manipulation, locomotion, and exploration. Erikson (1963, 1968) used the term *autonomy* to refer to the self-control the child acquires at this time. This sense of self-control is required if the child is to develop personal pride and to feel comfortable in self-expression. Mahler (1979) believed that a child acquires both a sense of separateness and a sense of relatedness to the world through the process of separation-individuation; the child emerges from a symbiotic relationship with the mother (separation) and acquires individual characteristics during the first three years of life (individuation). By age three, the child has a relatively independent, autonomous self.

The parents' role in the development of the child's sense of autonomy is to assist the child in achieving some sense of independence without allowing the child to attempt activities beyond his or her capabilities. At this stage, the child should be allowed to make choices (within reason) in order to learn this essential skill. If parents hinder the child's exploration, the resulting frustration may have enduring effects on personality and adjustment. If parents accept the child's need to explore and manipulate the environment, however, the child becomes more confident.

Aggression

Although it may have a biological origin, aggression is definitely a learned behavior. The precise timing, form, and intensity of aggression depend on the parental response to the behavior. During the first two years of life, the most common form of aggression or anger is the temper tantrum. Children may learn that crying, rolling on the floor, screaming, and holding their breath are the most effective ways to get what they want from their parents (Goodenough, 1931). It does not take long to learn that directed motor and language aggressions are equally effective. The child who wants a toy that another child has simply takes it; if the other child resists, the aggressor may strike the child to secure the toy. Since aggression is more likely to be accepted (perhaps even encouraged) in little boys, they tend to exhibit aggressive behavior more frequently than do girls (Goodenough, 1931).

Anger or aggression may occur when children are frustrated by parents who inhibit their autonomy or when children resist going to bed or sitting on the toilet. Because very young children lack socially appropriate alternatives or language facility to mediate the problem, they react with directed outbursts of motor activity.

Aggression may also occur because the child sees someone else behave aggressively. Bandura and Huston (1961) conducted research in which preschool children observed an adult attempting to solve a problem. During the task, the adult performed many irrelevant actions, including aggression toward dolls. The model did not exhibit aggressive behavior when performing before the control group. When the children were asked to solve a similar problem, 90 percent of the children in the experimental group imitated the aggression of the model. Not one child in the control group exhibited aggressive behavior.

Finally, aggression may result from the experience of some types of punishment, by which the parent is demonstrating to the child the potential effectiveness of aggression (Bandura, 1967). One long-term effect of punishment is that children become aggressive in the absence of the adult punisher.

Fears

All children have fears. Certain fears (e.g., fear of superhighways) are productive because they protect the child from harm. Other fears are counterproductive, however, and may even become so intense that they interfere with behavioral development. Many psychologists believe that fears are learned through observation or imitation learning. For example, children may learn to fear snakes by observing a similar fear reaction in their mother or father. Avoidance behavior in response to snakes becomes reinforcing because it reduces tension or anxiety. The child repeats the fear response until more mature patterns of behavior are learned as part of the socialization process.

Parenting Styles and Socialization

A child's social behavior can be greatly influenced by a particular parenting style. Armentrout and Burger (1972) reported that parents who exercise a high degree of psychological control over their children promote child behaviors that are regressive and dependent. If parents are overcontrolling, their children may be passive and inhibited. Yet, if parents do not exercise sufficient control, their children can be impulsive.

In an extensive research project on the relationship between children's social behaviors and parenting styles, Baumrind (1967, 1971) studied three groups of preschool children with different personality structures:

1. Pattern I children were found to be the most mature and competent of the three groups. Baumrind found them to be content, independent, realistic, self-reliant, self-controlled, explorative, affiliative, and self-assertive.
2. Pattern II children were rated moderately self-controlled and self-reliant, but they were also relatively discontented, distrustful, insecure, withdrawn, apprehensive, and uninterested in peer affiliation.
3. Pattern III children were classified as the most immature. They were extremely dependent and more withdrawn, tending to shy away from novel or stressful situations. The children in this group were also less self-reliant and less self-controlled than were the children in the other two groups.

After studying and rating the children, Baumrind studied the parents and rated them on four dimensions of child rearing: (1) control, defined as efforts to modify child behavior; (2) maturity demands, defined as pressures on the child to behave at a level commensurate with the child's intellectual, social, and emotional development; (3) clarity of parent-child communication, defined as the use of reason and solicitation of child input into the decision-making process; and (4) parental nurturance, defined as warmth (love) and involvement (praise and pleasure in the child's accomplishments). From this analysis emerged three distinct parenting styles:

1. Authoritarian parenting was described as punitive and restrictive. Parents placed severe limits and controls on the children. There was little verbal interaction between the children and the parents, and the parents were less likely to explain parental decisions or to allow the children to express disagreement with these decisions. Associated child behaviors included anxiety, failure to initiate activity, ineffective social interaction, discontent, withdrawing behavior, and distrust.
2. Permissive parenting, often called laissez faire, was warm, but included few demands for mature behavior and few limits placed on the child's behavior. Parents seemed unconcerned about training children to be self-reliant and independent. Associated child behaviors included

immaturity, poor self-restraint, and a lack of independence and self-reliance.

3. Authoritative parenting was seen as encouraging autonomy while placing limits and controls on the child's actions. There was a great deal of warmth and verbal interaction between parents and children. Authoritative parents were excellent models of mature and competent behavior. Associated child behaviors included social competency, self-reliance, social responsibility, independence, and self-control.

The warmth-hostility aspect of parenting has predictable effects on child behaviors. Parents who are hostile and show little affection to their children produce overtly hostile and aggressive children (Yussen & Santrock, 1982). On the other hand, altruistic children with a high self-esteem generally have parents who are warm, accepting, and affectionate (Coopersmith, 1967; Zahn-Waxler, Radke-Yarrow, & King, 1979). Yussen and Santrock suggested that parents who exhibit affection and warmth also tend to employ reasoning in the disciplining of their children. Such parents are usually firm in their positions but provide clear and explicit reasons for their rules. They "teach instead of preach," thus reducing anxiety and helping children to internalize social rules and understand social limits and structures.

THE ROLE OF THE FATHER IN CHILD DEVELOPMENT

Research interest in the role of fathers in child development is fairly recent. In the past, their role was largely ignored. LeMasters (1974) believed that a minimal role has been ascribed to fathers in the child development process for several reasons. First, parenting is a peripheral role for a father in our society. Despite changes in the employment pattern of families (i.e., working mothers), the mother is still seen as the "child rearer." The father is expected to display competence not in parenting skills, but rather in an occupation. Even with this arrangement, however, the father models many socially appropriate behaviors while fulfilling his role as a father.

LeMasters also stated that a father has no process equivalent to the physical and psychological bonding or attachment that occurs between mother and child. Even though a father may be included in the birthing, i.e., may be present in the delivery room, a father can never really share the biological events of pregnancy and childbirth. Because a father lacks this strong biological relationship, he is at a distinct disadvantage when trying to establish a bond with his child. Furthermore, loving, tender, nurturing behavior is still considered a feminine behavioral trait, and many men feel uncomfortable openly displaying this kind of "unmanly" behavior.

Finally, LeMasters maintained that, in order for a man to be a good father, he must be a good husband. In divorce actions, the mother is still routinely awarded child custody, while the father is obligated to provide economic support. This situation further perpetuates the father's role as a "breadwinner"—an economic rather than a nurturing role.

The Father as a Caregiver in Infancy

The father's preparation for competent caregiving is greatly restricted in our society. In fact, as young boys grow and mature, there is virtually no such preparation by their family or by society. On the other hand, young girls are encouraged and rewarded for appropriate doll play that reflects competent caregiving. Furthermore, adolescent and even preadolescent girls are encouraged to work as babysitters, thereby acquiring practical skills in the care of infants and toddlers. Despite the tremendous rise in the popularity of structured classes in both the process of childbirth (e.g., the Lamaze method in which the father is an active participant in the birthing) and care for an infant, the majority of men today do not receive formal training or experience in caregiving until their first child is born. Therefore, first-time fathers often undergo periods of anxiety and experience difficulties in adjusting to the role of caregiver.

According to Bigner (1979), most researchers have ignored the father's role in the development of infants. Erikson, for example, focused almost exclusively on the mother-child dyad as the source of both nurturance and the development of infant competence. It was not until the early 1970s that researchers began to show interest in the nurturing role of fathers. Parke and Sawin (1976) examined the results of several studies of father-infant interaction and concluded that fathers are both interested in and involved with their babies at the earliest stages of infancy. Furthermore, Parke and O'Leary (1976) found that fathers were as sensitive to the baby's cues as were mothers. Parke and Sawin (1980) reported that fathers can and do act both responsively and sensitively to their infants. Lamb (1977) even noted that infants became attached to their fathers at the same age that they became attached to their mothers.

The type of interaction between mother and child and between father and child has been studied by several investigators (Field, 1978; Lamb & Lamb, 1976; Redina & Dickerscheid, 1976). The researchers found that fathers spent more time in vigorous physical or play activities and other socializing experiences, and less time in routine caregiving activities than did mothers. The various authors concluded that the father plays a critical role, because he provides psychologically stimulating activities that are essential to the development of the infant's social competence.

The Father's Role in Sex Typing

The acquisition of gender-appropriate behavior is called sex typing. Today's emphasis on nonsexist attitudes both at work and at home has caused a change in traditional sex role differentiations. Nonetheless, there remain some firmly established sex differences in activities and abilities.

Fathers play a particularly prominent role in sex typing. Yussen and Santrock (1982) reported that according to sex typing research, fathers tend to behave toward sons and daughters in a way different from the way mothers behave toward them. Fathers appear to be more concerned that their children develop gender-appropriate behaviors. Fathers, especially, seem to abhor feminine behavior in their sons, so they encourage masculine identification. Kagan (1958) suggested that three conditions are necessary in order for a male child to acquire a strong masculine identity. The child must perceive that (1) the father (model) is dominant, powerful, and competent in tasks the son values; (2) the father is nurturant; and (3) there is a common basis or similarity between himself and his father.

Nurturant, warm, affectionate fathers also seem to contribute to sex typing of their daughters. Heilbrun (1976) hypothesized that fathers may behave in a typical masculine fashion toward everyone but their daughters. When interacting with their daughters, however, fathers often display warm, nurturing behavior, enhancing sex-appropriate female behaviors.

Mothers also have a role in sex typing. In point of fact, both parents encourage girls and boys to participate in different types of play, beginning in infancy. Although babies of both sexes would play with dolls if given the opportunity, many encourage doll play exclusively for girls. Boys are encouraged to engage in motor activities. Parents tend to play more physically and actively with boys, more quietly and tenderly with girls. Furthermore, it is generally acceptable for young daughters to cry, show dependency, and display affection, but boys who cry may be admonished—"Men don't cry!" Sons may also find fewer rewards for dependent and affectionate behavior. Parents also encourage their sons to fight back if struck by another child, but they may punish their daughters for doing so (Sears, Maccoby, & Levin, 1957).

Other factors influence the degree of identification that children have with their parents. Hetherington (1967) noted that children tend to imitate dominant, powerful adults rather than passive, weak ones. Same sex parents displaying these behaviors foster strong role development along appropriate gender lines. A dominant, nurturant father produces a very masculine son; a strong but feminine mother produces a very feminine daughter (Yussen & Santrock, 1982).

The Effect of Father Absence

The traditional family structure (nuclear family) of father, mother, and children, with father as breadwinner and mother as homemaker, no longer represent the majority of family situations. Today, there are many types of family structures, including the single parent family. Bane (1978) estimated that approximately 40 to 50 percent of the children born during the 1970s will spend some part of their childhood in a single parent (usually, the mother) home.

Studies of children who lacked a substantial fathering experience indicated that (1) adjustment is most problematic in personality and social development and (2) the father's absence seems to affect boys more adversely than girls (Bigner, 1979). The bulk of the research on the impact of father absence has focused on the sex role development of the son. Generally speaking, the boy whose father is absent is slightly more likely to show feminine behavior patterns. Hetherington (1960) found that males with absent fathers ranked somewhat lower, on the average, in masculine aggressiveness, preference for the male sex role, and interest in physical contact games and sports. On the opposite end of the continuum, Bronfenbrenner (1967) found that some males without fathers displayed "excessively male" behaviors, such as aggression or cruelty, and were more likely to engage in delinquent acts. Although most father-absent males develop normal, sex-appropriate roles, the problems that do occur are likely to fall at the extremes.

There is some evidence to suggest that father absence can have adverse effects on cognitive development (Santrock, 1972). This is particularly true for father-absent boys, whose quantitative skills appear to be lower than those of boys whose fathers are present in the home (Bigner, 1979).

Although the impact of father absence on girls has not been as widely studied, the effects do not seem as adverse. Bigner (1979) reported that preschool-aged girls whose fathers were absent were overly dependent on their mothers, who were seen as overprotective of their daughters. Hetherington (1972) did report, however, that girls with absent fathers occasionally find it difficult to relate satisfactorily to boys during adolescence.

EFFECTS OF FAMILIES ON EARLY LANGUAGE AND COGNITIVE DEVELOPMENT

Language Development

Children develop language through their active attempts to induce rule systems from the speech they hear around them. Yussen and Santrock (1982) maintained that "language development occurs because the human infant has a brain especially sensitive to the structure and rules of language, because the speech a child hears contains feedback about language rules, and because the child has a strong, built-in motivation to learn language" (p. 258).

Since children require a structured language environment to acquire speech, many investigators have studied the manner in which mothers talk to their children at different phases of language development (e.g., Furrow, Nelson, & Benedict, 1979). These investigators found that mothers used a number of strategies to reduce the complexity of language when talking to infants and young children. For example, mothers

- used shorter sentences
- simplified vocabulary
- used less complex grammatical structure
- paused longer and more definitely between sentences
- emphasized key words or phrases by both volume and stress changes

Cazden (1972) identified three other methods parents use to enhance language learning in young children: (1) prompting, (2) echoing, and (3) expanding. When a child fails to respond to a question, the parent who uses a variation of the same question is prompting. When the child says something that is only partially understandable, the parent may repeat what was understood and add a statement or request for more information; this is echoing. If the child speaks a short phrase, such as "Daddy go," the mother may follow it with an expanded version that expresses a complete thought, "Yes, Daddy went to work." Folger and Chapman (1978) demonstrated that young children were more likely to imitate parental speech if the parents had just imitated the child's speech or even expanded on it. In their study, mothers interacted with their one-year-old children in play sessions. When the mothers imitated or expanded upon their children's utterances, the children were more likely to try to reproduce the mother's speech than they were when the mother's speech was not an imitation or expansion of the child's earlier utterances.

Nelson (1980, 1981) and Nelson, Denninger, and Messe (1981) conducted research on mothers who reply to their children's speech by recasting it, defined as repeating the child's sentence in a way that retains the basic meaning but changes the syntactic structure (a strategy similar to Cazden's expansion). When the hypothesis that the child "compares" the two utterances with special attention to the mother's form was tested in a study, the researchers found that children acquired forms, both verbs and questions, from recast utterances.

Yussen and Santrock (1982) and Gardner (1982) suggested that such strategies help the child to gain a better grasp of grammar and syntax. Perhaps more significantly, they provide children with feedback regarding the success of their utterances in conveying a message. As Brown (1973) suggested, parents of children who acquire language earlier may be using these strategies with greater frequency than are parents of children who learn language more slowly. The exact nature of the impact of parents or other adults on the acquisition of language by children is summarized by Gardner (1982):

> Thus investigations have shown that at least some, though perhaps not all, components of what adults say to children influence the acquisition of syntax. We see that children are unlikely to acquire language without learning it in the context of social interaction, and we know that children are universally exposed to a very special form of speech. But whether any aspects of the speech children hear are necessary or sufficient in order for language learning to occur, or whether they simply render language acquisition somewhat easier for the child, is not yet known. Nevertheless, by examining the influences on the child, we can begin to document the various aids that children ordinarily use to grasp the language that they hear around them. (p. 184)

Cognitive Development

Many psychologists believe that the roots of early cognitive development are in the parents' playful social interactions with their children. Such interactions allow infants to satisfy their inherent curiosity about their environment. For example, Korner and Thomas (1970) suggested that babies who were crying in their cribs stopped crying quickly when they were picked up and placed on their mother's shoulders because this position allowed them to look around the room, providing an opportunity for visual exploration.

Rheingold (1973) suggested that restricting a baby's exploratory behavior by placing the baby in a crib or playpen often leads to signs of distress. She conducted an experiment in which mothers of 12- and 18-month-old infants placed them in rooms containing toys. All of the children left their mothers within seconds and explored the rooms. Rheingold observed that children displayed initiative in discovering and interacting with toys on their own.

Generally, children reared in deprived environments, such as institutions, score considerably lower on tests of infant development than do infants raised as part of a family. After reviewing all available data on the subject up to 1970, Thompson and Grusec (1970) concluded that the effects of raising children in institutions are negative because "children in institutions suffer from perceptual deprivation and restriction of learning opportunities" (p. 607). Ainsworth (1962) argued that it is not possible to make a distinction between maternal deprivation and lack of learning opportunities, since a parent supplies most of the stimulation for the infant.

White and Watts (1973) conducted a study to determine if certain experiences during the first six years of life could be structured so that children would be better prepared for formal schooling. After defining the abilities leading to competence (both socially and cognitively), these investigators observed families who had produced competent children. It was found that mothers of children who were rated as highly competent used the following child care techniques:

1. Talked to the child often and in understandable terms.
2. Made the child feel that what she or he was doing was interesting.
3. Provided many objects for the child to play with and arranged for the child to have access to a variety of situations.
4. Led the child to expect that help and encouragement would be supplied most, but not all, of the time.
5. Demonstrated and explained to the child primarily when the child asked for instruction and assistance. (pp. 242-243)

According to Biehler (1981), an analysis of the various infant care techniques leads to the conclusion that, during the first two years of infant-parent interactions, effective parents are particularly responsive to activities initiated by their children. An examination of the strategies used by the successful mothers studied by White and Watts suggests that, over the course of the first three years of life, effective parents encourage their children to explore and interact. Parents are most effective when they react to their children's responses with interest and support. It is of paramount importance that parents be sensitive to their children's feelings and help their children develop a sense of their ability to influence their world (Schaffer, 1977).

Many of the techniques that parents use to promote the development of cognitive competence in one-, two-, and three-year-old children are also effective with four- and five-year-old children. Biehler (1981) summarized those techniques as follows:

1. allowing children to initiate activities and then responding to their efforts in ways that extend and expand those activities
2. giving cognitively competent three- and four-year-old youngsters ample opportunities for self-expression
3. arranging conditions and providing responses so that children develop the feeling that they can affect consequences
4. seeing things from the child's point of view
5. establishing feelings of mutual delight in social interactions
6. talking, responding, enriching, encouraging, and explaining things to children

Baumrind (1967, 1971) found that the children of authoritative parents tended to become competent and self-reliant. Since competence is as much a function of cognition as it is of personality, it appears that the techniques of authoritative parents are likely to enhance intellectual development. Authoritative parents

1. permit and encourage their children to do things independently
2. encourage mature and skilled types of behavior
3. establish firm control but provide reasons for restrictions
4. while allowing for the egocentrism of preschool children's thought, respect their children's wishes but expect them to consider the needs of others
5. are warm, supportive, and loving
6. demonstrate admiration and appreciation for their children's accomplishments
7. model competence

Other researchers have studied the influence of parent behavior on child intelligence by using the IQ as a criterion. Schaefer (1975) reported that children whose parents (and early stimulation projects) provided them with books and toys, as well as verbal stimulation, have achieved higher scores on tests of intelligence.

As indicated earlier, the low mean IQ scores and slower language development of children reared in orphanages (Pringle & Bossio, 1958) suggest a definite relationship between cognitive development, language development, and the experiences provided by parents. Hess (1969) and Schaefer (1972) found that parent attentiveness, warmth, verbal interaction, effective teaching, diffuse intellectual stimulation, and demands for achievement correlate with subsequent intellectual development and academic achievement. Moore (1968) found that the language stimulation provided at the age of two and one-half years, experiences, toys, and books could be used to predict a child's reading level at seven years and IQ at eight years of age. This finding supports the hypothesis that early and continued parent-child interactions have a positive cumulative effect on the child's intellectual development and academic achievement (Schaefer, 1975).

Chapter 2

The Impact of a Handicapped Child on the Family

Most couples anticipate the birth of a child with eagerness and much happiness. The parents-to-be singly and together develop certain expectations about the child that is yet to be born. Since the child is most frequently a product of the parents' love for each other, the child is often idealized as the "perfect child." Sometimes the expectant mother views the child both as a gift to her husband, her parents, or herself and as the object of reinforcement and pleasure. The father may wish for a child to surpass his own accomplishments. When the child is finally born, all these dreams, expectations, and desires instantly come together and are invested in this dream child. If the child is handicapped, the psychological impact can be devastating.

The process by which a handicap is first suspected and then discovered has been the subject of much study. Although the bulk of the research has been conducted with parents of mentally retarded children, Karnes and Teska (1980) suggest that the process and subsequent parental reactions are similar, regardless of the child's handicapping condition. Roos (1975) suggests that the parents of seriously impaired children inevitably experience shock, disappointment, depression, and the feeling that life has been unfair. The frustrations and disappointments of the parents are intense. The emotional adjustments of the parents follow a pattern similar to that noted among those who are grieving over the death of a loved one or those who may be fearing their own imminent death. The concept of mourning is important to an understanding of the psychological trauma experienced by the parents of a handicapped child, for these parents are actually mourning the "death of the perfect child" of their dreams.

Those stages of adjustment are particularly well described in Kübler-Ross's 1969 book, *On Death and Dying*. Her model for the process of grief is clear, and it applies to families whose children are born with handicaps. In the Kübler-Ross model, there are periods of denial and isolation, anger, bargaining, depression, and acceptance as stages in grief. It is possible to see this pattern of suffering for any serious problem or a loss of a loved one.

The fact that many parents of newly identified handicapped children are subject to these feelings has been substantiated (Drotar, Baskiewicz, Irvin, Kennell, & Klaus, 1975; Wolfensberger, 1967). Of course, it is important to recognize that certain variables affect parental reaction to the diagnosis of a handicapped child. Schell (1981) and Marion (1981) have identified certain factors that influence parental feelings. Among those identified were

- severity of the child's handicap. Mildly handicapped children who look normal do not evoke the same parental response, either in duration or intensity, as a child who is profoundly impaired. Physical unattractiveness or signs of the impairment that are obvious to the public are generally less acceptable to the parents.
- social acceptability of the handicap. While the handicapped in general are, unfortunately, not particularly acceptable to the public, public reactions range along a continuum. Deaf-children (until they talk) or learning-disabled children are more socially acceptable than severely disturbed or multihandicapped children.
- socioeconomic level of the family. Parents in higher socioeconomic groups seem to react more adversely to the diagnosis of handicap, possibly because they view the child's handicap as destroying their dream of the "good life."

To these may be added

- the manner in which the parents are informed. Most professionals in early childhood special education have heard the horror stories about physicians who told parents, "Your child is a mongoloid who will never learn. It is best to put the child in an institution and forget him—anyway, he'll die at an early age." Since no one can predict with certainty what the future holds for handicapped children, even those who are severely handicapped, undue pessimism only serves to create a negative and unhealthy parental reaction. On the other hand, the professional who says, "Don't worry, he'll outgrow it," to the mother of an obviously impaired child is doing the family an equal injustice. Although reassurance is critical, false hope can lead a parent to delay seeking help for a handicapped child, thereby wasting precious time.
- age of onset or age of the child when the diagnosis is made. The older the child is when the diagnosis is made, the *more* difficult it is to accept

and the *more* intense are the parental reactions to the news. According to Barsch (1969), some parents of severely retarded children noted that, since the impairment was obvious at birth, they were better able to handle the feelings and emotions caused by the diagnosis.

PARENTAL REACTION TO THE DIAGNOSIS OF A HANDICAPPED CHILD

Parents of handicapped children are not a homogeneous group. Even though their reactions, emotions, and affective response capacities are diverse and complex, recurrent behavioral reactions occur with a certain predictability. These stages have been studied for well over 30 years, but investigators of these stages often differ on

- the number of stages parents pass through
- the names of the stages
- the sequence of the stages
- the precise nature of parental concern at each stage

Exhibit 2-1 shows the stages proposed by various authors.

Several consistent themes seem to emerge from the literature, however. Initially, parents experience shock, anguish, disbelief, hopelessness, mourning, self-pity, and sorrow (Wolfensberger, 1967). The early stages seem to consist of severe psychological disorganization. Parents may be overwhelmed and frantic; they may not know what to do next. The mother and father may be in conflict with one another, particularly if they blame each other for what has happened.

In the middle stages, parents seem to overcome the initial shock, but they may reject the diagnosis. Refusing to accept the fact that their child is handicapped, parents may feel that the physician or psychologist is in error. Marion (1981) calls this the denial stage. Denial can be a particularly destructive phase because (1) the child may not be placed in an intervention program and (2) the parent may refuse to talk about the problem, driving further inward the psychological problems that are likely to be bothering them. This produces a great deal of stress.

Another manifestation of the middle stages is "shopping behavior" (MacMillan, 1982). Parents may make repeated visits to the same or different professionals. Rosen (1955) identifies two types of shopping—one for a cause, the other for a cure. While searching for the cause, parents may be seeking a professional who will tell them what they want to hear,

Exhibit 2-1 Stages Experienced by Newly Informed Parents
of Handicapped Children

Hay (1951)	Rosen (1955)	Koegler (1963)
1. Bewilderment	1. Awareness of the problem	1. Shock
2. Suspicion	2. Recognition of its nature	2. Disbelief
3. Shock	3. Search for a cause	3. Fear and
4. Protest	4. Search for a cure	frustration
5. Education	5. Acceptance of the problem	4. Intelligent inquiry
6. Acceptance		

Grays (1963)	Kirk, Karnes, and Kirk (1968)
1. Guilt and shame	1. Disbelief
2. Knowledge and understanding	2. Fear
3. Acceptance	3. Intellectual inquiry
4. Help for the child	

Menolascino and Egger (1978)	Marion (1981)
1. Novelty shock crisis	1. Projection of blame
2. Personal values crisis	2. Guilt
3. Reality crisis	3. Denial
	4. Grief
	5. Withdrawal
	6. Rejection
	7. Acceptance

i.e., their child is normal. It should be noted, however, that parents sometimes shop for a cause of their child's handicap because the professionals with whom they have dealt to this point have been noncommittal or evasive about the diagnosis. When parents shop for a cure, they are usually being unrealistic; for example, neither severe mental retardation nor cerebral palsy can be cured at present.

The final stage, acceptance, is based on reality. Parents search their interactions with each other and with the child for those elements that make it possible for them to establish a nurturing relationship with the young handicapped child.

Parental reactions may be affected by the sex of the parent involved. Tavormina, Ball, Dunn, Luscomb, and Taylor (1977, as reported by Gallagher, Cross, & Scharfman, 1981) focused on the father's reaction to a handicapped child. They found that the father may divorce himself emotionally from the child, forcing the mother to provide all the care by herself.

The father then focuses on other activities, such as his job or social organizations. Tallman (1965) found fathers had more difficulty coping with mentally retarded children than did mothers. He believed that the fathers of severely retarded children were especially affected and vulnerable to social stigmas and extrafamilial influences.

In discussing their own reactions and responses to their retarded child, Turnbull and Turnbull (1979) identified practical problems as a recurring source of frustration. Moroney (1981) discussed the private troubles facing parents with handicapped children:

- additional financial hardships
- actual or perceived stigma
- extraordinary demands on time for personal care of the child
- difficulties in caregiver tasks (e.g., feeding)
- diminished time for sleeping
- social isolation from family and friends
- less time for recreational pursuits
- difficulties managing behavior
- difficulties performing routine household chores
- general feelings of pessimism about the future

Furthermore, having a handicapped child seems to intensify certain anxieties that already exist in most people (Roos, 1979, 1982):

1. The handicapped child's limitations diminish the possibility that the parents' own hopes and dreams will be fulfilled. By the time many people have reached adulthood, they have already experienced many disappointments in their lives, e.g., with their parents, their spouses, or their careers. The birth of a "defective" child instead of a "perfect" one could be interpreted as the "last straw."
2. With its many satisfactions, parenthood may be considered a way to develop intimate contact and transcend barriers of aloneness. Unfortunately, this elusive ideal is much more difficult to achieve with a child whose affective or psychomotor response capacities are limited. Some parents then feel that they have lost their only real chance for achieving intimacy and they may be overwhelmed by a feeling of aloneness.
3. Maturity brings with it constant reminders of our vulnerability. The birth of a handicapped child serves as a harsh reminder of exactly how little control we have over our destiny and of the fragile nature of human life itself.

4. There is a persistent myth in our culture that life is fair and just and that somehow right always prevails over wrong. When the physician or other professional tells the parent, "Your child is mentally retarded," or "Your child has cerebral palsy," the parent says, "Why me?" For some parents, a guilt reaction is inevitable. They ask themselves whether the birth of a handicapped child is a punishment for some misdeed. Parents may also challenge fundamental religious beliefs and question "God's judgment or fairness."

5. Many people believe that parenthood will give meaning and a sense of accomplishment to their lives. They see themselves as a wise guide, a good provider, and a source of inspiration to their children. When parents find out their child is handicapped, the purpose of their lives is challenged. Parental roles may be vastly curtailed and fundamentally changed from the parents' preconceived ideal.

6. Parents tend to fantasize about their child's future academic achievement, excellence in the arts or music, athletic accomplishments, and career successes. When the diagnosis is conveyed, the future suddenly seems bleak and full of stress-producing events. Instead of success, they may see academic failure, social rejection, emotional disturbance, sexual problems, inability to work and live independently, and a life of loneliness and isolation in their child's future. Therefore, parents of handicapped children tend to repress thoughts of the future and overemphasize the present and the past.

7. The birth of children (or grandchildren) gives parents a symbolic sense of immortality. The birth of a handicapped child threatens this fundamental need and intensifies anxieties related to death.

Not all parents react in the same negative fashion, nor are all parents under debilitating stress when their child is diagnosed as handicapped. Gallagher and associates (1981) found that some families were able to adapt and cope successfully. Stress-producing conditions were kept manageable.

PARENTAL ATTITUDES TOWARD AND INTERACTIONS WITH YOUNG HANDICAPPED CHILDREN

As they do with normal children, the important interrelationships between parents and children have a profound socializing influence on handicapped children. Some of the effects of the handicap on these interrelationships may be detrimental to the social and emotional development of handicapped children:

- The mother's expectations regarding the child's endowment are distorted (Cohen, 1966).
- Parents perceive the child as vulnerable (Green & Solnit, 1964).
- Parents' expectations for the child are not based on social norms for expected behavior (Roskies, 1972).
- The individual differences of infants and the way their mothers perceive them affect the attachment process (Fraiberg, Smith, & Adelson, 1969).

Lavelle and Keogh (1980) compiled an extensive review of the literature on the influence of parents' perceptions on their expectations and attributions. It was their opinion that parents' beliefs affect the subsequent behavior of the child. The attributions of parents were found to influence parental expectations about child performance, determine their opinion of the adequacy of the child's achievement, and affect the interaction between the child and the parents.

Lavelle (1977) reported significant differences in attributions and expectations among parents of educationally handicapped, retarded, and nonhandicapped children. The parents of educationally handicapped children attributed both success and failure to the child's effort (i.e., the child did or did not try hard enough). The parents of mentally retarded children attributed their child's success to sheer luck and failure to a lack of ability. In contrast, the parents of nonhandicapped children attributed success to ability and failure to a lack of effort or bad luck.

The child's appearance also affects parental expectations about the child's performance. Parents of mildly impaired (less visibly handicapped) children were found to overestimate the ability of their children (Jensen & Kogan, 1962; Tew, Laurence, & Samuel, 1974). On the other hand, more severe or visible physical handicaps can lower parental estimates of children's intelligence and future performance (Cohen, 1966).

Parental reactions to and interactions with young children are also influenced by the child's temperament. Thomas and Chess (1977) conducted a classic longitudinal study of temperament, which they defined as an infant's behavioral style. In the Thomas and Chess study, nine categories of behavior thought to be indicative of temperament were carefully studied:

1. activity level
2. rhythmicity
3. approach/withdrawal
4. adaptability
5. threshold of responsiveness

6. intensity
7. mood
8. distractibility
9. persistence

Using these nine categories, Thomas and Chess identified three common constellations of temperament: (1) difficult, (2) easy, and (3) slow to warm up.

In one study, 141 New York City children were rated on the nine Thomas and Chess dimensions (Thomas, Chess, & Birch, 1970). The experimenters found that 40 percent of the children could be classified as easy children. These children were cheerful, had regular sleep patterns, approached new situations with interest, and adapted readily to changes in the environment. Those children classified as difficult (10 percent of the group) had irregular sleeping and eating patterns, reacted with great intensity to frustrating experiences, had a generally negative mood, and withdrew passively from unusual events or people. According to the authors of the study, difficult children are likely to develop behavioral problems that require psychiatric attention in the preschool years.

The slow-to-warm-up group (15 percent of the sample) were inactive, quiet, and likely to withdraw (at least initially) when presented with novel events or strange people. If the slow-to-warm-up children are allowed to adapt to and interact with the environment at their own pace, they can function quite well. On the other hand, overly demanding parents who push their slow-to-warm-up child into new situations too quickly or too often may increase their child's natural tendency to withdraw. The result is a child who is lonely and has few interests.

The remainder of the sample (35 percent) could not be assigned to a group. They exhibited temperament characteristics that were associated with more than one of the three constellations.

Many psychologists believe that temperament results at least partially from biological factors. Yet the reaction of parents and caregivers to the infant's natural tendencies is an important determinant of temperamental quality. Thomas and associates (1970) noted:

> The paramount conclusion from our studies is that the debate over the relative importance of nature and nurture only confuses the issue. What is important is the interaction between the two— between the child's own characteristics and his environment. If the two influences are harmonized, one can expect healthy development of the child; if they are dissonant, behavioral problems are almost sure to ensue. (p. 109)

It also seems clear that children who are mentally retarded or who are affected by rubella syndrome do not differ from normal children with respect to the nine behavior categories indicative of temperament (Thomas & Chess, 1977). Nonetheless, Thomas and Chess noted that variations in temperamental characteristics influence parents. Ramey, Beckman-Bell, and Gowen (1980) suggested that parental response to a child is dependent on the particular characteristics exhibited by the child. Different children may induce, even require, different parenting techniques.

Ramey and associates (1980) reviewed the literature to determine the extent that differences in temperament influence interaction between parents and children. They found that certain infant characteristics, such as the amount of crying and the responsiveness to parental attempts to soothe the child, regulate the amount of contact that occurs between a parent and an infant. Parents cuddle, play, and talk to alert, visually oriented, responsive babies. In contrast, irritable or passive infants who fail to make eye contact or respond to cuddling make parents feel inadequate, resulting in less interaction (Moss, 1967; Moss & Robson, 1968). Beckwith (1972) reported that infants whose newborn neurological scores indicated organic abnormalities spent less time in interaction with their mothers. Furthermore, there was a significant and negative correlation between the degree of central nervous system involvement and the amount of time the mother and infant spent in interaction.

Ramey and associates (1980) suggested several ways in which handicapping conditions can influence mother-child interactions:

1. A child's handicap can alter the reward parents derive from parenting. When children are significantly impaired, they do not develop behavioral repertoires according to the parents' expectations, and the bonding or attachment process may be negatively affected.
2. Routine caregiving tasks (e.g., feeding) may be more difficult. Erikson (1963) stressed that the infant's needs must be met in a pleasant, warm fashion in order to establish trust. When these caregiving tasks are more difficult because of a handicap, the result is likely to be an increase in parental stress, which makes it difficult to establish a bond between the child and the mother.
3. The separations that may be caused by the need to hospitalize a handicapped child can disrupt parent-child interactions. Scandary (in Sirvis and Carpignano, 1976) pointed out that such hospitalizations and separations are stressful for both the child and the parents. The increased strain may make it even more difficult to establish attachment between the mother and the child.

4. Contextual variables may exert an indirect influence on interaction. Ramey and associates (1980) defined contextual variables as the reactions of friends, babysitters, and others to the handicapped baby; the financial resources available to the family; the mother's expectations for her child's development; and increased marital stress. These factors interact in a complex fashion to influence specific forms of parent-child interaction dramatically.

Hyperactivity also affects parent-child interactions. Campbell (1973, 1975) found that the mothers of hyperactive children exerted significantly greater effort to control and structure the behavior of their children than did mothers of nonhyperactive children. Hyperactivity is also associated with distractibility, a short attention span, clumsiness, emotional lability, antisocial behavior, and irritability (Langhorne & Loney, 1976; Whalen & Henker, 1976). As Bryan and Bryan (1978) note,

> the learning disabled child is confronted with a social world in which he is disliked, at worst, or ignored, at best, by his . . . parents. Moreover, there is evidence to suggest that he has difficulty in understanding subtle messages concerning adults' affective states, a deficiency which might well be expected to lead to social rejection. (p. 139)

CRITICAL EVENTS IN FAMILIES WITH YOUNG HANDICAPPED CHILDREN

A topic of great interest among professionals in early childhood education for the exceptional child is the identification of events in the family interaction that are likely to precipitate a crisis or major problem for the parents. Bray, Coleman, and Bracken (1981) surveyed 169 parents of handicapped children to document and categorize critical events that occurred in their families. A total of 660 events were identified on the questionnaires. The six areas named most frequently, in order, were

1. educational services. Circumstances surrounding the child's enrollment in school, such as appropriateness of placement, quality of related services, and the child's adjustment to the program were described as critical by almost 24 percent of the respondents.
2. initial diagnosis. Nearly 11 percent of the respondents identified this as a critical event. When the handicap was obvious by age two, 44 percent of the parents reported initial diagnosis as the first event.

3. family member impact. Events in this category, related to emotional reactions to stress, were found on 7.4 percent of the questionnaires.
4. medical management. Approximately 7 percent of the parents sampled identified the daily management of medication or adaptation to a prosthetic device as critical.
5. incomplete/inaccurate diagnosis. About 6 percent of the sample saw fluctuation, change, or constant refinement in the diagnostic process as a problem.
6. prognosis. Six percent of the sample said that descriptions of the child's future life chances were critical events.

Bray and associates (1981) further noted that the severity of the child's handicap, the disability category involved, the sex of the child, and the parents' social class all affected the way parents responded to the questionnaires. For example, parents of learning-disabled children seemed more concerned with educational issues, while parents of mentally retarded children saw the initial diagnosis as the most important event. When the child was a boy, 34 percent of the parents rated educational concerns as a problem. When the child was a girl, the percentage dropped to 10 percent.

Hammer (1972) also discussed critical events in the lives of parents of handicapped children. Hammer believed that parental stress is particularly intense when

- the child is born or the parents suspect the presence of a handicapping condition
- the diagnosis is being made and the handicap is being treated
- the child is ready to enter a school program
- the child reaches puberty
- the child reaches the age of vocational planning
- the parents grow old and worry that the child may outlive them

The role of professionals in all these events is critical, but it is particularly important in regard to the child's entry into an intervention or school program. Parents may show great concern, for example, if their handicapped children are going to be in classes with nonhandicapped children (Turnbull & Blancher-Dixon, 1980). Parents also worry about the quality of intervention services, whether their child will be accepted by teachers and peers, and "most importantly, whether the school will be able to 'understand' the child and to meet needs as perceived by the family" (Marion, 1981, p. 19).

EFFECTS OF A HANDICAPPED CHILD ON SIBLINGS

It is easy to overlook the impact handicapped young children have on their brothers and sisters. Siblings may repress their feelings for fear of adding to their parents' burdens or because they fear the answers to questions they have. Most of the research on the impact of a handicapped child on siblings has involved retarded children. It may be assumed that many of the findings apply to siblings of any handicapped child.

Parents, especially those at higher socioeconomic levels, are often concerned that the retarded child may have a detrimental effect on the normal siblings. Appell and Tisdall (1968) reported that retarded children admitted to institutions had a greater number of siblings at home than did children not admitted. Farber (1968) indicated that parental concern over the effect of a mentally retarded child on normal siblings is most pronounced when the child is severely retarded.

Farber (1959, 1960) found that normal sisters showed more personality disorders than did normal brothers when the retarded child was in the home. He concluded that girls, especially older sisters, must frequently assume homemaking and child care duties, thus increasing demands on them. Graliker, Fishler, and Koch (1962) reported, however, that teenaged siblings of the mentally retarded children they studied seemed happy, well adjusted, unashamed of their retarded brother or sister, and unburdened with respect to their responsibilities toward that sibling, even though there is evidence that siblings of retarded children must often assume more advanced age roles than would otherwise be the case. Carr (1974) summarized studies of the impact of moderately and severely retarded children on their siblings as follows:

> Many of the studies of the effect on the siblings of a retarded child have suffered from methodological drawbacks, in particular those of small selected samples. Nevertheless, what emerges from the studies is a consistent lack of support for the still widely-held view that normal children will suffer from the presence of a retarded child in the home. (p. 829)

Rather than assume negative impacts, it might be better to examine the needs of siblings of handicapped young children. Marion (1981), using the Maslow (1962) hierarchy of needs, suggested that siblings of handicapped children have a need

1. to belong
2. for working through feelings and emotions
3. for truth in communication

To these would be added

4. to become involved in the handicapped child's program at whatever level the sibling can tolerate
5. to live their lives free of excessive demands to care for their handicapped sibling

Need to Belong

Parents of young handicapped children may devote so much time and energy to the needs of their handicapped child that they inadvertently neglect the emotional needs of their normal children. Even if the normal siblings adjust well, they still have feelings, anxieties, and questions about their handicapped sibling. Normal siblings may interpret the parents' attention to the needs of the handicapped child as a lack of concern by their parents for their needs. Normal siblings may lack a sense of belonging to the family.

Parents can do much to address their normal children's need to belong by planning quality "alone time" for each normal sibling in the family. It does not matter what the activity is; in fact, the normal siblings should be allowed to select the activity that they wish to share with their parents.

Need for Working through Feelings and Emotions

Often normal siblings' innermost feelings and emotions with respect to their handicapped brother or sister are in turmoil. Siblings not only may feel excluded from the parents' love and attention, but also may resent the time and money spent on the handicapped child. This resentment produces guilt feelings.

Normal siblings may also feel fear and embarrassment. Young siblings fear that they, too, may become crippled or blind. Even more frightening for adolescent sisters is the fear that they may produce a child like their handicapped sibling. Some normal siblings do not want their friends to come to their home for fear of being ridiculed or excluded from their circle of friends. Strong feelings of shame may conflict with feelings of embarrassment, particularly when the siblings see their peers interact with the handicapped child in a positive and accepting manner.

Many intervention projects extend support services to siblings to assist them in working through emotional problems.

Need for Truth in Communication

Honesty between professionals and parents is vital to the establishment of the parent-professional partnership. In the same fashion, parents must be open and honest with their normal children about their handicapped child. Siblings may hear superstitions and myths about the handicap from their friends, and the only solution is for parents to include siblings in family discussions about the handicap.

Need to Become Involved in the Handicapped Child's Program

The involvement of *all* family members is now a goal of many intervention projects. It must be remembered, however, that siblings have varying tolerance levels regarding the intensity of their involvement. Frequently, parents fail to determine what, if any, involvement siblings want in the handicapped child's intervention program.

It may be extremely beneficial if parents and professionals work cooperatively to provide siblings with information about the handicapped child's intervention program, current level of functioning, and anticipated progress. Parents can hold regular family meetings to share information and provide siblings with a forum for expressing their feelings and concerns. Siblings may volunteer to participate in the handicapped child's program in the home. Schools and agencies should make provisions for training siblings to work with young handicapped children under their parents' supervision.

Need to Live Their Own Lives

Sometimes beleaguered parents make excessive demands on older siblings, expecting them to share in child care duties for the handicapped child and to devote themselves to the handicapped child in the same way that the parents do. This is not only unfair, but also causes the sibling to resent the parents and the handicapped child. In the long run, it is far more productive to involve siblings at their tolerance levels and allow them to choose how intensely they wish to become involved with the care of their handicapped brother or sister.

Chapter 3

Helping Families Deal with Practical Problems

For many years, it has been assumed that effective parenting comes naturally. Professionals now recognize that skillful parenting is a composite of learned behaviors that can be directed to provide optimum development for any child. Why then are many parents failing to develop these skills? White (1975) cites three major barriers to the development of optimum parenting skills:

1. ignorance. The majority of parents are ill-prepared for the demands and responsibility of parenting. Many do not recognize developmental milestones and thus do not provide appropriate experiences, nor are they aware of the need for early stimulation to satisfy the child's natural curiosity or social development. Furthermore, parents may be unsure of themselves in their role as caregivers.
2. stress. The stress of having an active 8- to 24-month-old child in the home is tremendous. A child at this age is a whirlwind of activity— driven by intense curiosity, the child becomes involved in dangerous situations, frequently with objects of some value to the parents or siblings. Frequently, tension arises between the parents over the neatness of the house.
3. lack of assistance. The mobility of the American people has all but eliminated the physical and psychological relief provided by the extended family of grandparents, aunts, uncles, and others.

In addition to these obstacles, there are changes in the relationship between the parents in terms of companionship, sexual adjustment, and new role expectations (e.g., the father as a caregiver); changes in the relationships between parents and siblings; reaction of siblings to the newborn; and, often, financial problems. Parents of a newborn handicapped child face all

33

these problems, magnified, as well as problems specifically related to the handicapped child.

FAMILIES AND COMMUNITY INTERVENTION SERVICES

Once parents recognize that their child is "different," they begin an interaction with their community's network of services. Frequently, this interaction is totally unsatisfactory to the family.

Medical Services

A family's initial involvement with community services is generally with a medical professional, a family practice physician or a pediatrician. In the not too distant past, the physician was a "passive" participant in the process of community treatment or educational interventions. The pediatrician or family practitioner generally performed a routine physical examination to detect medical problems, e.g., seizure disorders, sensory deficits, clear-cut neurological problems, and genetic disorders such as Down's syndrome. From there, the child moved to services in psychological or educational areas. At this point, the physician's further participation in the intervention system was limited to any ongoing medical treatment required by the child's disorder. As Levine (1982) pointed out, this traditional pediatric role has several shortcomings. For example, since few of the problems affecting learning have a medical origin, a physical examination may not be particularly useful in planning educational interventions.

Recent modifications in the training of pediatric residents have changed the role of the physician as a member of an interdisciplinary treatment team and a provider of long-term management (Guralnick, Richardson, & Kutner, 1980). The physician has become more cognizant of family dynamics, including the impact of environmental problems on learning, and can assess a family's coping styles and those interactions that have a direct bearing on a child's learning and overall development. The physician can also identify underlying neurodevelopmental factors, such as the maturation of the central nervous system, motor function, and various aspects of information processing and output (Levine, 1982).

The treatment of handicaps places added pressures and demands on the pediatrician or family physician. Because of the natural psychological trauma associated with the identification of a handicapped child, families are particularly vulnerable and in need of an empathic, informed pediatrician. Parents are often unable to accept the relative permanency of handicaps and may project anger toward the physician during the initial diagnostic evaluation. Many families report dissatisfaction with the manner in which they were first informed of the child's handicap, as well as the lack of support immediately thereafter (Tarran, 1981). These initial contacts are important, however, because they may determine the long-range success of intervention programs aimed at helping families achieve a healthy emotional state.

What is the role of the pediatrician at this point? Certainly, the physician must be a good listener. Parents may request further medical opinions or resign themselves to the initial findings. This is a time of difficult transition as parents attempt to design a plan for their child's future course. The primary physician may help the family to secure further medical input; however, the pediatrician must know when to assist the parents in moving from a diagnostic phase to a planning phase for future daily living (Howard, 1982).

This is often a time of great confusion in the family. Parents are concerned not only with the present but also with the future. As Howard (1982) notes,

> Present concerns include thoughts about care for the infant, readjustment, family routines, possible neglect of other family members, cost of providing the necessary help for the child, and disruptions of family harmony and integration. Future concerns deal with socialization opportunities and eventual self-sufficiency. (p. 317)

Frequently, the physician can help the parents feel more competent in their parental roles. Counseling can lead the family to recognize the strengths and positive behaviors of the handicapped child. Parents can then gain confidence in their own positive feelings and expectations for the child's development (Howard, 1982).

As the initial contact, the pediatrician is an obvious source of further referrals. The attitudes of each family unit must be considered individually, however; many families are not ready to accept intervention services, which they view as additional substantiation of their child's handicap. Pediatricians must be tolerant and understanding of a family's viewpoint if they choose not to participate.

Families that originally resist referrals to other agencies may come to view intervention more positively as the child's delays become more pronounced or the family becomes more accepting of the child. When this occurs, the physician or pediatrician must be able to identify the appropriate community agency so that an effective referral can be made (Guralnick, Richardson, & Heiser, 1982; Howard, 1982).

Referral to Community Agencies

The agencies that provide diagnostic and intervention services for young handicapped children may be threatening places for families in transition. Parents who are not well informed require information on the medical, educational, and financial impact of a handicapped child (Schell, 1981). Parents also need answers to questions regarding day care facilities, the attitudes of others toward them and their child, their role in the child's intervention program, and long-term medical management of the impairment.

Areas of Conflict

Relations between the family and the service agency may be marred by conflict (Foster, Berger, & McLean, 1981). Agency professionals focus their energy on the needs of the handicapped child, but parents have their own needs and must also attend to the needs of the handicapped child and other children in the family (Minuchin, 1974).

Many parents expect a community agency to provide something for or to their child. When the professionals place heavy demands on the parents and expect them to become intensely involved in the child's program, particularly in a home-based program, parents may become guilty or resentful. Parents may feel guilt if they do not spend a great deal of time working with the child; they may feel resentment because the "helping" agency is not helping. If parents choose not to participate, agency professionals may view it as lack of commitment to the child.

The trainer-trainee relationship between professionals and families may also lead to conflict. Many agencies assume parents know little or nothing about the developmental and educational needs of their children. This is not only inaccurate but also inappropriate if a true spirit of cooperation is to be established. The optimum climate for the parent-professional relationship is characterized by mutual respect, honesty, and an egalitarian attitude on both sides (Enzer, 1976).

Many agencies treat the families of handicapped children as homogeneous units. Public Law 94-142, the Education for All Handicapped Children Act, requires individualized education programs (IEPs) for children in special education, but does not require them for parents. Thus, it is important for agency professionals to view and treat each family individually.

Levels of Family Involvement

Since it is known that effective parent-child interactions can improve child performance (Bronfenbrenner, 1974) and that parents will become involved in intervention programs for their children, provided the level of involvement is appropriate (Karnes, 1973), it is important to build constructive, cooperative parent-professional relationships. It is essential to establish good lines of communication. Professionals must learn to become active listeners, accepting in a nonjudgmental fashion what parents have to say and avoiding the use of jargon. In addition, the program must be organized to ensure that parents are active participants in all facets, including decision making.

In Bronfenbrenner's (1974) analysis of preschool programs, he noted that

> the involvement of the child's family as an *active participant* [emphasis added] is critical to the success of any intervention program. Without such family involvement, any effect of intervention . . . appears to erode fairly rapidly once the program ends. In contrast, the involvement of the *parents as partners* [emphasis added] in the enterprise provides an on-going system which can reinforce the effects of the program while it is in operation, and help to sustain them after the program ends. (p. 55)

Professionals must be aware of the rights of parents to remain in control of the intervention sessions, whether they occur in the agency or in the home. Parents who have this sense of control are more likely to become active participants in the intervention and less likely to become overly dependent, passive observers of the action (Bromwich, 1981).

It must also be recognized that family involvement in any intervention or educational program is developmental in nature. Families are individual units, and every family cannot be expected to participate in a program with the same intensity or at the same level. Therefore, program developers must plan a continuum of options for family involvement that permits families to progress from one level to the next. The following continuum categories were adapted from the levels identified by Karnes and Lee (1978):

1. Level I: Passive Receptivity to Program Involvement for the Child. At this level, families agree to allow the child to participate in the program. They also adhere to minimal program requirements for parental involvement, such as mandatory parent-professional conferences, but are reluctant to go beyond this interaction.
2. Level II: Minimal Involvement in Program for the Child. Families have more personal contact with professional staff at this level. There are discussions about the child's program and alternatives for family

involvement in other aspects of the program, e.g., parent groups or training sessions.

3. Level III: Involvement as Trainee in Intervention Strategies. Training may take many forms. Parents may be trained to assist in educational activities with the child in the home. This training must be "hands-on" and allow the family members to work with the child immediately in one or more curricular areas. Other training could involve support areas such as physical therapy (for home carry-over), medical practices, or speech therapy.

4. Level IV: Involvement as Fully Participating Member of Interdisciplinary Team. The training of families is both a developmental and ongoing process, but a family member(s) can eventually function as an active member of the interdisciplinary team, exchanging meaningful information with professional team members. Training and experience working with the child allow the family member to work closely with the education professional to select program goals, teach certain skills, measure progress, and even evaluate program effectiveness.

5. Level V: Involvement as Counselor of Other Families of Handicapped Children. Skilled parents can be effective counselors of other parents, especially those of recently identified handicapped children (Karnes & Lee, 1978; Mori & Olive, 1980). Parents at this level can provide emotional support and encouragement to new families, because they accept a handicapped child as an individual capable of developing to the maximal limits imposed by the impairment. The parent counselor can also help the new family by sharing experiences and explaining the program's benefits for the child as well as the family members (Shearer & Shearer, 1977).

6. Level VI: Involvement as Advocate and Policy Maker. As advocates, parents, families, and their allies organize to fight for handicapped children's needs and rights by causing schools, agencies, and branches of government to make necessary changes (Biklen, 1974). Biklen noted that advocacy involves appraising oneself, building alliances with appropriate groups, identifying community needs, knowing and responding to those who resist change, learning how to use power, and, finally, taking action (e.g., demonstrations, demands, or letter writing). In order to become policy makers, parents must have been so thoroughly integrated into the agency program that there is a high level of mutual trust and respect. If this occurs, parents actually help formulate agency/program policy and can interpret that policy to the community at large.

7. Level VII: Involvement as Program Initiator and Developer. Parents can and do operate their own intervention programs for handicapped children (Lillie, 1976; Wiegerink & Parrish, 1976). When these programs are well organized, operated according to carefully stated objectives, and guided by a strong documentation of progress and evaluation plan (Sheehan, 1981), handicapped children can be efficiently and effectively served.

The categories are not strictly hierarchical, although most families would be at Level III for some period prior to moving to Level IV and beyond. Once Level IV has been reached, parents may move quickly to Level V and simultaneously function at Levels VI and VII.

Parents must feel that their priorities and concerns are being addressed. They should be involved as much as possible in the planning of activities and selection of goals and objectives for their child. This establishes a parent-professional partnership in which objectives can be pursued cooperatively. Furthermore, when there is joint planning and decision making, professionals can openly and honestly discuss any unrealistic parental expectations or inconsistencies in parenting techniques (Bromwich, 1981).

Support Services

Every program should include support services for families with a handicapped child. Frequently, agency professionals become so involved in the provision of services to children that they fail to see the need of the entire family for services. Families may be frustrated in their dealings with other agencies or in their day-to-day problems. Knowing someone cares and is interested in the entire family is crucial to the ongoing parent-professional partnership. Yet, care and encouragement are not enough; parents also want professionals to be well informed about other community services that could be of assistance to them (Giacobbe, Carlton, Blanton, Fallen, & Clarke, 1978). Information services vary from lists of babysitters willing to take handicapped children to national and state agencies serving handicapped children and families, and local social service agencies such as welfare or mental health/mental retardation agencies (Hanson, 1981).

Parents also need social and emotional support (Lillie, 1976) to strengthen and bring stability to the family situation (Enzer, 1976). It is not uncommon for parents to devote time and resources to the handicapped child while forgetting about their own needs or the needs of other children in the family. The skilled professional can help the family to achieve both balance and harmony, thus avoiding the pitfall of becoming a "handicapped family."

Frequently, parents' groups can provide support, information, and even counseling. Many parents with similarly handicapped children may meet informally or formally to discuss common concerns, problems, and frustrations, or to receive training in areas such as discipline or behavior management (Hanson, 1981; Mori & Olive, 1980).

Parent Training

Professionals frequently fail to recognize and use constructively the strengths of families with a handicapped child. It is not atypical for the service provider to view the parent as a trainee "in need" of something that only the professional can provide. It is important, however, for the professional to determine existing positive parenting behaviors and use them as a foundation for further intervention strategies (Bromwich, 1981). Recognizing a family's strengths is not only a part of individualized programming, but also a signal to the family that their contribution is respected. Furthermore, it enhances a family's self-confidence, encourages further positive interactions, and models the appropriate family-child interaction, i.e., recognizing the child's strengths and building on those (Bromwich, 1981).

Parent education or training must be based on a family's needs and provided at a level that is within that family's capacity to respond. Professionals must not assume that they know what the family needs in the way of training. The appropriateness of working cooperatively with families to determine needs is well documented (Cansler, Martin, & Valand, 1975; Enzer, 1976; Lillie, 1976; Northcott & Fowler, 1976). Parental training is most effective if professionals work with families to "determine needs, to define and prioritize goals, and to plan training activities that will assist each family member to reach those goals" (Karnes & Teska, 1980, p. 98).

Once the initial needs assessment and goal selection have been completed, the professional staff and the family should develop a written plan for the family similar to the IEP used to guide the child's program. A written plan ensures a better beginning to the parent-professional partnership and a greater degree of accountability by all parties concerned.

Another important aspect of training involves the sharing of information with parents. Accurate information free of professional jargon should be provided to the parents. In this fashion, parents can be meaningfully involved in the treatment program from the initial diagnosis through the treatment and on to the placement or referral phase.

Although it is necessary to determine training goals and content individually for each family, there are some goals and content areas that are applicable to most families served in intervention programs for preschool handicapped children. Quick, Little, and Campbell (1974) elaborated general goals for parent training in the Project MEMPHIS program:

1. To increase the parents' knowledge and understanding of the human development process.
2. To increase the parents' knowledge and understanding of exceptionality and handicapping conditions.
3. To increase the parents' knowledge and understanding of desirable child-rearing practices.
4. To increase the parents' acceptance of their own handicapped child as well as handicapped children in general.
5. To enhance the child care-effecting techniques of the parents.
6. To enhance the child-teaching techniques of the parents. (p. 29)

Karnes and Teska (1980) suggested that families need training in relations with community service agencies, advocacy skills, and methods and techniques for enhancing the development of the handicapped child. The specifics of their recommendations overlap those implied by Quick and associates (1974), but Karnes and Teska include education in the provisions of Public Law 94-142; state rules and regulations; and the availability of special programs, financial assistance, counseling services, and relevant parent organizations. In order to become competent in direct teaching of a child in the home, family members also need to (Karnes & Teska, 1980)

- interact with the handicapped child in ways that promote positive behavior acquisition or change
- reinforce desirable behavior
- determine through observation or assessment a child's level of development
- establish a home milieu that is supportive and conducive to learning
- use appropriate direct teaching procedures
- determine child progress or mastery of instructed skills
- keep meaningful records on child progress
- communicate effectively with the treatment team

COMMUNICATING WITH FAMILIES OF YOUNG HANDICAPPED CHILDREN

Effective communication is the cornerstone of a meaningful parent-professional relationship. Parents and families are in an excellent position to share vital information with professionals and to participate fully as members of the interdisciplinary team. Frequently, however, parents do not express their perceptions, needs, and goals; they assume a passive or submissive role relative to the professional (Welsh & Odum, 1981).

One means to encourage full communication and prevent miscommunication is to create a climate conducive to the exchange of information and ideas. Much has been written about effective interpersonal communication. Gordon (1970) has developed a systematic program for communication skills improvement.

Components of Effective Communication

In order to communicate, one person (the sender) conveys a message either verbally or nonverbally to another person (the receiver). The receiver must decode, or interpret, the message and usually responds by sending a message back to the original sender. If the receiver interprets the message to the satisfaction of the sender, communication is correct. A problem in communication occurs when the receiver incorrectly interprets the message and the sender is *unaware* that this has happened.

Gordon (1970) offers two strategies to prevent communication problems: active listening and "I" messages. The first strategy, active listening, has also been called reflective listening (Rogers, 1963), effective listening (Dinkmeyer & McKay, 1976), and responsive listening (Chinn, Winn, & Walters, 1978). Active listening is really a process of perception checking in which feedback is used to confirm the receiver's interpretation of a message. Active listening should be used only during the discussion of a problem, not during the exchange of information in normal conversation. Active listening requires the receiver to

1. care about the person sending the message
2. believe that what the sender is saying is important
3. spend the time to listen to the message

The receiver practicing active listening must be careful to avoid introducing an interpretation of feelings into the message or simply parroting what the sender said. The purpose of active listening is to understand the message and the attendant feelings, and to share this understanding with the sender. In discussing this process, Rutherford and Edgar (1979) caution the active listener to avoid lagging behind the sender by responding to earlier statements, overshooting the message by assigning more emotion than the sender intended, or undershooting the message by assigning less emotion than intended.

"I" messages are sent as statements of fact and feeling, not conjecture and blame. Senders of "I" messages state how a particular action makes them feel. For example, a parent might say, "I get really frustrated when I can't understand my child's needs." This statement expresses a feeling and does not blame others or imply guilt. "I" messages can be extremely effective, since they allow the receiver to modify a specific problem for the sender. Sometimes, however, even good "I" messages produce no results or changes; they may be ignored or cause the receiver to feel threatened. When this occurs, the parties move to a technique Gordon calls conflict resolution.

Conflict resolution has five distinct phases or stages:

1. determining ownership of the problem. Both parties use "I" messages and active listening to discuss the problem thoroughly and decide exactly who has or "owns" the problem. Gordon (1970) suggests that the one with the problem is the one who is uncomfortable about a specific situation.
2. agreeing on problem definition and on willingness to solve it. No resolution is possible unless both conditions are met.
3. generating possible solutions. Both parties again use active listening and "I" messages to produce a series of options. The parties must participate equally, and each must have the opportunity for unrestricted input. All solutions suggested should be written down, along with a statement describing each party's rights and responsibilities for the solution.
4. implementing solutions and selecting one. The solutions are implemented, tested, and given sufficient time to produce results. The most workable solution, as determined by the parties, is selected and written into a formal contract between the parties.
5. evaluating the solution. The parties must discuss the selected solution, using both "I" messages and active listening, if necessary. If everyone is satisfied, the solution remains in effect. If not everyone is satisfied, the conflict resolution process is repeated until the parties arrive at a workable solution.

Clearly, conflict resolution is a complex process with many prerequisites for success. As Rutherford and Edgar (1979) noted,

> First, the participants must value bilateral decision making since the entire process is based on this concept. Unless individuals truly believe in bilateral decision making, this system will probably fail. Second, participants must possess the basic skills nec-

essary for engaging in the process. Third, they must accept joint ownership of the problem. Fourth, the participants must be truthful and open. Dishonest "I" messages result in inaccurate information. Finally, as in all participative systems, the participants must truly desire a solution to the problem. (p. 84)

This process can greatly facilitate communication between professionals and parents, but it may require the parties to participate in a formal training program to develop the skills.

The Parent-Professional Conference

The conference between parents and professionals is a valuable forum for sharing information, "clarifying issues, searching for answers, deciding on goals, determining mutual strategies, and forming a team in the education of the student" (Berger, 1981, p. 114). Unfortunately, while parent involvement is mandated by Public Law 94-142, meaningful family-professional interactions are still not widespread. Karnes and Teska (1980) attribute this to the fact that many professionals are not trained to interact with parents; lack of training generally leads to apprehension and even feelings of incompetence. Conferencing skills are learned, and staff members must be provided with sufficient in-service education to gain the skills necessary to prepare, conduct, and evaluate contacts with families.

Preparing for the Conference

Effective conferencing begins with good planning and preparation. The first step is to schedule the conference at a time that is convenient for the family. It may be necessary to schedule meetings in the late afternoon or at night because both parents are working. In most circumstances, it is desirable to meet with both parents, particularly when both are willing to become involved in their child's program. Joint involvement is not always desirable, however; it is not wise, for example, when severe marital conflict is occurring, especially when it involves the child (Kelly, 1974).

Once the scheduled appointment has been confirmed, the professional must specify objectives for the contact. Without specific objectives, conferences can become merely conversations that cannot be evaluated for effectiveness. With objectives clearly delineated, the professional can guide the conference to a successful conclusion.

Although objectives for the conference vary according to the individual needs of the child and the family, as well as the level of involvement at which the family is functioning, certain universal objectives can be identified. Included among these are the following:

- to establish a climate conducive to ongoing effective communication
- to understand the family dynamics and determine parental expectations for the child
- to explain the child's intervention program
- to provide documentation of the child's progress
- to gather information on the family's efforts to work with the child at home
- to allow parents to express feelings and concerns or to ask questions
- to establish future goals for the child's program or the family's involvement

Before the actual conference, the professional must gather data pertinent to the objectives of the conference. Such data include anecdotal records and reports of assessments, both formal and informal. If possible, a videotape of a child can be valuable and enjoyable as a record of child performance.

Conducting the Conference

Where the conference is conducted is as important as how it is conducted. Conferences should be held in private, but comfortable, rooms with all parties seated in adult-sized chairs. A relaxed, open atmosphere is essential to the success of the conference.

Professionals should be careful about consciously or unconsciously establishing physical or psychological barriers between themselves and the families. For example, the professional who sits behind the desk during the conference is suggesting that the family is subordinate to the professional. In contrast, sitting in a circle in comfortable chairs or around a table in adult-sized chairs facilitates face-to-face, meaningful interaction.

The professional can further enhance communication by adhering to the following guidelines:

- Show respect and concern by being attentive to the family.
- Maintain eye contact at all times.
- Do not use jargon or acronyms in explanations.
- Be specific and objective when presenting information.
- Answer any and all questions honestly, but sensitively.

- Use active listening skills as necessary.
- Plan future goals (and meetings) cooperatively with the parents.
- Clarify and summarize the results of the conference, including any joint decisions that may have been reached.

Evaluating the Conference

The conference does not end when the parent leaves. The effectiveness of the conference must be evaluated. The professional may use the following questions as a basis for such an evaluation:

1. Did I plan ahead by specifying goals and objectives for the conference?
2. Did I gather enough data to inform parents about their child and the program?
3. Was the conference held in a comfortable room free of physical (and psychological) barriers?
4. Did I use active listening when appropriate?
5. Was I attentive and open to parents' feelings, concerns, and questions?
6. Did I respond honestly and sensitively in jargon-free terms to the parents' questions?
7. Did we plan the child's future program and the family's involvement together?
8. Did I clarify and summarize the conference and subsequent decisions?

If satisfied with the answers to these questions, the professional can feel more confident regarding the quality of the conference. Parents may also be asked to evaluate the conferences they have with professionals.

Evaluation is useful only if it is employed to improve program services. Professionals should use evaluation data to improve their conferencing skills by planning in-service training in this area.

EXTENDED FAMILIES AND THE ATTITUDES OF OTHERS

Professionals in the many disciplines that serve young handicapped children and their families frequently forget that parents of handicapped children must interact not only with professionals, but also with their own parents, other relatives, neighbors, friends, and the public at large. Many of these interactions can be particularly painful for the parents, especially if someone they value reacts negatively to their handicapped child. Michaelis (1981) wrote of neighbors and friends who neither asked to hold nor play with her Down's syndrome baby. Eventually, her fear of nonacceptance by her friends caused her to lose touch with them.

Extended Families and Young Handicapped Children

Gabel and Kotsch (1981), in summarizing psychoanalytic and clinical data, indicated that the effect of grandchildren on grandparents is considerable. Grandchildren are often a source of joy and satisfaction to their grandparents, reviving their feelings of importance and giving them a new purpose in life. All of these highly positive elements may be seriously affected when the grandchild is handicapped.

Obviously, grandparents expect that a normal, healthy child will be born, which will somehow enhance their sense of survival and lessen their awareness of mortality. Thus, as it does in the parents, the arrival of a handicapped child may trigger in the grandparents a mourning process that includes the stages of denial, grief, and anger (Gabel & Kotsch, 1981). Denial may be seen in the grandparents' refusal to accept the diagnosis that the grandchild is handicapped (Gayton & Walker, 1974), which may delay the parents' own acceptance of the situation. Gabel and Kotsch (1981) reported that some grandparents even discouraged the handicapped child's parents from participating in intervention programs because they felt "special" help was not necessary.

Pieper (1976) suggested that there is a grief reaction for grandparents because they feel that the grandchild will never fulfill their needs as grandparents. Grandparents want to be proud of their grandchildren, to baby them, to spoil them, to care for them, and, perhaps above all, to love them without the burden and responsibility of raising them. Grief often becomes anger because grandparents blame either the son-in-law or daughter-in-law for having the "bad blood" that caused the child to be defective. Pieper (1976) reported that her mother-in-law felt her son's well-being, including his financial future, emotional makeup, community position, and independence, was threatened.

Grandparental reactions may be sufficiently negative to preclude their support or assistance at first. The grandparents and the parents must come to recognize the support that they can give each other. Many grandparents do not help or contribute because they are never really asked to do so. Parents must be open with grandparents, sharing the information they receive from professionals and letting grandparents know their help and guidance are needed.

Grandparents can be extremely helpful to the parents of handicapped children in at least two ways (Pieper, 1976). For example, they can encourage the parents to renew some social contacts with their peers. Grandparents may volunteer to be babysitters, but this may be a problem when the medical care needs are complicated (Gabel & Kotsch, 1981). Grandparents can also help by providing a different perspective. Parents are often too emotionally involved to render adequate solutions to the problems that occur. Very often, the grandparents can suggest simple, direct solutions to seemingly insoluble problems.

Professionals can help extended families, especially grandparents, to become knowledgeable about the child's handicap. If possible, grandparents should be included in training sessions so that they can acquire the skill to assist the child and can develop the feeling that their counsel and assistance are of value.

Siblings of Young Handicapped Children

Siblings of handicapped children face special problems in trying to cope with the problems in family relationships. It is normal for siblings to feel anxiety, guilt, anger, fear, and frustration over the time, money, and attention their parents give to the handicapped child. Siblings, especially adolescents, also may fear that their children "will turn out that way" or that their friends will not like them anymore. These feelings can then cause the normal sibling(s) to feel guilty because of their emotions. Unless the parents are cognizant of these feelings, a conflict can arise that may result in the siblings displaying antisocial behavior (Marion, 1981), or other serious problems.

Parents can prevent many problems by providing open, honest information to the siblings at a level they can comprehend. The siblings need to be informed of the nature of the handicap, the type of intervention program the child is in, and they should be given an honest appraisal of the perceived impact on the family constellation. Further, parents must be conscious of the fact that the siblings have needs that must be met. Adequate attention and involvement at the siblings' level of tolerance may help ease the tension that is likely to exist. Parents must also be cautious that they do not thrust too much responsibility on the siblings for the care of the handicapped child. Siblings should be allowed to be involved in the care and education of the handicapped child at a level they feel comfortable with. Involvement in training programs at the intervention site, agency, or school should be strictly voluntary. If siblings do become interested, they can provide extremely valuable assistance to their families.

One final caution for the professional is in order. Some parents may become martyrs for the handicapped child (Ross, 1964) and create a "handicapped family." Family counseling may be necessary to help all members to readjust to the altered family relationships.

Family Social Life

The birth of a handicapped child restricts the family members' social lives, relationships with friends, and the relationship between husband and wife. Many families of handicapped children withdraw into a tight circle when they find out the child is handicapped. It is not uncommon for the parents to stop seeing their old friends or to stop going out for an evening; they may be uncomfortable facing their friends, or they may not want to or may be unable to leave the child with a babysitter. This very normal situation may change as the parents become more accepting of the child, but it may take some encouragement by professionals before parents resume normal social activities.

Gordon (1976) noted that the stress of having a handicapped child in the family is often exacerbated by a lack of communication between the spouses about their feelings and their need for emotional support. Open, honest communication can be the beginning of a more healthy marriage relationship. Marriage counseling as an option should not be discussed, since some couples may see it as an admission of failure. Rather, the couple should be encouraged to seek out all options that may help them work out and discuss their problems.

Parent Organizations

Many authorities (Giacobbe et al., 1978; Gordon, I., 1976; Lerner, Mardell-Czudnowski, & Goldenberg, 1981) point out the value of the support that local, state, and national parent organizations can give to families of handicapped children. These groups are usually comprised of parents of like-handicapped children. They were formed initially to disseminate information to the public, secure needed services for children and families, and serve as advocates for legislative actions. Giacobbe and associates (1978) indicated that parent programs now address objectives that include

- developing public awareness relative to handicapping conditions and service needs
- representing the needs of children

- disseminating information to parents and professionals relative to a variety of critical issues, i.e., legal rights, program implementation, placement
- creating appropriate and necessary educational, vocational, and recreational programs
- supporting state and national associations

Table 3-1 provides a listing of national organizations that provide some or all of these services.

Table 3-1 National Organizations for Parent Services

Name	Address	Service
Alexander Graham Bell Association for the Deaf	3417 Volta Place, N.W. Washington, DC 20007 202/337-5220	National organization for parents and teachers interested in hearing-impaired children. Provides information on home training, amplification; has a large library on deafness.
Allergy Foundation of America	801 Second Avenue New York, NY 10017 212/876-8875	Provides a listing of allergy clinics available across the United States, as well as informational pamphlets describing different allergies (pamphlets cost 50¢ each).
Association for the Severely Handicapped	7010 Roosevelt Way, N.E. Seattle, WA 98115 206/523-8446	New national organization. Publishes a monthly newsletter for parents and professionals concerned with children having great needs for special assistance.
American Foundation for the Blind	15 West 11th Street New York, NY 10011 212/924-0420	Private agency. Provides information and referral services for the public.

American Speech, Language, and Hearing Association	1801 Rockville Pike Rockville, MD 20852 301/897-5700	Educational and professional organization for speech, language, and audiology. Provides clinical services. Free public information literature is available on request from the association.
Association for Children and Adults with Learning Disabilities (ACLD)	4156 Library Road Pittsburgh, PA 15234 412/881-1191	National organization within every state. Provides information on advocacy, publications, and new developments related to children with learning disabilities.
Closer Look	Box 1942 Washington, DC 20013 202/833-4160	National information center to help parents find out about rights, how to get services, and locate a local group. Publishes a free newsletter, *The Closer Report*, with much helpful information.
Down's Syndrome Congress	Ms. Betty Buczynski 16470 Ronnies Drive Mishawaka, IN 46544	National information service for and by parents of Down's syndrome retarded children. Publishes a monthly newsletter on new information of special interest ($5/year).
Epilepsy Foundation of America	1828 L Street, N.W. Washington, DC 20036 202/293-2930	National agency for people with epilepsy. Provides free information on epilepsy and educational materials to individuals and groups dealing with seizure disorders; provides referral service; monitors related legislative activity; is a strong advocate to help obtain needed services and rights for those with epilepsy.

Mental Health Association, National Headquarters	1800 North Kent Street Arlington, VA 22209 703/524-3352 703/524-4230	Provides referral services for parents; holds workshops and seminars on the various aspects of mental health; makes available to the public a large collection of free literature.
National Association for Retarded Citizens	2709 Avenue E East P.O. Box 6109 Arlington, TX 76011 817/261-4961	Has over 1,900 state and local chapters; promotes programs for retarded children and their families.
National Association for Visually Handicapped	305 East 24th Street New York, NY 10010 212/889-3141	Provides free learning materials for parents to help their children, including large print books and a monthly newsletter to keep families informed on the new techniques used with visually handicapped.
National Easter Seal Society for Crippled Children and Adults	2023 West Ogden Avenue Chicago, IL 60612 312/243-8400	National organization with local societies throughout the United States. Provides rehabilitation services to persons with physical handicaps.
National Hemophilia Foundation	25 West 39th Street New York, NY 10018 212/869-9740	Provides free literature on hemophilia and the handicapping conditions that can result from it; provides referral services; was directly responsible for the establishment of 23 centers for hemophilia that provide diagnostic services, training, and rehabilitation.
National Society for Autistic Children	169 Tampa Avenue Albany, NY 12208 518/489-7375	National organization. Provides information on the education and welfare of children with severe needs in communication and behavior.

Spina Bifida Association of America	343 S. Dearborn Chicago, IL 60604 312/662-1562	National association. Distributes information to parents and professionals; has local chapters throughout the United States.
United Cerebral Palsy Association, Inc.	66 East 34th Street New York, NY 10016 212/481-6300	National association. Provides information and services to families with a child with cerebral palsy.

Chapter 4

Rights and Responsibilities of Families of Young Handicapped Children

The long history of special education services for handicapped children is marked by many struggles, legislative initiatives and mandates, and court battles and victories that finally created the impetus for vital program services. Although it was not initiated by advocates for the handicapped, *Brown v. Board of Education* (1954) had a significant impact on the handicapped because it was the first Supreme Court case that focused on exclusionary practices of the schools, and the importance and protected status of education under the Fourteenth Amendment of the U.S. Constitution (Turnbull & Turnbull, 1978).

The basic argument in *Brown* was that the equal protection clause protected a class of persons, in this case, black children, and entitled them to education on equal terms with all other children. Looking back on *Brown* many years later, proponents of handicapped children's right to education realized that the handicapped were a "class" in the same way the Court had held that a racial minority was a class. Later court cases clarified the impact of *Brown* and made it meaningful for the handicapped.

EARLY LEGISLATION AND LITIGATION

The Handicapped Children's Early Education Assistance Act

According to LaVor and Krivit (1969), the Handicapped Children's Early Education Assistance Act (HCEEAA) was a landmark because it was the first piece of legislation in history designed exclusively for the handicapped; earlier legislation had always been attached as a rider to some other act. Harvey (1977) noted that the intent of the act, Public Law 90-538, was to encourage planning, experimenting, and innovating with replicable models for educating young handicapped children. The essential provisions of Public Law 90-538 were summarized by LaVor and Krivit as follows:

1. research—the provision of a sound knowledge base relative to preschool handicapped children and programs designed to serve them
2. development—the design of curriculums and strategies to meet the unique needs of preschool children with handicaps
3. demonstration—the creation of excellent programs that could be replicated in other communities
4. training—the development of a body of professionals and ancillary service personnel to staff new programs
5. implementation—the development of quality programs disseminated throughout the United States

While the HCEEAA was instrumental in demonstrating the impact of early intervention services, it did not mandate that states provide the services. As a result, many handicapped children remained unserved by public education.

Litigation on Behalf of the Handicapped

Among the many court cases filed on behalf of handicapped plaintiffs, two stand out as especially meaningful to the educational rights of handicapped children: *Pennsylvania Association for Retarded Children (PARC) v. Commonwealth of Pennsylvania* and *Mills v. D.C. Board of Education.* In the first, a consent decree (a final order entered by consent of all parties and approved by the court) established a right to a publicly funded education for all school-aged mentally retarded persons, regardless of the nature of the handicap. The consent decree included the following provisions:

> Having undertaken to provide a free public education to all of its children, including its exceptional children, the Commonwealth of Pennsylvania may not deny any mentally retarded child access to a free public program of education and training.
>
> It is the Commonwealth's obligation to place each mentally retarded child in a free, public program of education and training appropriate to the child's capacity—among the alternative programs of education and training required by statute to be available, placement in a regular public school class is preferable to placement in a special public school class and placement in a special public school class is preferable to placement in any other type of program of education and training.

The Secretary of Education shall be responsible for assuring that every mentally retarded child is placed in a program of education and training appropriate to his learning capacities, and to that end—he shall be informed as to the identity, condition and educational status of every mentally retarded child within the various school districts.

Insofar as the Department of Public Welfare is charged to "arrange for the care, training and supervision" of a child certified to it, the Department of Public Welfare must provide a program of education and training appropriate to the capacities of that child.*

Every retarded person between the ages of six and twenty-one years as of the date of this order and thereafter shall be provided access to a free public program of education and training appropriate to his capacities as soon as possible but in no event later than September 1, 1972.

Wherever defendants provide a pre-school program of education the training for children less than six years of age, whether kindergarten or how so ever called, every mentally retarded child of the same age as to the date of this order and hereafter shall be provided access to a free public program of education and training appropriate to his capacities.

With the acceptance of this decree, the Commonwealth of Pennsylvania assumed responsibility for providing education for all its mentally retarded individuals aged 6 to 21. If there was any weakness in this decision, it was that no constitutional principle was used to decide the case. Therefore, although it is a landmark case, *PARC* did not establish a constitutional or judicial precedent.

The second case, *Mills v. D.C. Board of Education,* was not settled by a consent decree, but by a judgment against the defendant board of education. *Mills* also differed from *PARC* in that all handicapped children, not just the retarded were the plaintiffs. Using the due process guarantees of the Fifth Amendment, the court in *Mills* ordered the District of Columbia Board of Education to provide each handicapped child of school age with a free and suitable education, regardless of the degree of physical, emotional, or mental disability.

---

*This provision was altered in the course of the implementation of the decree. A School Administrators' Memorandum issued in the summer of 1972 announced that, for a period of one year, education would be provided to children in institutions by the Department of Public Welfare, under the supervision of the Department of Education, but thereafter it was to be the responsibility of the Department of Education itself.

Many subsequent court cases during the early to mid-1970s established that education is essential if handicapped children are to function in society. Although the opinions seemed to establish clearly that *all* children could benefit from an education, it was not until the passage of Public Law 94-142 that the right to an education for all children became a national reality.

PUBLIC LAW 94-142: EDUCATION FOR ALL HANDICAPPED CHILDREN ACT

In November of 1975, President Gerald R. Ford signed into law the broadest federal legislation regarding education of the handicapped ever passed by the Congress of the United States. The purpose of this law is simple:

> It is the purpose of this Act to assure that all handicapped children have available to them, within the time periods specified, a free appropriate public education which emphasizes special education and related services designed to meet their unique needs. (Public Law 94-142, 1975, Sec. 3, C)

Several aspects of this act are critical from the parent-professional perspective.

Testing and Classification

Under the Education for All Handicapped Children Act,

(a) Tests and other evaluation materials
  (1) Are provided and administered in the child's native language or other mode of communication, unless it is clearly not feasible to do so;
  (2) Have been validated for the specific purpose for which they are used;
  (3) Are administered by trained personnel in conformance with instructions from the producer;
(b) Tests and other evaluation materials include those tailored to assess specific areas of educational need and not merely those which are designed to provide a single general intelligence quotient;
(c) These are selected and administered so as best to insure that when a test is administered to a child with impaired sensory,

manual or speaking skills, the test results accurately reflect the child's aptitude or achievement level or whatever other factor the test purports to measure, rather than reflecting the child's impaired sensory, manual, or speaking skills (except where those skills are the factors which the test purports to measure);

    (d) No single procedure is used as the sole criterion for determining an appropriate educational program for a child and placement;

    (e) The evaluation is made by a multidisciplinary team or group of persons, including at least one teacher or other specialist with knowledge in the area of suspected disability;

    (f) The child is assessed in all areas related to the suspected disability, including, where appropriate, health, vision, hearing, social and emotional status, general intelligence, academic performance, communicative status, and motor abilities.

The intent of the law is to ensure that individual variability is taken into account in the testing of any child with a suspected handicap. Furthermore, the law is designed to sensitize special educators to the fact that significant differences in child-rearing techniques, familial expectations and aspirations, linguistic experiences, availability of formal and informal learning experiences (Oakland & Matuszek, no date), and other factors important in a pluralistic society can influence the manner in which a child responds to a test instrument.

Parents should be aware that, under the law, certain basic requirements regarding testing must be met:

- The examiner must be skilled in establishing rapport, administering and scoring the tests, analyzing the results, and performing any other functions commonly assigned to the role.
- The sample of behaviors observed must be adequate in amount and clearly representative of the area (e.g., motor skills, language, or self-help) being tested. Furthermore, instruments that are used must be valid (that is, they must measure exactly what they are supposed to measure and not penalize a child for the handicap).
- The approach of the assessment must be multimeasure and multisource (Bagnato & Neisworth, 1981).

The term *multimeasure* indicates that a variety of assessment devices and approaches must be utilized to obtain a full and accurate profile of the child's strengths and weaknesses. Tucker (no date) maintains that there are at least nine areas of information that are essential to a comprehensive individual assessment:

1. observational data
2. other data available
3. language dominance
4. educational assessment
5. sensori-motor and/or psychologistic assessment
6. adaptive behavior
7. medical and/or developmental
8. personality assessment
9. intellectual assessment (p. 43)

The term *multisource* indicates that information must be gathered from an interdisciplinary team that includes school psychologists, early childhood special educators, parents, physicians, speech/language therapists, and physical or occupational therapists.

When these requirements have been met, parents and professionals can feel more confident that a child will be appropriately placed in an intervention program. As Tucker (no date) maintained,

> Only when all sources of data are considered in concert is an assessment truly comprehensive and only then do decision makers have the necessary information to make appropriate decisions about the educational placement and programming of a child referred for special education consideration. Placement on less data than this is to deny a child his civil rights as an individual. The assessment techniques used may be as nonbiased as presently possible, however, until all relevant data was available, a nonbiased decision is not possible. (p. 51)

Least Restrictive Appropriate Placement

The Education for All Handicapped Children Act makes it incumbent on service providers to ensure that

> To the maximum extent appropriate, handicapped children, including children in public or private institutions or other care facilities, are educated with children who are not handicapped; . . . special classes, separate schooling or other removal of handicapped children from the regular educational environment occurs only when the nature or severity of the handicap is such that education in regular classes with the use of supplementary aids

and services cannot be achieved satisfactorily. (Federal Register, 1977, 121.550)

While the more popular term *mainstreaming* is not used in either the law or the regulations, the implication is clear—the handicapped child is to receive services in integrated programs whenever feasible. As Vincent, Brown, and Getz-Sheftel (1981) noted, "Segregated programming has to be demonstrated to result in greater gain to the young handicapped child for it to be implemented" (p. 23).

From a judicial standpoint, mainstreaming is preferred "because the existence of separate, self-contained special education programs and schools was found to be equivalent to the establishment of separate but unequal systems of education" (Turnbull & Turnbull, 1978, p. 140). In the not too distant past, certainly prior to the passage of the Education for All Handicapped Children Act, it would not have been uncommon for special education facilities and programs to be inferior, funded at a lower level than regular education programs, and managed by the least capable professionals. Perhaps mainstreaming is viewed as a way of redressing the wrongs of the past while providing a means for children to progress to more normal educational experiences. As Turnbull and Turnbull (1978) noted, special education programs often become terminal placements for children with no place to go.

"Least restrictive" may be relatively easy to define, but a definition of "appropriate placement" is somewhat more difficult. The law does not define appropriate placement; rather, it says that the placement decided on by the individualized education program (IEP) committee is appropriate. Placement decisions are extremely difficult because the committee must determine how restrictive the placement must be.

This act clearly mandates that a range of placements be available so that each child can be placed in the least restrictive setting that is appropriate to the child's needs as determined by the IEP committee. The first such continuum of services was provided by Deno (1970), who used a cascade model of special education service. Unfortunately, this continuum may not be appropriate for preschool children, since many regular preschool programs are still outside the public school (i.e., in the private sector). In those states where preschool programs are mandated, they are required *only* for preschool children who are handicapped, which makes mainstreaming impossible. Further complicating the least restrictive environment concept is the fact that many of the most effective early intervention models are markedly "special" with one-to-one strategies, carefully designed and conducted contingency management programs, and ongoing assessment (Safford & Rosen, 1981).

Figure 4-1 Continuum of Alternative Placements for Preschool
Intervention Programs

Home-based services or family-child instruction in a central location

---

Regular program with consultation services

Regular program with modification

Regular program with support services

Integrated classroom

Segregated classroom in an agency or
neighborhood school

Segregated classroom in a special
school, center, or agency

Residential early
intervention programs

A continuum for preschool intervention programs appears in Figure 4-1.

The home-based approach is viewed as least restrictive, mainly because in our society it is "normal" for a child of preschool age to be cared for in the home. Because current economic and social changes have created many two-job and single parent families, the day care center is also a "normal" place for a child and may be considered a proper setting for the home-based approach. In this approach, a team member visits the home to provide training to the parent and family so that they can help to meet the child's needs. This same approach could be used with the parent and family going to a central location to receive training.

The regular program with consultant services involves a consultant or itinerant teacher who works with a teacher (but not directly with the child), e.g., to improve service delivery or develop materials. This may occur in a program such as Head Start or any other program serving handicapped children for day care, respite, or some other type of care. In the regular program with modification, an itinerant consultant and the teacher work together directly with the child. As is the case with the second option, the service to the child may be broad and may occur in virtually any type of facility. A child in a regular program with support services receives direct services from an itinerant consultant, such as physical therapy or speech therapy.

The integrated classroom is a specially designed early education program in which identified handicapped children are integrated with nonhandicapped children for education. This approach may involve child care facilities and preschools, but the central purpose is education.

When the segregated classroom in a neighborhood school or other agency is used, handicapped children are educated and receive support services only with other handicapped children. Nonhandicapped children are nearby, but they are not typically integrated for educational purposes. In the self-contained classroom in a special center, school, or agency, the child receives services in a location where only handicapped children are located for education and support services.

The child who is placed in a residential early childhood program for educational purposes never leaves the facility. Furthermore, this facility is not the domicile of the child's parents.

Individualized and Appropriate Education

The Education for All Handicapped Children Act uses the language "appropriate education" to mean an education that is suitable to and individualized for each handicapped child's unique needs. The tool for achieving the individualized education is the IEP, about which the act says:

> The term "individualized education program" means a written statement for each handicapped child developed in any meeting by a representative of the local educational agency or an intermediate educational unit who shall be qualified to provide, or supervise the provision of, specially designed instruction to meet the unique needs of handicapped children, the teacher, the parents or guardian of such child, and whenever appropriate, such child. (Sec. 601 cc)

The IEP in early intervention programs has several purposes:

1. The IEP meeting facilitates communication between parents and school personnel and enables them, as equal participants, jointly to determine the child's needs, services to be provided, and anticipated outcomes.
2. The IEP itself serves as the focal point for resolving any differences between the parents and the professionals, either through the meeting or through the procedural protections that are available to parents.

3. The IEP sets forth in writing a commitment of the resources necessary to provide a handicapped child with special education and related services.
4. The IEP is a management tool to ensure that each handicapped child is provided special education and related services appropriate to that child's special learning needs.
5. The IEP is a compliance/monitoring document that may be used by monitoring personnel from each government level to determine whether a handicapped child is actually receiving the free appropriate public education agreed to by the parents and the school.
6. The IEP serves as an evaluation device for use in determining the extent of the child's progress toward the projected outcomes. (*Note:* The law does not hold teachers or other professional personnel accountable if a handicapped child does not achieve the goals and objectives set forth in the IEP.)

The law further mandates in Sec. 121a.346 that the IEP be written to include the following elements:

(a) A statement of the child's present levels of educational performance;
(b) A statement of annual goals, including short term instructional objectives;
(c) A statement of the specific special education and related services to be provided to the child, and the extent to which the child will be able to participate in regular educational programs;
(d) The projected dates for initiation of services and the anticipated duration of the services; and
(e) Appropriate objective criteria and evaluation procedures and schedules for determining, on at least an annual basis, whether the short term instructional objectives are being achieved.

Components of the IEP

The IEP is truly the cornerstone of the Education for All Handicapped Children Act. It is not only crucial to the eventual success of the intervention process, but also facilitates meaningful parental participation. The law mandates that it be written to include the following components.

Summary of Present Levels of Performance. The results of the assessment process are included in the summary of the present levels of performance. By means of up-to-date, relevant, and reliable assessment data from all members of the interdisciplinary team, including the parents, the child's most pressing education or intervention needs are analyzed. The current levels of performance for handicapped preschoolers may include data on

- fine motor development
- gross motor development
- receptive language development
- expressive language development
- cognitive development
- self-help skills development
- social and emotional development
- individual temperaments and learning styles
- specific health problems (e.g., seizure conditions, allergies, medication needs)

Annual Goals. The IEP committee must address the basic question "What do we want the child to be able to do after one year of education or intervention services?" Again, this is linked to the assessment process; sound decisions as to priority educational goals can be made only from sound assessment data. Parents are an important source of information regarding the actual content of the goals, but the agreement of the team in regard to the annual goals is the real guarantee of the appropriateness of the IEP.

For each annual goal developed from the summary of present levels of performance, there must be accompanying short-term objectives. These are intermediate instructional steps that must be taken to accomplish the stated goals. In order to be meaningful, these short-term objectives should be stated in terms of observable or measurable child behaviors with specific criteria of acceptable performance.

Specific Special Education and Related Services. Each IEP must contain a list of all the special services that are needed to meet each child's individual needs. Special education is defined in the law as follows:

1. . . . specially designed instruction, at no cost to the parent, to meet the unique needs of a handicapped child, including classroom instruction, instruction in physical education, home instruction, and instruction in hospitals and institutions.
2. The term includes speech pathology, or any other related service, if the service consists of specially designed instruction, at no cost to the parents, to meet the unique needs of a handicapped child, and is considered "special education" rather than a "related service" under State standards. (Sec. 121a.14)

Related services are defined as

> transportation and such developmental, corrective, and other
> supportive services as are required to assist a handicapped child
> to benefit from special education, . . . speech pathology and
> audiology, psychological services, physical and occupational
> therapy, recreation, early identification and assessment of dis-
> abilities in children, counseling services, and medical services
> for diagnostic or evaluative purposes. The term also includes
> school health services, social work services in schools, and par-
> ent counseling and training. (Sec. 121a.13)

This component must also contain a statement of the amount of time
the child will participate in regular programs—the least restrictive environment. Although the term *mainstreaming* is not used in the law, it is
very clear that both Congress and the courts intended for handicapped
children to be educated with nonhandicapped children to the maximum
extent feasible. Therefore, the IEP committee must determine:

1. Is integration for the handicapped child appropriate?
2. If appropriate, is integration possible? As indicated earlier, there
   may be preschool programs only for children who are handicapped,
   thus affording no means for integration.
3. If appropriate and possible, how much integration can be provided?
   This may be a percentage of time, or a number of hours per day.

Dates for Initiation and Duration of Services. The IEP must clearly
indicate when the special education or related services will be initiated
and how long they are to continue. These requirements are intended both
to ensure accountability of the service provider and to imply that services
or any form of special education need not be terminal in nature.

Evaluation Criteria and Timelines. If the objectives are written in measurable terms with specific criteria of acceptable performance, it is much
easier to determine whether objectives (and goals) have been achieved.
The law requires that the IEP contain information on the exact method,
criteria, and person responsible for evaluating each objective.

The IEP must be finalized prior to placement of the child in a program.
Furthermore, the IEP must be in effect before special education and related
services are provided. The IEP is to be reviewed and revised at least once
a year by the IEP committee or at the time a program change is recommended. Less formal reviews may be held as frequently as a committee
may consider appropriate.

IEP Format

The law does not specify the format of the IEP, only that it must contain the preceding components. Thus, a variety of formats is possible. Exhibit 4-1 is a sample IEP format for young handicapped children.

Composition of the IEP Committee

The law stipulates that the following people must be involved in the development of an IEP:

1. a representative of the agency or other service provider (not the teacher), or a designee who is qualified to provide or supervise the provision of special education. This representative must have the authority to commit the agency's or school district's resources for the provision of services.
2. the teacher.
3. the child's parent(s), guardian, or surrogate.
4. when appropriate, the child.

The law allows other individuals to be present at the discretion of either the family or the service provider. When a child's abilities are being evaluated for the first time and the committee is meeting to determine the child's initial placement or service, the law mandates that the primary diagnostician or evaluator be a member of the committee or that the agency representative or teacher be knowledgeable about evaluation procedures and qualified to interpret results.

Besides the letter of the law that requires parental participation in the IEP process, the spirit of the law promotes the parent-professional partnership for the child's best interests. The law stipulates that the public agency take steps to ensure parent participation in the IEP, including

- advance notice of meetings
- mutually convenient scheduling of meetings
- arrangement for interpreters for deaf or non-English speaking parents
- other means, such as conference telephone calls, to involve the parents

If these steps have been taken and the parents are still unwilling to participate, the agency may hold an IEP meeting without the parents. The agency must, however, document the attempt to notify parents with a record of telephone communication, written correspondence, and visits to the home or parents' place of employment. When possible, a signed waiver verifying parental refusal to participate in the IEP development should be obtained.

Exhibit 4-1 Sample Individualized Education Program (IEP)

NAME _____ DATE OF BIRTH _____

PARENT(S) NAME _____ ADDRESS _____

TELEPHONE (Home) _____ (Work) _____ FOR EMERGENCIES _____

PRIMARY LANGUAGE OF CHILD AT HOME _____ CHILD ALLERGIC TO _____

PRESENT LEVEL OF PERFORMANCE/CHILD'S SKILLS IN FOLLOWING DEVELOPMENTAL AREAS:

DATE OF EVALUATION _____ INSTRUMENT(S) USED _____

_____

_____

_____

ACADEMICS/COGNITIVE _____

LANGUAGE/COMMUNICATION _____

SELF-HELP _____

SOCIAL/EMOTIONAL _____

PSYCHOMOTOR/GROSS/FINE MOTOR _____

OTHERS _____

LONG-TERM GOALS:	Increase/Decrease	Desired Amount	Desired Accomplishment Date
1.			
2.			
3.			
4.			
5.			

(Use additional pages as necessary.)

SHORT-TERM INSTRUCTIONAL OBJECTIVES: Observable behavior, criterion	Initiation Date	Staff Responsible
For GOAL # 1		
For GOAL #2		
For GOAL #3		
For GOAL #4		

Page 2

NAME _____   PRIMARY LANGUAGE OF HOME _____

PERSONS RESPONSIBLE FOR IMPLEMENTING THIS IEP _____

(Parent)   (Teacher)

RELATED SERVICES PROVIDED: (By whom, how often)

1. _____

2. _____

EXTENT OF PARTICIPATION IN EXPERIENCES WITH NONHANDICAPPED CHILDREN: _____

COMMITTEE SIGNATURES:

TEACHER _____
            Name   Title

AGENCY REPRESENTATIVE _____
                         Name   Title

Exhibit 4-1 continued

TEAM MEMBERS _____
Name   Title

_____
Name   Title

_____
Name   Title

The IEP is not a binding contract. No agency, teacher, or any other person may be held accountable if a child does not achieve growth projected in the objectives.

DATE OF IEP DEVELOPMENT _____

I have had the oppportunity to participate in the annual development/review of this IEP. I have had my rights and responsibilities explained to me in my primary language. I understand that there will be at least an annual review of my child's progress.

Please check one:
☐ I agree with this IEP.
☐ I do not agree with this IEP.
☐ I refuse permission for any special education or related services at this time.

_____   _____
Parent/Guardian/Surrogate   Date

DUE PROCESS PROCEDURES FOR FAMILIES AND CHILDREN

Due process protection—the right of any individual to protest prior to the initiation of government action—is a constitutional guarantee under both the Fifth and Fourteenth Amendments. The constitutional safeguard that no one shall be deprived of life, liberty, or property without due process of law is extended to handicapped children and their families in educational matters because education is viewed as a property right. Thus, handicapped children, through their parents, have the right to protest actions of state or local education agencies. As Turnbull and Turnbull (1978) noted,

> Without a means of challenging the multitude of discriminatory practices that the schools had habitually followed, the children would have found that their right to be included in an educational program and to be treated nondiscriminatively (to receive a free appropriate education) would have a hollow ring. (p. 171)

The procedural safeguards are designed to produce both correct and fair results. Abeson and Zettel (1977) summarized the required due process elements of the Education for All Handicapped Children Act as follows:

1. Written notification before evaluation. In addition, the right to an interpreter/translator if the family's native language is not English (unless it is clearly not feasible to do so).
2. Written notification when initiating or refusing to initiate a change in educational placement.
3. Opportunity to present complaints regarding the identification, evaluation, placement, or the provision of a free appropriate education.
4. Opportunity to obtain an independent educational evaluation of the child.
5. Access to all relevant records.
6. Opportunity for an impartial due process hearing including the right to:
   a. Receive timely and specific notice of the hearing.
   b. Be accompanied and advised by counsel and by individuals with special knowledge or training with respect to the problems of children with handicaps.
   c. Confront, cross examine, and compel the attendance of witnesses.

    d. Present evidence:
      1. Written or electronic verbatim record of the hearing.
      2. Written findings of fact and decision.
  7. The right to appeal the findings and decisions of the hearing.

Notification

Prior to passage of the Education for All Handicapped Children Act, Public Law 94-142, agencies providing services to young handicapped children could, and often did, initiate or terminate placement or intervention before they notified the parents of their intentions. Thus, such actions were often taken without the parents' knowledge or consent. Public Law 94-142 changed that, however, since it requires any agency providing education to young handicapped children to give prior written notice to the family whenever it proposes to initiate or change, or refuses to initiate or change, identification, placement, assessment, or the provision of a free appropriate public education. Such notices must contain

(1) A full explanation of all the procedural safeguards available to the parents . . .;
(2) A description of the action proposed or refused by the agency, an explanation of why the agency proposes or refuses to take the action, and a description of any options the agency considered and the reasons why those options were rejected;
(3) A description of each evaluation procedure, test, record, or report the agency uses as a basis for the proposal or refusal; and
(4) A description of any other factors which are relevant to the agency's proposal or refusal. (Sec. 121a.505)

It also requires that the notice be

(1) Written in language understandable to the general public, and
(2) Provided in the native language of the parent or other mode of communication used by the parent, unless it is clearly not feasible to do so. (Sec. 121a.505)

If the native language or other mode of communication of the parent is not a written language, the state or local education agency must take steps to ensure

(1) That the notice is translated orally or by other means to the parent in his or her native language or other mode of communication;
(2) That the parent understands the content of the notice; and
(3) That there is written evidence that the requirements (of oral translation and parent understanding) have been met. (Sec. 121a.505)

Access to Records and an Independent Evaluation

Although previously schools and other agencies providing educational services had routinely denied parents access to their child's records, Public Law 94-142 is clear in its stipulation that parents have a right to read and review any and all records on the child's identification, evaluation, placement, or the provision of a free appropriate public education. Furthermore, the agency must give the family a copy of the IEP if requested to do so.

The law provides that parents may request an independent evaluation of their child's abilities, that is, an evaluation by someone who is (a) not employed by the agency providing services to the child and (b) qualified—having met certification, licensure, or other requirements of the service-providing agency—to administer tests or conduct procedures to determine if a child is handicapped and the nature and extent of the special education and related services needed. The law requires that, if asked, the service provider must inform the family regarding where independent evaluations can be obtained. In some instances, the hearing officer in a due process hearing may require the service provider to pay for an independent evaluation. If parents obtain an independent evaluation at their own expense, the law requires that it be considered among the evidence presented at a due process hearing or used in the IEP process.

Complaints, Due Process Hearings, and the Right to Appeal

The right of families to register complaints is tied closely to their right to a fair and impartial due process hearing. The law stipulates that parents must be given the opportunity to present complaints about their child's identification, evaluation, placement, or free appropriate public education. In the event of a parental complaint, the school district may initiate mediation to redress the complaint without a due process hearing. Nonetheless, it is required to take the initial steps toward a hearing that would result in a decision within 45 days after the complaint is received.

Exhibit 4-2 shows the steps involved in a request for a due process hearing following a parental complaint.

Exhibit 4-2 Due Process Hearing

FAMILY

Registers, in writing, a request for a hearing. Typical is a complaint about the child's identification, evaluation, placement, or free appropriate public education.

⇨

AGENCY

Informs parents about any available free or low-cost aid in the area.

⇨

⇨

May enter into mediation with family.

⇨

Appoints or arranges for the appointment of a qualified, impartial hearing officer for the case. The law provides that this person *may not* be employed by the agency involved in providing the service, nor may the person have a personal or professional interest that might interfere with objectivity in the hearing.

⇨

HEARING OFFICER

Contacts parents to determine if they (a) have been informed of their rights under the Education for All Handicapped Children Act, (b) prefer a particular time and location for the hearing, (c) need an interpreter, and (d) want an open or closed hearing.

Contacts the agency to determine a time and location preference.

Arranges for the hearing, notifies the parties, and provides for a verbatim record of the proceedings.

Ensures that both parties disclose all evidence and witnesses at least five days before the hearing.

⇨

THE HEARING

⇨	⇨	⇨
Family	Hearing Officer	Agency
Has the right to	Presides over the hearing and may question witnesses; also must rule on any objections filed by either party.	Has the right to
● be accompanied by an attorney or by other experts in special education.		● be represented by legal counsel.
● present evidence and confront, examine, and cross-examine witnesses.		● present evidence and confront, examine, and cross-examine witnesses.
● compel the attendance of witnesses.		● compel the attendance of witnesses.
● make written or electronic verbatim record of the hearing.		● make written and oral arguments.
● receive a written decision by the hearing officer,		● receive a written or electronic verbatim record of the hearing.
		● receive a written decision.

Exhibit 4-2 continued

Family	Agency
including findings of fact, no later than 45 days after the initial request for a hearing. (The hearing officer may grant an extension.)	● appeal the decision of the hearing officer.
● have the child present.	
● have the hearing open or closed to the general public.	
● appeal the decision of the hearing officer to the State Board of Education or to a state or federal district court.	

✧

THE DECISION

Hearing officer provides all parties with a written decision, including findings of fact, based solely on the evidence presented during the hearing. Unless one of the parties appeals the hearing officer's decision or begins a court action after an appeal, the decision of the initial hearing is final.

✧

THE APPEAL

✧   ✧

Either party may appeal the decision of the hearing officer. If the hearing is being held by a local school district, the appeal is filed with the State Board of Education, which has 30 days to review the case, reach a decision, and send a written decision to both parties. If there is no further appeal, the decision of the State Board would be final.	When there is no appeal to the State Board of Education, the parties may file a civil action in either a state court or a federal district court.

✧

THE CHILD

Remains in current placement during the hearing process or the time of the appeal, unless *both* parties agree otherwise.

RESPONSIBILITIES OF PARENTS OF YOUNG HANDICAPPED CHILDREN

Professionals who work with parents of young handicapped children should identify the responsibilities that they expect parents to assume. Of course, the empathic and knowledgeable professional must know *when* to introduce these expectations into the parent-professional relationship. As in all other aspects of the relationship, the professional must judge the level of acceptance, tolerance, and readiness of the parent before introducing new demands.

Understanding the Child

During the preschool years, nonhandicapped children use many trial-and-error behaviors to establish their sense of belonging and trust within the family. Since a family environment is generally dynamic, the children are frequently actively involved in attempting to shape or mold that environment. If a behavior works and fits into the children's goals, they will incorporate it into their repertoire. While handicapped children may attempt to operate in the same fashion in their environment, limitations of the disability, whether motoric, cognitive, or sensory, may affect the manner in which they "learn" what works and what does not work.

Parents must attempt to understand their handicapped child. They must ask themselves such questions as

- How does the child act on the environment?
- What limitations, if any, has the impairment imposed?
- What compensations, or even overcompensations, has the child developed?
- What are the child's strengths or assets?
- What kind of family atmosphere is being presented to demonstrate a pattern of family relationships?
- Where does the handicapped child fit into this atmosphere?

Intervention programs can help parents answer these and other questions. If parents assume the responsibility of understanding their child, parent-child interactions can become more positive and healthy.

Showing Respect for the Child

Parents of a young handicapped child sometimes view the child as handicapped first and a child second. Parents must regard their handicapped child as a *child first,* however, with the same rights and needs that all human beings have. Professionals should model this behavior for parents and help them to develop confidence in their child and to recognize the abilities that the child does possess. When the parents are able to show respect for the child, they can promote optimum growth of the child.

Building on the Child's Strengths

A natural tendency of parents (and, unfortunately, some professionals) is to focus on what the child cannot do, on the disability and the weaknesses. Instead, parents must build on the child's strengths. By encouraging parents to focus their energy and attention on what their child does well, professionals help them to minimize what the child is unable to do.

Handicapping conditions are labels, and "when we label a child, we see him as we have labeled him" (Dreikurs, 1964). The mentally retarded are thus "too dumb," the behavior-disordered are "brats" and so on. In this fashion, parents perpetuate certain behaviors rather than encouraging their children to overcome disabilities and move in a constructive direction.

Establishing and Maintaining a Routine

For whatever reasons, some parents of young handicapped children fail to provide a routine for their children, a structure that clearly identifies the boundaries of their lives. Routine and structure permit families to function effectively while promoting children's socialization, self-sufficiency, and independence. Without the routine, children become self-indulgent, unsocialized, and dependent on others. A lack of structure also invites noncompliance, a behavior pattern that prevents the meaningful integration of many handicapped preschoolers into mainstream service delivery patterns that require compliance for child success.

When parents shun the responsibility of establishing and maintaining a routine, they invite serious disruption of the family atmosphere. Handicapped children who have no structure in their lives frequently infringe on the rights of other family members, thereby adding to the already negative image that parents and siblings may hold.

Making Time for Training

Professionals frequently become disillusioned when parents refuse or fail to work with their handicapped children on important educational goals or skills in the home. While many nonhandicapped children learn through imitation or observation, most handicapped children require specific and systematic instruction to acquire daily living and other skills. Parents must set aside the time to provide this training for their handicapped child, incorporating it into the daily routine. They need to be alerted to the many moments that occur in the course of a day (e.g., feeding time, dressing time, bathing time) during which important social, self-help, language, and motor skills can be taught.

While parents are responsible for taking the time to train their child, professionals are responsible for teaching parents to observe and record behavior, perform a task analysis of selected target skills, reinforce appropriate behaviors, use correct instructional strategies, and document progress. Parent responsibilities for instruction can and should be written into the IEP, further ensuring the meaningful participation of parents in the intervention process.

With the current government budget cuts, it becomes even more urgent for parents to shoulder some of the responsibility for educating their young handicapped children. Professionals cannot afford to allow parents "to drop off children for something to be done." Rather, professionals must encourage parents to function as equal partners in the educative process.

Avoiding Overprotection

It is not uncommon for parents of young handicapped children to overprotect their children. This reaction seems to be most common among parents of physically handicapped, Down's syndrome, and visually impaired children. Robinson and Robinson (1976) identified four factors in mentally retarded children suggestive of overprotection: (1) adaptive behavior ratings lower than those expected in view of the mental age, (2) continual requests for assistance, (3) poor large muscle coordination in the absence of physical impairments, and (4) problems in separating from their mothers.

Dreikurs (1964) identified two major reasons for parental overprotection: (1) a need to be dominant and keep children submissive so that they are helpless and dependent; and (2) feelings of inadequacy that are projected onto the child. Dreikurs presents an example of parental overprotection that could make a child feel helpless and in need of protection from life's problems:

> Two months ago it was discovered that Joe, six, has diabetes.
> He is given a daily dose of oral insulin which Mother calls his
> "vitamins." Joe has not been told anything about his condition.
> Mother justifies her actions on the basis that she doesn't want

Joe to become "odd." All discussion of the disorder with the doctor is done out of Joe's presence. She reminds him daily that he must eat only what she gives him so that the "vitamins" will work. (p. 189)

The child in this example is old enough to be told about his problem, and the appropriate parental attitude could establish a healthy attitude in the child. The child, while aware of his medical problem, can learn to manage it, to prevent it from becoming a great handicap, and to live a normal or near normal life.

Linde and Kopp (1973) describe a number of ways professionals can help parents face the day-to-day problems of having a mentally retarded preschooler in the family. First, the professional can be a sounding board and ally. In this capacity, the professional communicates to the parents a respect for the capabilities of the child, something that the parents may not recognize or may have forgotten during trying times. Second, the professional can become a role model, demonstrating a respect for the right of the handicapped preschooler to take ordinary risks. The professional can help parents realize that "overprotection endangers the . . . [child's] human dignity, and tends to keep him from experiencing the risk taking of ordinary life which is necessary for normal human growth and development" (Perske, 1972, p. 195). Third, the professional can urge parents to become involved with parent groups. If overprotecting parents can meet with other parents whose children have taken some risks, over-protection may dissipate.

Encouraging Independence

Dreikurs (1964) notes that parents should "never do for a child what he can do for himself" (p. 193). This is an extremely important concept that must be conveyed to parents of young handicapped children. In the case of handicapped children, it may be wise to modify the rule to read, "never do for a child what he can be taught to do for himself." Many times parents of a young handicapped child become frustrated and discouraged when their child takes a long time either to acquire or to perform a skill. The parent may find it easier to feed the child or dress the child than to wait for the child to learn to do it or watch as the child takes a long, sometimes struggling path to the completion of the skill.

Children enjoy having things done for them. If parents reinforce this behavior, they are really conveying two things to the child: (1) they do not trust the child to do the skill and, thus, do not respect the child; and (2) the child's natural desire to do things independently is stifled.

Parents must assume the responsibility for promoting independence in their handicapped child. As young children strive to explore their environment, as facilitated by the parents if necessary, they experience success and competence. As young handicapped children succeed in and on more complex environments, they develop the skills to solve problems and become more self-sufficient. When parents "let go" and allow this to occur, they show not only respect for the child but also a willingness to build on the child's strengths.

Being Consistent

Parents must be consistent with their young handicapped child. As indicated earlier, it is extremely important for children to develop a sense of order. It is imperative for them to know that certain behaviors will routinely result in certain consequences—either pleasant or unpleasant—and that behavior rewarded by their father will also be rewarded by their mother. As I. Gordon (1976) noted, children "need the comfort that parents do not operate from whim, but some sense of consistency, both within the individual parent and between the parents" (p. 136).

The theory and principles of behavior modification indicate that consistency is important to behavior acquisition or extinction. While it is not possible to be consistent at all times, parents must follow through on consequences for appropriate and inappropriate behavior. According to Dreikurs (1964), children learn from interactions in the environment with the use of natural consequences (those that follow an event without parental intervention) and logical consequences (those that parents structure logically to follow a misdeed). As is the case with reinforcement or the withholding of reinforcement, "accurate and consistent application of logical consequences is often remarkably effective and may result in amazing reduction of friction and an increase in family harmony" (Dreikurs, 1964, p. 85).

Being Honest with Professionals

Parents must be honest in their relationships with professionals. Unfortunately, the history of parent-professional interactions in early intervention programs has not always been positive and facilitating. Many professionals view parent input suspiciously or negatively. Marion (1981) talks about the "uneasy truce"; Blatt (1979), in describing the reasons that the parent-professional relationship has not really been a partnership, argues that parents "refuse to remember that people are people, that all are in need of something and someone" (p. 6).

When both parties trust and respect each other, when lines of communication are established, and when the relationship is characterized by honest sharing of feelings, values, concerns, and objections, the parent-professional relationship can become a real partnership.

ALLOWING PARENTS TO BE FREE

Sometimes professionals fail to allow parents to be free of the awesome burdens and responsibilities of raising a handicapped child. Certainly, parents of handicapped young children are entitled to some of the freedoms (Gordon, 1975) in today's society:

- freedom to feel that they have done the best they could
- freedom to enjoy life as intensely as possible, even though they have an exceptional child
- freedom to let their handicapped child have privacy
- freedom to have hostile thoughts once in a while without feeling guilty
- freedom to enjoy being alone at times
- freedom to tell people about their child's progress and achievements with a real sense of pride
- freedom to have their own hobbies and interests
- freedom to tell teachers and other professionals what they really feel about the job the professionals are doing and demand that their opinions be respected
- freedom to devote as much time as they want to the handicap cause; to get away from it for a while and return if they want
- freedom to tell their child when they are displeased with the child, even though their child has a handicap
- freedom to refrain from praising their child gratuitously, even though they have been told to offer much praise
- freedom to lie once in a while and say everything is fine; not to feel compelled to tell the truth to everyone who asks
- freedom to say at times that they do not want to talk about their problems or their handicapped child
- freedom to have an annual vacation without the children, to have dates, celebrations, weekends away, time together to enhance their marriage
- freedom to spend a little extra money on themselves, even though they feel they cannot afford it

Part II

Families with Special Needs

Young children with special needs are a heterogeneous group. Thus, the problems of definition, characteristics, and treatment approaches vary widely. This section and the chapters in it are organized to reflect answers to seven common questions that parents ask about their exceptional children:

1. What is *(the name of the category)?*
2. What are the characteristics of *(name of category)* children?
3. How many children are likely to be *(category)?*
4. How are *(category)* children identified?
5. What is the impact of *(category)* on families?
6. What is the impact of *(category)* on the future lives of children?
7. What intervention strategies can be used for *(category)* children?

The section is organized strictly along categorical lines; the labeling versus nonlabeling argument is largely a sham battle. Programs are funded by category; current laws, both federal and state, are categorical; professionals use categories to facilitate communication; and parents want answers specific to their child's category.

This book has been written mainly to help professionals facilitate communication with parents and even other professionals. The preponderance of evidence points to the need for categories, despite what the author (or the reader) personally feels about labeling. Thus, Chapter 5 contains the answers to the questions about children who have sensory, physical, and learning disorders. In Chapter 6, mental retardation is discussed; in Chapter 7, emotional disturbance. Chapter 8 presents information on gifted and talented young children.

Families of Children with Sensory, Physical, and Learning Disorders

Grouping the sensory impairments (e.g., blindness, deafness) with the physical or crippling conditions and health impairments is not unusual, because in toto they are often referred to as low-incidence handicapping conditions. Although they occur infrequently in the population, they nonetheless require the assistance of special educators and other professional personnel.

Learning disabilities, by virtue of definition and practice, remain essentially a problem of academic or school-related failure. Estimates of the incidence of learning disabilities in *school-aged* populations can run as high as 30 percent (Lerner, 1976). Most mildly mentally retarded children escape detection until they enter school, when their academic or social inadequacies set them apart from their peers. Even with a strict definition of learning disabilities, i.e., severe and pervasive learning problems, most truly learning-disabled children will not be identified until school age. Because of the variability in child growth and development, and the lack of predictive validity for infant intelligence measures, only the most severely involved young children will be recognized as learning-disabled during the preschool years. There remains a dearth of research on the validity of predicting later school-related academic performance on the basis of *presumably* related behaviors in the infant and toddler years.

WHAT ARE THE COMMON SENSORY, PHYSICAL, AND LEARNING DISORDERS?

Sensory Impairments

Visual Impairments

Many definitions of visual impairments have been proposed by many disciplines for various purposes. For a variety of reasons, primarily legal ones, the definition of blindness proposed by the Social Security Board in 1935 (with modification) is used in literature describing blindness. Historically, then, those with visual impairments have been divided into two major categories:

1. the legally blind: corrected vision in the better eye is 20/200* or less, or the widest diameter of the visual field subtends an angle no greater than 20 degrees
2. the partially sighted: corrected vision in the better eye is 20/70 or less

These legal definitions have virtually no value for educational purposes, however, because they emphasize the disability of the person. Furthermore, the term *blind* conjures up an image of the person who can see "nothing" when, in fact, an extremely small percentage of people labeled blind actually have *no* useful vision (Ward, 1979).

The emphasis on using and stimulating low vision, as well as on early educational intervention, was spurred by research demonstrating that children with low vision could learn to use the vision they had more effectively (Barraga, 1964). Educators became more concerned then with definitions that stressed functional visual efficiency (DuBose, 1979a) and the alterations necessary in the learning environment to maximize achievement.

Barraga (1976) proposed the use of the umbrella term *visually handicapped* to refer to all children requiring special education programs because of visual problems. A child with a visual handicap is "one whose visual impairment interferes with his optimal learning and achievement, unless adaptations are made in the methods of presenting learning experiences, the nature of the materials used, and/or in the learning environment" (p. 16). This includes children who are blind, have low vision, or are visually limited, defined as follows:

---

*A 20/200 distance visual acuity means that an individual must be at a distance of 20 feet to read the letters or symbols on a chart that the person with normal vision could read at a distance of 200 feet.

- blind. Children with no vision at all and those with only light perception and no light projection are considered blind.
- low vision. Children with low vision usually have little distance vision. When provided with adequate lighting and carefully selected materials, these children can see objects held from a few inches to several feet away from the eyes.
- visually limited. Children with visual handicaps may still have useful vision. They are treated as seeing children who may need special lighting, prescription lenses, or other optical aids (e.g., magnifiers, large print).

Hearing Impairments

Numerous terms and definitions are used to describe children with hearing impairments. An authoritative statement on definition was jointly proposed in 1975 by the Conference of Executives of American Schools for the Deaf and the Convention of American Instructors of the Deaf. This report suggested the following:

- Hearing Impairment: A generic term indicating a hearing disability which may range in severity from mild to profound: it included the subsets of deaf and hard of hearing.
- A deaf person is one whose hearing disability precludes successful processing of linguistic information through audition, with or without a hearing aid.
- A hard of hearing person is one who, generally with the use of a hearing aid, has residual hearing sufficient to enable success for processing of linguistic information through audition. *(Report of the Ad Hoc Committee,* p. 509)

Since age of onset of the hearing loss affects language and speech aquisition and thus is significant for educational intervention purposes, two other terms included in the report must be considered:

- Prelingual deafness: Deafness present at birth, or occurring early in life at an age prior to the development of speech or language.
- Postlingual deafness: Deafness occurring at an age following the development of speech and language. (p. 510)

Physical Impairments

Much of the literature on the subject of physically handicapping conditions describes orthopedically and health-impaired children. Public Law 94-142 defines this broad, yet numerically small, category of special education as follows:

> Orthopedically impaired means severe orthopedic impairment which adversely affects a child's educational performance. The term includes impairments caused by congenital anomaly, impairments caused by disease, and impairments from other causes such as fractures, or burns that can cause contractures. Other health impaired means limited strength, vitality or alertness due to chronic or acute health problems such as a heart condition, epilepsy, tuberculosis, rheumatic fever, nephritis, asthma, sickle cell anemia, hemophilia, lead poisoning, leukemia, or diabetes, which adversely affects a child's educational performance.

Gearheart's (1980) classifications of crippling conditions and health impairments illustrate the diversity of this category of special education. The four classifications suggested by Gearheart (1980) are

1. neurologically related disabilities: cerebral palsy, spina bifida, epilepsy
2. musculoskeletal and orthopedic disabilities: muscular dystrophy, osteogenesis imperfecta, arthritis
3. cardiovascular and respiratory system disabilities: cystic fibrosis, asthma, congenital heart defects
4. disabilities of metabolic origin: diabetes

Learning Disorders

Among the many definitions of learning disabilities, the most commonly accepted is that endorsed by the federal government and incorporated in Public Law 94-142:

> Specific learning disability means a disorder in one or more of the basic psychological processes involved in the understanding or in using language, spoken or written, which may manifest itself in an imperfect ability to listen, think, speak, read, write, spell, or to do mathematical calculations. The term includes such conditions as perceptual handicaps, brain injury, minimal brain dys-

function, dyslexia, and developmental aphasia. The term does not include children who have learning problems which are primarily the result of visual, hearing, or motor handicaps, of mental retardation, or of environmental, cultural, or economic disadvantage.

This definition attempts to differentiate between truly learning-disabled children and those who are remedial readers or slow learners. Wallace and McLoughlin (1979) stress that the federal definition applies to "children and youth who have very severe and specific learning disabilities" requiring special education intervention (p. 7).

Several basic dimensions cut across most definitions of learning disabilities. Wallace and McLoughlin (1979) have identified four such dimensions:

1. a discrepancy between potential and actual performance
2. indications in academic subjects or language of strengths and weaknesses in learning
3. intactness of sensory modalities, i.e., no deafness or blindness
4. a focus on an explanation for the learning problem

Hallahan and Kauffman (1976) have listed five major ideas included in most definitions of learning disabilities:

1. There is academic retardation.
2. There is an uneven pattern of development.
3. There may or may not be evidence of central nervous system involvement.
4. Environmental disadvantage is not the cause of the learning problem.
5. Learning problems are not caused by emotional disturbance or mental retardation.

WHAT ARE THE CHARACTERISTICS OF CHILDREN WITH SENSORY, PHYSICAL, AND LEARNING DISORDERS?

Sensory Impairments

Visual Impairments

In reporting the results of various studies of visually impaired persons, Bryan and Bryan (1979) noted that there was no psychology of blindness per se. Yet the visually impaired do evidence certain differences in various areas.

Intellectual/Cognitive Characteristics. Visual impairments do not automatically result in lower scores on standardized intelligence tests. On the other hand, there is considerable evidence to suggest that the development of conceptual abilities in blind children does lag behind that in sighted children (e.g., Stephens & Simpkins, 1974), particularly on tasks that require abstract thinking. Children with visual impairments tend to deal concretely with the environment, perhaps owing to early divergences in the acquisition of sensorimotor schemata. As Piaget and Inhelder (1969) observed,

> The sensory disturbance peculiar to those born blind has, from the outset, hampered the development of sensory-motor schemes and slowed down general coordination . . . action learning is still necessary before these children develop the capacity for operations on a level with . . . the normal child. (pp. 88-89)

Personality Characteristics. Social maladjustment and personality disorders do not automatically result from visual impairments. While some research with older visually impaired youngsters indicates that they are not always well accepted by peers (Bateman, 1964), other research suggests no concomitant lowering of the visually impaired child's self-concept (Schindele, 1974). It has been noted, however, that appropriate parental interactions with the visually impaired infant are essential to later social development, positive self-concept development, and the establishment of independence or self-reliance (DuBose, 1976; Lowenfeld, 1964).

Motor Characteristics. DuBose (1979a) noted that children who are blind "experience their world differently, resulting in selective lags in developing certain motor and locomotor behaviors" (p. 337). In older preschool children with visual impairments, Folio (1974) noted delays in running, hopping, jumping, and skipping. Masters, Mori, and Lange (1983) observed that, if the blind individual does not receive orientation and mobility training (including attention to posture, coordination, freedom of movement, and overall physical fitness), serious motor problems may develop. When visually impaired children are trained appropriately, they can learn to swim, ski, ride horses, and participate in many other forms of vigorous physical activities.

Hearing Impairments

Children with a hearing impairment suffer their most serious disability in the area of language development, comprehension, and production. Language in this sense is the language used by most people who are part of the hearing world. Deaf children raised by parents who use manual language can and do learn manual language expertly (Schlesinger & Meadow, 1972). Children born hearing-impaired do not naturally develop normal language comprehension and production, however, and may never do so. Hallahan and Kauffman (1982) suggested at least three reasons that language acquisition is impaired. Hearing-impaired children

1. receive inadequate auditory feedback for sounds they produce
2. receive inadequate verbal reinforcement from adults
3. are unable to profit from adult language models

Other areas are also affected by a hearing impairment.

Intellectual/Cognitive Characteristics. The results on a standardized intelligence test (specifically, a nonverbal test of intelligence such as the Leiter International Performance Scale or the Nebraska-Hiskey Learning Aptitude Test) suggest little evidence of intellectual retardation, since hearing-impaired persons score within normal limits on these tests. Lennenberg (1967) noted that "with preschool deaf children . . . individual performances on the Leiter Scale (1936-1955) . . . [do not] . . . differ . . . from those of hearing children" (p. 360).

In the area of concept development, Furth (1961) noted that the cognitive abilities of hearing-impaired children are not negatively affected by the impairment unless the particular concept is language-dependent. Since actual language-dependent concepts are relatively few in number, overall cognitive development is generally not retarded in hearing-impaired children. Furth also concluded that any cognitive deficiencies may be the result of inadequate parental stimulation or educational training.

Personality Characteristics. While there is no evidence that deaf persons have a higher incidence of emotional disorders than would be expected in the hearing population, Meadow (1975) found that deaf children describe feelings of social isolation and difficulty in establishing interpersonal relationships. Castle and Warchol (1974) noted that deaf children enrolled in private nursery schools were essentially social isolates; they played alone, chose their own play activities, and were generally uninterested in teacher-initiated activities.

As adults, the deaf tend to have higher arrest rates and greater adjust-ment problems in social, marital, sexual, and vocational areas than do hearing adults (Ranier, Altshuler, & Kallmann, 1969). Their need for social interaction often causes them to associate only with other hearing-impaired individuals in what Furth (1973) called the "deaf community."

Motor Characteristics. In the absence of other impairments, hearing impairments alone do not delay motor development or cause persistent motor problems. When the hearing impairment affects the semicircular canals (the sense of balance) or the vestibule (sensitivity to the pull of gravity and acceleration), however, there may be gross motor problems related to balance and equilibrium.

Physical Impairments

Because the nature and severity of physical impairments are so diverse, generalizations regarding characteristics are almost impossible; however, certain broad characteristics can be seen.

Intellectual/Cognitive Characteristics. In the absence of mental retar-dation or other neurological problems that affect learning, there is no difference between the intellectual abilities of physically and nonphysically impaired children. Differences in academic achievement often found in older physically impaired children are frequently caused by irregular school attendance as a result of illness or hospitalization.

Personality Characteristics. Newman (1980) maintained that children with physical impairments have the same range of personality character-istics that the children without such impairments have. Physically impaired children are subject to certain psychological reactions, however. Sirvis and Carpignano (1976) noted that among the major psychological problems faced by the physically impaired child is overdependence on caregivers that interferes with the development of self-sufficiency and self-esteem. Furthermore, normal social relationships may be impaired because of the reactions of parents and peers, as well as the limitations on physical activity that prevent normal exploratory experiences.

Motor Characteristics. Obviously, the major manifestations of a physi-cal impairment are generally physical or motor in nature. Following are several common conditions resulting in physical disabilities with their typical motor or physical characteristics:

- cerebral palsy. Grove (1976) defined cerebral palsy as a movement or posture disorder resulting from an abnormality of the brain. In addition, cerebral palsy can cause abnormalities in sight, hearing, speech, sensation, as well as mental retardation and convulsions. Table 5-1 provides a description of the motor disability involved in the various types of cerebral palsy.

Cerebral palsy is caused by damage to the brain prenatally, perinatally, or soon after birth. The damage can be caused by infections, disease, trauma before or during birth, a difficult or complicated labor, prematurity, anoxia, or high fever.

In addition to types of cerebral palsy, there are patterns of involvement (Table 5-2). Denhoff (1976) notes that the patterns of involvement apply to all types of motor impairments, not just cerebral palsy.

- epilepsy. Some children with physical impairments may also have convulsive disorders. Epilepsy is a condition marked by seizures or convulsions and rapid muscular contractions caused by an abnormal discharge of electrical energy in the brain. The seizures are usually classified into four types (Table 5-3).

- juvenile rheumatoid arthritis. Generally manifested by pain and swelling in the joints, such as wrists, elbows, hips, knees, ankles, and the joints of the foot (Grove, 1976), juvenile rheumatoid arthritis may also be manifested by eye inflammation, skin rashes, and problems with the liver, heart, and kidneys (Gearheart, 1980).

- muscular dystrophy. Thompson and O'Quinn (1979) noted that muscular dystrophy is a hereditary (sex-linked transmission), progressive disease that begins early in childhood. The principle manifestations in the motor area (e.g., early clumsiness, tiptoeing, frequent falling, and general motor problems) may be mistaken for learning disabilities or laziness (Langley, 1979). Duchenne variety is both the most common and most serious of the dystrophies. As the disease progresses, muscular weakness and scoliosis make a wheelchair necessary for mobility. Further deterioration leads to loss of respiratory function or cardiac failure and eventually death between the ages of 15 and 25 (Langley, 1979).

- spina bifida. When the spinal column fails to close completely during fetal growth, spina bifida results. Depending on both the form of the condition and the location of the opening, various neurological manifestations can occur, for example, paralysis in the lower extremities, lack of bladder and bowel control, and hydrocephalus (enlargement of the head caused by excessive accumulation and pressure of cerebrospinal fluid). Treatment, including surgery during the first few days of life, can improve mobility. Children with spina bifida often can walk with braces and crutches. If the child's only problem is spina

Table 5-1 Categories and Motor Characteristics of Cerebral Palsy

Classification	Characteristics
Spasticity	Flexor (bending) and extensor (straightening) muscles contract simultaneously. The limbs are rigid and movement jerky. There may also be trembling and unsteadiness. Approximately 50 percent of persons with cerebral palsy manifest spasticity.
Ataxia	Balance is affected. Lack of coordination results in a staggering, awkward gait. Approximately 25 percent of the cerebral-palsied are in this category.
Athetosis	Movements appear to be in a random or circular pattern. Movement is also extremely slow, uncontrolled, and involuntary. Approximately 25 percent of these individuals experience athetosis.
Hypotonia	Flaccid muscles give child appearance of "looseness." There is a lack of muscle strength.
Tremor	Movements are spontaneous, alternating, and involuntary (rare). Muscular tension and stiffness is continuous (rare).
"Mixed" types	More than one of the above.

Table 5-2 Patterns of Involvement in Cerebral Palsy

Pattern	Limbs Involved	Percentage of Cerebral-Palsied Persons Affected
Hemiplegia	Arm and leg, same side	35 to 40
Paraplegia	Legs only	10 to 20
Quadriplegia	Both arms and legs	15 to 20
Diplegia	Legs more involved than arms	10 to 20
Double hemiplegia	Arms more involved than legs One side more involved	Rare
Monoplegia	One limb involved	Rare
Triplegia	Three limbs involved	Rare

bifida, intelligence usually falls into the normal range; however, spina bifida can be associated with "retarded physical, mental, or emotional development; dislocated hips; scoliosis, equinovarus; cleft lip and palate, soft tissue contractures; and eventual skeletal deformity due to unopposed muscle action, gravity, and posture" (Langley, 1979, pp. 94-95).

Table 5-3 Types of Epileptic Seizures

Type	Description
Grand mal	The most severe of the types, involving a loss of consciousness, falling, and involuntary muscular contractions. Such seizures are sometimes preceded by an aura or a signal that a seizure is about to occur. During the seizure, the person may foam at the mouth and lose bladder or bowel control. On awakening, the person may be confused and disoriented.
Petit mal	The most common seizure in children. Although the child loses consciousness, there is no motor activity. There is usually no aura preceding this type of seizure, and it is frequently misdiagnosed as daydreaming or laziness.
Psychomotor	The most complex of the four types of seizures. It affects both cognitive and motor processes, sometimes resulting in bizarre or purposeless behavior, as well as confusion, anger, and abusive behavior.
Jacksonian	A partial seizure that affects only one part of the body with rhythmic, twitching movements.

Cardiovascular and Respiratory System Disabilities

Two of the most common respiratory system disabilities that result in chronic health problems are asthma and cystic fibrosis. Asthma, a common childhood disorder, is an allergic condition characterized by excessive mucus in the bronchial tubes or lungs and spasms of the bronchial musculature. When an asthma attack occurs, the child exhibits extremely labored breathing and wheezing. One physical manifestation of asthma is a large, barrel chest.

Cystic fibrosis is the most common fatal hereditary disease of childhood. It is characterized by a buildup of abnormally thick mucus in both the intestinal and respiratory tracts. In physical appearance, the child with cystic fibrosis has a large, barrel chest; thin extremities; and a protruding, distended abdomen (Harvey, 1975).

Learning Disorders

The procedures designed to determine the characteristics of children with learning disorders are often methodologically unsound. In an attempt both to define learning disorders and to describe the symptoms and signs that can be used to identify learning-disabled children, Task Force I was cosponsored by the National Society for Crippled Children and Adults and the National Institute of Neurological Diseases and Blindness of the National Institutes of Health (Clements, 1966). Task Force I identified some 99 characteristics reported in the literature about learning disorders. The 10 most frequently reported were

1. hyperactivity: excessive motor behavior in the absence of stimulation to cause such behavior
2. perceptual-motor impairments: difficulty in coordinating eye-hand movements in activities such as copying a geometrical shape
3. emotional lability: frequent and unpredictable changes in mood or emotional behavior
4. general coordination deficits: awkwardness in activities involving gross motor (large muscle) skills
5. attentional deficits: distractibility or extremely short attention span; perseveration, the inability to change activities or refocus attention to a new task
6. impulsivity: behavior or actions that occur without forethought or regard for consequences
7. disorders of memory or thinking: inability to recall information or difficulty in comprehending abstract concepts
8. specific learning disabilities: problems learning academic skills in reading, spelling, writing, or arithmetic
9. disorders of language: problems in understanding, recalling, or expressing language; deficits in speech, grammar, and vocabulary
10. equivocal neurological signs: signs such as clumsiness, poor visual-motor coordination, and poor balance, sometimes called "soft" signs because they are not clearly related to classic signs of neurological problems but are not within normal limits

Intellectual/Cognitive Characteristics. Most authorities agree that, as a group, the learning-disabled possess normal or near normal intelligence. Research has documented, however, that these children are deficient in concept development and problem-solving strategies (Keogh & Donlon, 1972; Torgesen & Kail, 1980). Memory problems, perhaps owing to language inadequacies, also affect these children's ability to think.

Disorders of thinking and memory are probably affected by the learning-disabled child's attentional deficits. Tarver and Hallahan (1974) reviewed more than 20 studies on this subject and concluded:

1. Learning-disabled children tend to be more easily distracted than control children by figure-ground distractors.
2. Learning-disabled children tend to be more impulsive than control children.

3. Hyperactivity is more likely to occur in social situations in which motoric inactivity is required.
4. Learning-disabled children find it difficult to sustain attention over time.

Personality Characteristics. The behavior of learning-disabled children often parallels that of children with emotional disturbance. Learning-disabled children often have low self-esteem, perhaps because of rejection by peers. These children often become social isolates, avoiding interaction with others and pulling back into themselves. Other personality characteristics reported for learning-disabled children include

- dependency. As a group, the learning-disabled show excessive dependence on parents, teachers, and other adults. Overdependence manifests itself most frequently as the need for constant help, approval, and encouragement.
- disruptive behavior, including aggressive behaviors (e.g., hitting and fighting)
- social perception problems, such as poor social judgment, lack of sensitivity to the feelings of others, and irrational behavior.

Motor Characteristics. Wallace and McLoughlin (1979) reported that children with learning disabilities are frequently "awkward" or "clumsy" in activities requiring gross motor skills, such as walking, running, hopping, jumping, skipping, catching, throwing, and the like. Additionally, the child with learning disorders may have problems of balance, rhythm, body image, and other sensorimotor integration areas. Finally, the learning-disabled child may manifest problems in fine motor activities and eye-hand coordination.

HOW MANY CHILDREN HAVE SENSORY, PHYSICAL, AND LEARNING DISORDERS?

Sensory Impairments

Visual Impairments

The visually impaired are the smallest group of learners with special needs. The figure most often cited for the incidence of visual impairment is 0.1 percent. This U.S. Office of Education figure accounts for those persons classified as legally blind. Hewett and Forness (1977) noted that

1 in 500 school-aged children has a visual problem serious enough to warrant some intervention, particularly corrective lenses.

Hearing Impairments

Approximately 0.575 percent of school-aged children have hearing impairments, with 0.5 percent considered hard of hearing and 0.075 percent considered deaf. The U.S. Office of Education estimates do not include another 3 or 4 percent of the school-aged population with conditions that could lead to a hearing loss.

Physical Impairments

The U.S. Office of Education suggests that approximately 0.5 percent of school-aged children have health disabilities severe enough to warrant special education services. Half of these children have cerebral palsy and other crippling conditions; half have chronic health problems (Hallahan & Kauffman, 1982). Table 5-4 summarizes prevalence data on the conditions discussed earlier.

Learning Disorders

It is not surprising that estimates of the percentage of children with learning disorders vary widely in view of the confusion regarding the definition of such disorders. Lerner (1976) noted that estimates of the prevalence of learning disorders vary from a low of 1 percent to a high of 30 percent. Reid and Hresko (1981), in their review of research studies on the prevalence of learning disorders, indicated that an estimate of 1 to 3

Table 5-4 Prevalence Data on Physical Impairments

Condition	Percentage of Child Population
Cerebral palsy	0.15
Epilepsy	0.5
Juvenile rheumatoid arthritis	0.08
Muscular dystrophy	0.004
Spina bifida	0.02
Asthma	2.5[a]
Cystic fibrosis	0.1

[a]Only a very small percentage of children with asthma are in need of special education; the remainder are maintained in regular classes.

Source: U.S. Office of Education, 1979.

percent of the school-aged population is a satisfactory figure, particularly when this includes only *severe* cases that require special remedial help.

HOW ARE CHILDREN WITH SENSORY, PHYSICAL, AND LEARNING DISORDERS IDENTIFIED?

Sensory Impairments

Visual Impairments

A number of children with visual impairments are identified at birth. If no impairment has been discovered, parents and professionals must still be sensitive to behavior in a child that may indicate a visual problem. Some visually impaired children use mannerisms or self-stimulating behaviors to provide the sensory stimulation lacking because of visual defects. These include

- rocking the body excessively
- inappropriate tongue clucking or hand clapping
- flicking the fingers in front of the eyes
- constant tapping of objects
- rapid, seemingly random, turning of the head

Other indicators of possible eye problems have been suggested by the National Society for the Prevention of Blindness (1972):

- appearance of eyes
  recurring sties
  inflamed or watery eyes
  crossed eyes
  red-rimmed or swollen eyelids
  encrusted eyelids
- complaints by the child
  headaches, nausea, or dizziness after close visual tasks
  itching, burning, or scratchy eyes
  poor vision
  blurry or double vision
  pain in eyes caused by lights
- behaviors
  rubs eyes excessively
  blinks, frowns, scowls, squints, or makes other facial distortions
    when doing close work

covers one eye; tilts head or thrusts head forward
confuses letters of similar shape
holds books close to eyes
cannot see distant objects clearly

While these indicators are not conclusive evidence of a visual impairment, their existence mandates further observation and visual screening or examination.

DuBose (1979a) recommended the following screening tests for use with young children:

- *A Flash-Card Vision Test for Children* (1966). Using three symbols (apple, house, umbrella) presented in Snellen acuity notation, this test measures visual acuity of children as young as two years, three months of age.
- *The Home Eye Test* (Boyce, 1973). This test, using an E chart, has been successful with children as young as three years of age.
- *The Snellen Symbol Chart* (National Society for the Prevention of Blindness). This scale contains symbols that are read at a distance of 20 feet.
- *Stycar Vision Tests—Screening Tests for Young Children and Retardates* (Sheridan, 1973). Children are asked to name (or match) familiar objects at a distance of ten feet.

Children who have difficulty on these or other screening instruments should be referred for a complete eye examination by an eye care specialist. The ophthalmologist is a physician with specialized training in the diagnosis and treatment of diseases, injuries, or birth defects that affect vision. Treatment may include surgery, medication, or corrective lenses. The optometrist is a health care professional trained to examine the eyes for visual problems or disease. The optometrist may prescribe corrective lenses, optical aids, or special teaching modification to increase visual efficiency. The optometrist may also refer the child to the ophthalmologist if eye disease is suspected.

Hearing Impairments

Routine screening for hearing problems in neonates has not been particularly reliable (Shah & Wong, 1979). A neonate is considered at risk for hearing impairments and eligible for a complete audiological assessment, however, in the presence of

- a medical history of hereditary childhood hearing impairment
- fetal infection, e.g., rubella or herpes
- defects of the ear, nose, throat, cleft lip or palate
- birthweight less than 1500 gm
- bilirubin level greater than 20 mg/100 ml serum (DuBose, 1979b)

Since early detection is both vital and possible, parents must be made aware of signs of hearing problems in infants. Parents need to know how young children react to sounds or use language at certain ages. For example, the 12- to 18-month-old child should have a vocabulary of several words (e.g., mama, dada, bye-bye) and respond to simple spoken commands with understanding (e.g., "kiss me" or "wave bye-bye"). The two-year-old child should speak in two- or even three-word sentences. Included among the things that parents can do to check their child's hearing are

- Clap hands within four to eight inches of a neonate's head. Observe if the baby is startled, e.g., throws out hands or shakes.
- Call out the child's name at 3 to 6 months. Observe whether the baby ceases crying or movement.
- Call out the child's name from behind at 8 to 12 months. Observe whether the child turns toward the person who called.

If the child does not react as expected to these simple tasks, there may be a hearing problem, and a more complete hearing assessment is needed. Often, the parent does not notice a problem, particularly if there is no other child to use as a comparison. Professionals and day care workers also must be aware of behaviors that *may* indicate a hearing problem and require a referral for special testing. A hearing impairment may be present when the child

- fails to follow simple directions
- does not respond to loud noises
- cannot locate the source of a sound
- frequently turns up volume on record player or radio
- talks too loudly or too softly
- watches others for cues as to what to do instead of listening to teacher's directions
- has limited speech or poor vocabulary
- has extremely poor articulation; nasal, high- or low-pitched speech

- maintains high noise level even during "quiet" activities (e.g., naptime)
- complains of earaches, dizziness, or a "ringing" in the ears
- has persistent colds or upper respiratory congestion
- cocks head to one side or turns head in an apparent effort to use "better ear"
- requests repetitions or says "Huh?" or "What did you say?" to excess

The presence of any high-risk or behavioral indicator of a potential hearing loss is reason to do a more intensive screening or assessment of hearing function. Even neonates can be assessed by behavior-observation audiometry or the Crib-O-Gram; a motion detector attached to the infant's crib records the baby's reactions to sounds sent over a loudspeaker. Hearing acuity is assessed by means of changes in the child's activity level when sound is presented.

For children 18 months to 3 years of age, conditioning techniques may be used to determine hearing ability (Sweitzer, 1977). This involves pairing a sound or signal sent through earphones with a flash of light. After several presentations of the paired stimuli, the sound is presented alone. If the child turns toward the light source, the child can hear. If the child fails to turn toward the source of light, the child may have a hearing problem.

Once children reach three years of age, they are usually able to respond to pure tone audiometric procedures. The audiometer is a machine that presents pure tones at different intensities and frequencies. Responses are recorded to air conduction (directly through the ear) and bone conduction (bypassing the middle ear and going directly to the bones behind the ear). Using standardized symbols and notation, the audiologist records the results of the examination on an audiogram.

The degree of hearing loss is measured in decibels (dB). A loss can range from slight (16 to 29 dB, in which case little difficulty will occur) to extreme (80 dB or more, in which case only some loud sounds are heard and vision is the primary avenue for acquiring information).

Physical Impairments

Hart (1979) noted that medical advances have decreased the incidence of or eliminated many acquired conditions that previously caused debilitating physical impairments. These same advances have also extended the life span of children who in the past would not have survived birth or would have died during the first few years of life. Therefore, many of the physical impairments are now congenital in origin.

Many physical impairments are identified at birth or soon after. Such impairments often result from damage to the central nervous system, primarily to the brain and spinal cord. Severe damage is observable either as paralysis or lack of motor function and/or the presence of a seizure disorder.

Musculoskeletal and orthopedic impairments may be apparent at birth because they affect the movement of the limbs. Others, such as muscular dystrophy, involve progressive deterioration and may not be identified until the child begins to manifest signs of muscle weakness (frequently between the ages of five and seven years). Still others are identified during early infancy when the child fails to reach important developmental milestones, such as head control in the prone position (usually at three to four months) or rolling supine to prone (usually four to six months).

Both parents and day care providers should be aware of normal motor development. While motor skills develop in an orderly sequence (Table 5-5), they do so at an individual rate for each child. Most children acquire motor milestones within certain specified periods, however. If young children are periodically checked for the milestones, the parent or professional can determine if the child's motor development is proceeding within normal limits.

Table 5-5 Normal Motor Developmental Patterns

Age	Motor Development
Birth to two months	Holds head up in prone position; exhibits stepping reflex with support; rolls onto side
Two to four months	Holds chest up in prone position; reaches for objects
Four to six months	Rolls supine to prone; holds head erect in sitting position; sits with some support
Six to nine months	Moves from prone position to crawl; pulls self to standing position; handles and inspects objects; walks with adult assistance
Nine months to one year	Walks with feet spread (wide base); uses inferior pincer grasp (thumb and index finger) to secure small objects; explores objects with finger tips
One to two years	Walks well alone; stacks two and three blocks; copies a vertical stroke holding a crayon; uses superior pincer grasp
Two to three years	Runs and jumps; climbs stairs; walks a balance beam

Cardiovascular and respiratory conditions, as well as metabolic disorders, are often diagnosed early in life because of the impact that these conditions have on normal development. Children with chronic medical conditions often fail to gain weight or to grow adequately, causing parents to seek medical advice and a formal diagnosis.

Learning Disorders

Because learning disabilities are generally defined in terms of academic tasks, there is great difficulty in identifying children with learning disorders during the preschool years (Keogh & Glover, 1980; Mercer, Algozzine, & Trifiletti, 1979). Essentially, it is a question of *predicting* a possible problem rather than identifying an actual one.

Among the many problems inherent in the task of identifying learning problems in the preschool years are the following:

- Children with a learning disorder, unlike children with physical impairments, look "normal." Most of these children appear to be of normal intelligence and competent in development or social tasks of early childhood.

- Frequently, an apparent learning disorder or developmental delay is actually just slow maturation. Owing to the variability of human development, some children may seem to lag behind in certain developmental milestones; they frequently catch up to their age peers, however.

- Attempts to predict school failure on the basis of performance on individual tests of intelligence during the preschool years are of limited value. For children birth to two years of age, the instruments used are largely sensorimotor in nature. As Mori and Olive (1980) note, "Only in those cases where severe retardation is detected do the infant tests have acceptable predictive validity" (p. 29). Keogh and Becker (1973) suggest that even for the older preschool child (except in the care of extremely low scores), "prediction of school failure on the basis of intelligence test scores alone appears tenuous" (p. 6).

- The results of preschool tests designed to predict school failure usually do not lead to appropriate educational intervention. Because the relationship between the findings of these tests and later school achievement "are too low to allow definitive prediction about individual children" (Keogh & Becker, 1973, p. 7), the critical link between assessment and curriculum or program intervention is missing.

- The prediction of learning problems, even when they do not actually exist, may result in a "self-fulfilling prophecy" (Keogh & Becker, 1973). Parents and professionals may inadvertently elicit inappropriate child responses and trigger the onset of "behaviors" that constitute the misidentified deficit condition.

Despite these obvious and serious problems, it remains important to attempt identification of learning disorders at as early an age as possible. Mercer and associates (1979) suggested that preacademic skills are presently the most accurate predictors of school success or failure. Yet these skills (e.g., identifying shapes, colors, letters) are found in tests that may lack predictive validity. Furthermore, not all authorities agree that learning disabilities can be predicted from failure on tests of preacademic skills. They suggest that such failures may result from lack of exposure to structured learning experiences and opportunities designed to facilitate the acquisition of these skills. Nonetheless, the problem remains—How do we identify the young child with learning problems?

It appears that certain high-risk factors and behavioral factors may be useful in the early detection of learning disorders:

1. high-risk factors
    prematurity
    low birth weight
    fetal anoxia
    high and prolonged fever in infancy
    difficult delivery
    seizure disorder
    reflex abnormalities
    history of diagnosed learning disorder in parents or siblings
    meningitis or encephalitis during preschool years
    failure to thrive

2. behavioral factors
    hyperactivity (extreme restlessness or motor activity in excess of
       stimuli present)
    impulsiveness
    short attention span
    inability to follow directions
    extreme awkwardness
    distractibility
    perseveration

In addition, failure to achieve certain preacademic skills within an appropriate time period (Table 5-6) may indicate a learning disability.

Children who have a high-risk factor, manifest the behavioral indications, or display problems in the preacademic area *may* be evidencing a learning disorder. These children should undergo a thorough diagnostic workup, including a complete medical and psychological evaluation, as well as

- intelligence testing
- perceptual testing (essentially visual-motor functions)
- language testing (including auditory discrimination, comprehension, and expression)
- further preacademic testing, particularly prereading

WHAT IS THE IMPACT OF A SENSORY, PHYSICAL, OR LEARNING DISORDER ON THE FAMILIES?

Effects of Sensory and Physical Disorders

When parents discover their child is handicapped, whether it is a sensory or physical handicap, they may succumb to the overwhelming need to make the child like them, to make the child normal (Schlesinger & Meadow, 1972). While intervention efforts may reduce the impact of the impairment and perhaps lessen the handicap, they cannot make a blind child see or a crippled child walk. Too often, parental demands for "more normalcy" make handicapped children feel rejected as they are.

Table 5-6 Normal Development of Preacademic Skills

Age	Preacademic Skill
Two years	Names common objects in picture book; matches associated objects (e.g., cup and saucer); stacks rings on peg in order of size
Three years	Matches colors; stacks blocks in order of size; copies circle
Four years	Names four to six colors; copies cross and square; matches pictures of familiar objects; rote counts to 5
Five years	Names some numbers and letters; rote counts to 10; copies triangle; handedness (either right or left) is well established; sorts objects by single characteristics, e.g., color, shape, size

The psychological impact of bearing a handicapped child, regardless of the nature of the condition, is profound. Roos (1975) maintained that it is inevitable for the family of a seriously impaired child to experience shock, disappointment, depression, and the feeling that life has been unfair. As Mori and Olive (1980) noted:

> As a result of those realities, parents often become very depressed. They sense such loss—loss of the child they hoped for and loved, loss of their fantasies of family fun and honor, loss of money, loss of time, even loss of a sense of worth. They are overwhelmed by the challenges ahead. They are afraid they cannot meet all of the child's needs. They fear failure, criticism, loss of esteem in the eyes of others. They fear poverty as the costs of care are so great. They even feel guilty because they fear they can no longer fulfill all the social activities they enjoyed before. They also may feel guilty because they resent the tremendous disturbance the child has created in their living patterns. (p. 88)

Dubose (1976) felt that the single most influential factor in the development of a blind child is the parents' ability to cope with the dilemma the child presents. Along that same line, the reactions of the family of the child with a physical impairment can either worsen or offset the reactions of others (Hallahan & Kauffman, 1982). Parents of a sensorily and physically impaired child may find their child frightening, even repulsive. Compounding this problem is the fact that handicapped babies often react to parental affection in more subtle ways thus diminishing "rewards" to the parents.

Some parents prevent their physically or sensorily impaired children from engaging in the same number and quality of social interactions as nonhandicapped children. This understandable, but nonetheless counterproductive, reaction is seen as necessary to shield the child. Unfortunately, overprotection deprives sensorily and physically impaired children of the opportunity to learn important skills and role expectations, as well as to learn to cope with negative social reactions. In other words, as DuBose (1976) noted, a blind child needs to be protected from those who would overprotect him and "make him a blind man" (p. 52).

Other parents withhold any emotional investment in the child. They care for the child's needs, but they refuse to love the child for fear that the child will die or the love will not be returned. Still others are unable to love the child because they refuse to believe that they could have given birth to such a child. They overcompensate in areas not related to the establishment of a meaningful attachment. This failure to discharge infant care duties with warmth, regularity, and affection results in a child unable to develop a trusting attitude toward others (Erikson, 1968).

Schell (1981) described two particularly pervasive problems in the family's development of a nurturing relationship with the handicapped child. The first concerns the parents' expectations for the child's development. When the condition is discovered early in the child's life, parents know they must alter their perception of child development, but they do not know exactly how much to change their expectations. This uncertainty can lead to a crisis of confidence as a parent and cause parents to focus exclusively on what the child is not doing or is not able to do. If progress remains slow or differs greatly from the norm, parents "may simply give up the struggle" (Schell, 1981, p. 22). Furthermore, parents who fail to develop realistic and accurate expectations may extend the child's training beyond the child's emotional or physical capabilities. When the child cannot respond, parents may become abusive (Frodi, 1981).

The second area of difficulty described by Schell deals with the parent-child relationship. The attachment is certainly more tentative and fragile when motor, perceptual, or language systems are so impaired that parents cannot interpret a baby's signals or the infant appears unresponsive to the parents' attempts at play or intervention. Thus, "the infant may be unable to elicit the kind of . . . nurturing . . . needed . . . [and] a negative interaction pattern will develop" (Schell, 1981, p. 23).

Parents who must cope with extraordinary physical demands for care, extended hospitalization or medical care, or unusual, extended efforts to communicate with their child may suffer parental burnout (Hagen, 1981). Parental burnout can be

- psychological . . . when people begin to feel tired, drained;
- social . . . when people become irritable;
- intellectual . . . when the burnout starts to affect the mind;
- psycho-emotional . . . when the person begins to perceive himself/herself as always meeting someone else's need;
- introspective . . . when the person begins to question his or her own value systems. (Hagen, 1981, p. 5)

Effects of Learning Disorders

Parents of children with learning disorders generally face somewhat different problems than do parents of physically and sensorily impaired children. In the first place, their child looks "normal." Often, the parents do not find out about the child's problems until much later. The child progresses through the milestones of development, but at a slightly different pace. Parents have a vague idea of a problem, but not the exact nature of it. Furthermore, the child's disabilities are not readily apparent, even compared with the abilities of so-called normal children. This often leads parents to entertain the false hope that the child will eventually catch up with peers, and the learning disability will disappear. Almost daily coverage of miracle diets, drugs, or esoteric therapeutic regimens (e.g., megavitamin therapy) may delude parents into seeking unproved treatment and thus may delay educational intervention that could ameliorate the problem; even worse, failure of such unorthodox treatments could lead to parental frustration, surrender, or child abuse.

If the parent rejects the diagnosis because the child's performance in the home is not as "deviant" as the professional who has evaluated the child's condition has determined, other positive benefits of parental interaction in the intervention program may be seriously delayed. Furthermore, the parent may begin to focus on what the child is not able to do, or to magnify the problems. Some parents refuse to accept the learning disability diagnosis because they fear the child is really mentally retarded.

Parents of a learning-disabled child are often confused and frustrated by the inconsistencies they see in their child's behaviors. In some areas, the child's performance is normal or near normal; in others, it is atypical. McCarthy and McCarthy (1969) called the patterns of normal behavior a "taste of honey" for parents of the learning-disabled child. Humphries (1979) noted that parents who see signs of normalcy are driven to find other typical or normal behavior patterns. When the typical patterns are not found, the parents become further confused and frustrated.

This constant state of uncertainty is stressful for all concerned. Humphries (1979) suggested that helping the family form realistic expectations about the child's performance is of critical importance in the early stage of the coping process. Parents need a reduction or elimination of the uncertainty so that they may confront the problem directly as soon as a diagnosis is confirmed (Dembinski & Mauser, 1977). Of course, reducing uncertainty is not easy when a problem is being predicted rather than diagnosed.

Rates of divorce, separation, and desertion are generally higher for couples with handicapped children than for the general population (Love, 1973; Reed & Reed, 1965). Other problems include higher rates of depression (Richman, 1977), suicide (Love, 1973), sexual dissatisfaction (Gath, 1979), and general marital conflict (Humphries, 1979).

WHAT IS THE IMPACT OF SENSORY, PHYSICAL, AND LEARNING DISORDERS ON THE FUTURE LIVES OF CHILDREN?

Sensory Impairments

Visual Impairments

Children with a visual impairment and no other handicapping conditions may be expected to experience certain delays in early development. As indicated earlier, visually impaired children, particularly those born blind, are likely to perform poorly on tasks that require abstract thinking. Since early experiences with the environment tend to be concrete, these children tend to deal with the world in more concrete terms. Yet it has been demonstrated that appropriate learning experiences can greatly improve the conceptual abilities of blind children.

Hallahan and Kauffman (1982) noted that "the most important ability for the successful adjustment of most visually impaired individuals is their mobility—their skill in moving about in their environment" (p.294). Motivation to learn mobility and early training in the prerequisites of the skill, including strength, endurance, balance, coordination, and agility, can certainly facilitate the acquisition of this most important behavior.

From a strictly educational standpoint, "the similarities between visually handicapped children and so-called normal children outweigh the differences. The basic needs of both groups in school are the same" (Ward, 1979, p. 346). With appropriate intervention in the early childhood years and meaningful educational and social experiences during the school years, the visually impaired learn to function effectively in most areas. Parents and teachers must expose visually impaired children to a wide variety of early experiences, allowing thorough exploration of objects and translating unusable visual stimuli into another form of sensory input that can be used.

Much greater emphasis is being placed on career education (not only for the visually impaired but for all handicapped children) as a lifelong educational process that spans the preschool to the adult years. Given appropriate career education experiences starting early in life, the entire range of occupational choices is possible. As Brolin and Kokaska (1979) noted,

> Blind persons have been known to be successful in a wide array
> of occupations, such as sales (including real estate and insur-

ance), cooking (chef), nursing, television repairs, medicine, court reporting, typing, and receptionist. (p. 72)

Hearing Impairments

Even with extensive training, the hearing-impaired child does not develop normal language comprehension and speech production. The education of deaf children has not been highly successful. In fact, as Furth (1973) noted, "even a moderate criterion of success, such as a reading level of better than grade four, is only achieved by about 25 percent of all deaf children when they finally leave school after 12 or more years" (pp. 32-33).

This lack of school success is usually coupled with the well-documented social integration problems of the deaf (Furth, 1973). For many deaf children, accepting their impairment is a commitment to the deaf community (Furth, 1973), in which they socialize with people like themselves.

Early studies of the vocational adjustment of the deaf (Boatner, Stuckless, & Moores, 1964; Kroneberg & Blake, 1966) showed that young deaf adults suffered high rates of unemployment, were paid lower wages than hearing persons for equivalent work, and had limited upward mobility—despite the fact that deaf persons were rated superior workers by their immediate supervisors. With advancements in postsecondary educational opportunities in the mid-1960s and 1970s, Moores, Fisher, and Harlow (1974) found that significant gains had been made in the training and placement of deaf workers. Increased training opportunities increased upward mobility, although initial choice of occupation remained somewhat limited.

Preschool programs for the hearing-impaired have certainly become far more prevalent in recent years, but the long-term impact of early intervention on "graduates" of preschool programs remains to be determined. Preschool or early intervention is overwhelmingly supported in the literature, however (Moores, 1978, 1979).

Physical Impairments

In the absence of mental impairments, the greatest impact of a physical impairment is on psychosocial adjustment and self-care (independent living skills). As noted earlier, a child's response to a handicap is dependent on the reactions of parents, teachers, and peers; however, many physically impaired persons display adverse reactions to their physical differences. Jourard (1958) noted the following:

- denying or refusing to acknowledge that the disability exists or that it imposes any limitations whatsoever

- resigning or "giving up"—seeing the situation as hopeless and refusing to help oneself or to be helped
- regarding oneself as the victim of injustice perpetrated by others and punishing the "others" by hostility or withdrawal
- showing arrogance and rebellion, rejecting help or empathy, making aggressive demands, and remaining aloof
- viewing the disability as a punishment for real and imagined infractions of family or societal rules
- becoming dependent and demanding because remaining helpless seems the only way to ensure attention, affection, and care

Scandary (in Sirvis & Carpignano, 1976) adapted a model to show how patterns and intensities of stress vary in the lives of children at different ages. The major source of stress for a handicapped infant (birth to two years) is parental reaction to the impairment. Further stress may be caused by hospitalization, separation from the family for treatments, and a limitation of physical activity that retards experiential learning and development.

The toddler and preschool years are stressful because the child typically attempts to gain independence through movement and exploration of the environment. If the child's physical impairment prevents this, the child may experience frustration and anger. Medical treatment and restrictions add to the stress and interrupt the course of development. Social interaction with others may be impeded by limitations imposed by the impairment or by overprotecting parents. Even without these particular obstacles, the physically impaired child does not have the same number and quality of social relationships.

An important subarea in the psychosocial domain is the self-concept. As Sirvis and Carpignano (1976) observed,

> For the young physically disabled child, restricted ability to explore the environment and barriers to "normal" relationship goals may present difficulties in self-acceptance. Body image becomes a crucial factor when the disabled youngster begins to compare himself with age mates who are not disabled. Warm acceptance must be available at times when the positive self-concept is being challenged. (p. 87)

Self-care directly influences psychosocial development. If young physically impaired children do not learn to care for their own needs at an early age, "they will become unnecessarily dependent adults" (Bigge, 1976, p. 137). By learning to care for themselves, these children are learning to survive in society. They can feel independent, which contributes to their feelings of adequacy and confidence. This dimension has a direct bearing on success in both educational and occupational endeavors.

The occupational outlook is as varied as the types of physical impairments. Children with mild problems or problems that can be controlled (e.g., diabetes or asthma) may be virtually unaffected as far as career choice is concerned. Those with more severe impairments require intensive career and vocational preparation to make optimal use of their intelligence, decision-making ability, and social and residual physical abilities to secure economic, social, and personal fulfillment.

Learning Disorders

Programs are so few, data so sparse and inconclusive, that it is not possible to say with any certainty that early intervention with the learning-disabled child results in fewer subsequent referrals for special education. It is not even possible presently to say that early intervention can remediate the learning disability, particularly if the learning disability is not identified until the child enters school (Wallace & McLoughlin, 1979).

The impact of a learning disability is determined by its nature. Most learning-disabled children have what Gallagher (1966a) called developmental imbalances (i.e., low in some areas of development, high in others). Once young children with a presumed learning disability reach school age they may realize for the first time that they are different from their peers in areas of academic competence. The impact of academic deficits can be great.

Initially, instructional strategies for the school-aged child with a learning disorder focused on process deficits, that is, a failure in basic systems that interpret the input from the senses (perception). Early tests measured processes such as figure-ground perception or auditory discrimination that professionals believed were inherent prerequisites to the acquisition of reading or arithmetic skills. If the child exhibited a deficiency in a basic process, the remediation was designed to improve perceptual functioning so that academic functioning could be improved. Newcomber and Hammill (1975) found that training in auditory processing skills did not significantly improve academic achievement, however.

Recently, more learning disability specialists have been focusing on product deficits, which are simply failures to achieve in reading or arithmetic. The remedial approach is to attack the child's failure directly by determining the subskills the child has not mastered. Unfortunately, in 30 years of research on teaching reading, no approach has been found to eliminate or reduce reading disabilities in first-grade children (Lohnes, 1973). Remediation programs in arithmetic do not produce a more promising picture, unfortunately.

This may seem to be a very pessimistic view of the educational future of learning-disabled children. Obviously, since learning disability is a relatively new area, there is a critical need for additional research into improved methods of instruction. In the meantime, current efforts to educate younger learning-disabled children continue to focus on the remediation of academic deficits.

At the secondary level, there has been a great deal of recent interest in compensatory programs (Deshler, 1978) and career education (Mori, 1980). Compensatory programs are designed to teach basic skills but use different procedures to meet the child's special needs (e.g., use of "talking" books). Career education focuses on preparation for life's roles, including specific vocational skill acquisition. At the present time, there are few empirical data to support the efficacy of either of these approaches.

In some ways, the social problems faced by learning-disabled children may be more difficult to deal with than the academic ones. Research suggests that learning-disabled children are viewed negatively by parents, who described them as more impulsive, more anxious, less considerate, and less able to receive affection than normal children (Owen, Adams, Forrest, Stolz, & Fisher, 1971; Strag, 1972). In addition, teachers perceive learning-disabled children as lacking adequate social skills and behavior control. Behaviors reported included lack of cooperativeness, little tact, inability to accept responsibility, and high aggressiveness (Keogh, Tchir, & Windeguth-Behn, 1974; Myklebust, Boshes, Olson, & Cole, 1969). Peers are also likely to reject learning-disabled children. Bryan (1974) reported that peers judged these children to be more worried, less clean and neat, less physically attractive, and more ignored socially than normal children.

These disturbing data make for a rather gloomy conclusion. It appears that learning-disabled children are "likely to be rejected by or in conflict with parents, teacher, and peers. Some may well be rejected by virtually all of the significant people with whom they come in contact" (Bryan & Bryan, 1979, p. 133).

A promising approach for reducing the impact of the social problems of learning-disabled adolescents was described by Zigmond and Brownlee (1980). Called the School Survival Skills Curriculum, it focuses on assessing and teaching social perception skills and socially appropriate behaviors by working with significant others in the child's life.

WHAT INTERVENTION STRATEGIES CAN BE USED FOR CHILDREN WITH SENSORY, PHYSICAL, AND LEARNING DISORDERS?

Sensory Impairments

Visual Impairments

Carroll (1961) noted that preschool blind children require a special intervention approach so that they can acquire independence at an early age. Mori and Olive (1978) and Fraiberg, Smith, and Adelson (1969) described specialized intervention techniques designed to reduce the impact of the visual impairment. Early training focuses on the mother-child interaction, not only to facilitate the bonding process (Fraiberg et al., 1969) but also to assist the mother in learning "to attend to, and communicate by means of tactile, kinesthetic, and auditory signals" (Safford, 1978, p. 86).

Mori and Olive (1978) suggested that developmental programs of blind infants should include:

• stimulation of primitive reflexes (supervised by a physical therapist) to increase the child's mental memory of the processes involved
• stimulation of the child's other senses—touch, taste, smell, and hearing—to lay a foundation for later cognitive development
• enhancement of language development by recognizing the child's attempts to communicate with others and reinforcing them, as well as by talking to the infant often and in a meaningful way

Other critical accomplishments of infancy (Fraiberg et al., 1969) include

• establishment of human-object relations
• development of a bimanual exploratory manipulative skill
• development of object permanence concept
• gross motor mobility

Infant programs for the visually impaired are usually provided by a home visitor. Later preschool educational experiences may be provided in integrated settings with special instruction by an itinerant specialist. The emphasis of instruction for the toddler and older preschool blind child is development and refinement of the remaining senses (DuBose, 1979a), training in cognitive functioning (especially classification, reasoning, and conservation skills), and social development (including mobility and self-care skills).

There are no magic methodologies that have proved to be more successful than others in teaching skills to visually impaired children. Behavior modification techniques have been successfully used to reduce blindisms or stereotypic behaviors in blind children. Lowenfeld (1952) has identified five necessary components in an instructional program for visually impaired children.

1. individualization: need for careful assessment to identify individual differences among pupils
2. concreteness: multiple opportunities to explore real objects kinesthetically to discover shape, size, texture, and so on
3. unified instruction: careful regard for sequencing, demonstrating relationships, and providing structure to a series of activities
4. additional stimulation: purposeful and systematic planning of experiences that broaden the children's awareness of their world
5. self-activity: enhanced opportunities for independent, self-initiated exploratory experiences

Hearing Impairments

Moores, Weiss, and Goodwin (1976, 1978) conducted a major longitudinal evaluation of preschool programs for the deaf over a five-year period. Included among their findings were the following:

- Children functioned in the normal range of intelligence as measured by the Piagetian tasks of classification, conservation, and seriation, as well as by the performance subtests of the Wechsler Intelligence Scale for Children.
- Children scored at age norms for hearing children on four of five tests of the Illinois Test of Psycholinguistic Abilities.
- Children at age seven possessed decoding skills for reading readiness equivalent to those of children with normal hearing; however, they exhibited difficulty in processing complex linguistic structures, such as passives and negatives.
- Children at age seven were below norms for hearing children in arithmetic.
- It is possible to integrate strong programs in auditory training, speech, and manual communication at very early ages.
- The single most effective means of communication was simultaneous manual communication and speech.

- The most effective programs had both social and cognitive-academic components from the beginning; if the cognitive-academic components were not introduced until after age four, the children fell steadily behind in all academic measures.

The results of this study are the basis for recommended procedures for early intervention programs for the hearing-impaired. Moores and associates (1976) urge the following:

- Intensive teacher inservice programs in techniques, methods, and curriculum.
- Teachers trained and certified in the education of the hearing impaired.
- Preparation of individual cumulative files containing general background information, audiological and ontological evaluations, medical information, educational history, and school achievement data.
- Recruitment of deaf teachers to teach young hearing-impaired children.
- Programs with a cognitive-academic emphasis from the beginning of training, because this emphasis results in superior academic achievement, at least through eight years of age.
- Mathematics should receive attention equal to that given to other academic and language-related areas.
- Manual communication should be coordinated with oral communication.
- Intensive auditory training should be conducted daily.
- Teachers should be videotaped and audiotaped periodically to ensure consistency of program goals.
- Parent counseling should involve helping parents cope with the reality of deafness in the family.
- Programs mainstreaming hearing-impaired children into regular classes should have a consistent system of related services, including speech and language therapy, sign language interpreters, and academic tutoring.
- Children must be provided opportunities to express and receive complex grammatical and semantic relations including passive voice, subject-verb agreement, negation, and spatial relationships.
- Academic curriculum should parallel the regular classroom as much as possible. Content at present seems to be sacrificed for greater concentration on speech and language.

Preschool programs for the deaf have served as trend-setters in early intervention. According to DuBose (1979b), the John Tracy Clinic in Los Angeles used parent training and the home-based mode of service delivery as early as the 1960s. Other programs, such as the Central Institute for the Deaf in St. Louis, the University of Kansas Medical Center, and the Bill Wilkerson Hearing and Speech Center, initiated similar programs.

Horton (1974) described the program at the Bill Wilkerson Center and presented evidence of the significant language growth and auditory development for children in the preschool program. Horton noted that 18 children from the program entered regular first- and second-grade classes and maintained a satisfactory performance. The parent program at the center has five basic objectives:

1. to teach parents how to optimize the auditory environment
2. to teach parents how to talk to their children
3. to teach parents the principles of normal language development and the application of the information to language stimulation
4. to teach parents behavior management
5. to provide parents with emotional support to help them cope with their children and the stresses on the family

Northcott and Fowler (1976) described the UNISTAPS Project in Minnesota, a joint parent-staff program that emphasizes assessment of parental needs, a statement of objectives for parental participation, participation activities, and ongoing evaluation. Parents are not only involved in a home/preschool program but also provide support to a center-based kindergarten nursery school. A major focus is helping parents create a supportive, stimulating home environment.

Physical Impairments

Early intervention services for physically impaired children are now commonplace. Many children are served in United Cerebral Palsy or Easter Seal Rehabilitation Centers, especially in states where there is no mandate to serve the under five population. Because of the multiplicity and complexity of their problems, these children are usually served by many professionals in a transdisciplinary approach (Connor, Williamson, & Siepp, 1978). The team ideally works with physically disabled children toward fulfillment of the four basic developmental goals (Sirvis, 1982):

1. Physical independence, including mastery of daily living skills
2. Self-awareness and social maturation
3. Academic growth
4. Career education, including instructive leisure activities (p. 392)

By virtue of the fact that physically impaired children have significant motor problems, early intervention initially focuses on handling and positioning to facilitate motor development and other learning activities. Finnie (1975) and Utley, Holvoet, and Barnes (1977) described in detail the need to support the child's body at various points and in various postures to enhance muscle tone and movement. The key points are the neck and spine, shoulder girdle, and pelvic area; pressure on these points controls muscle tone in the extremities and influences voluntary motor movement.

Connor and associates (1978) and Langley (1979) stressed the crucial importance of motor development programming as a prerequisite to later cognitive, communication, and social independence skills. Included in their recommendations for specific programming are:

- changing abnormal postural patterns by blocking them through handling techniques that change tone and allow the child to move with greater ease
- providing range of motion activities to maintain joint flexibility and prevent contractures
- normalizing tactile and kinesthetic input
- emphasizing symmetry of body postures and movements
- inhibiting the deteriorating influence of associated reactions
- avoiding abnormal compensatory movements

For those children who can develop locomotion skills, it is essential to discourage abnormal, exaggerated crawling (e.g., "commando crawling") and teach more appropriate locomotion (e.g., the use of a scooter board). Motor skills are taught in the sequence of normal motor development, beginning with head control, back extension, and reaching with the arm activities. By means of adaptive equipment, such as a bolster, a child can be taught good sitting balance with normalized tone. The next task is to teach the child to stand. Parents or professionals working with a child who is attempting to pull to a standing position must stress as normal a movement pattern as possible. Later, walking may be encouraged, employing techniques to ensure good balance, proper weight transfer, and appropriate gait. Children who are unable to walk may be encouraged to develop sufficient upper body control to sit in a wheelchair and use their arms to propel the chair.

As indicated earlier, the acquisition of independent self-care skills promotes independence and encourages the development of a positive self-concept. Using task analysis procedures (Bigge, 1976), preschool physically impaired children can be taught eating, dressing, and toileting skills. Adaptive devices, such as prone boards, wedges, spill-proof cups, plate guards, buttonhooks, or special grip spoons and utensils, may facilitate these tasks. Most preschool programs for physically impaired children employ the services of an occupational therapist to select and design adaptive devices of all kinds.

With consistent, individualized educational programs, most physically impaired preschoolers can be well prepared to enter regular school programs in the first grade. As Reynolds and Birch (1977) noted, "there is no justification for assembling children with health and crippling impairments into one group for schooling" (p. 403). When transportation problems are not insurmountable, the physically handicapped child who is not also severely mentally retarded can be educated in regular schools and regular classes.

Learning Disorders

Preschool programs for the learning-disordered child are very rare. Because of the extreme difficulty of early identification of learning disorders and the lack of programs to remediate these problems in early childhood, there are few data on the effectiveness of early intervention. The results of preschool intervention with disadvantaged and mentally retarded children may shed some light on the possible long-term effects of intervention with learning-disordered children. Two reports, one by Bronfenbrenner (1974) and the other by Lazar and Darlington (1979), substantiate the benefits of early education for disadvantaged populations.

Bronfenbrenner (1974) presented many findings; among those were several of extreme significance:

- Children in preschool programs evidenced significant IQ gains. These gains tended to diminish when the children entered school, although the decline could be offset by continuation of the intervention programs.
- Children in cognitively oriented, structured programs made more significant gains than children in play-oriented programs.
- Children made greater and more enduring gains when parents were part of the intervention effort.

Lazar and Darlington (1979) reported on "graduates" of early intervention programs as they continued into elementary school. Included among their findings were the following:

- Graduates of early intervention programs were placed in special education less often than control group children who did not receive early intervention.

- Regardless of program, failure patterns were reduced and fewer children were retained at a grade level.
- Children who had been in early intervention programs were much less likely to be identified as underachievers than control group children who had not been in such programs.
- Children who had been in early intervention programs scored higher on achievement tests in arithmetic than did control group children.

Similar gains have been reported for handicapped preschool children (Stock, Wnek, Newborg, Schenck, Gabel, Spurgeon, & Ray, 1976). Unfortunately, until more reliable means to identify the young child with a learning disorder are available, efficacy of programs for learning-disordered preschoolers must be inferred from research conducted on other children with special needs.

Chapter 6

Families of Mentally Retarded Children

While mental retardation has probably been in existence almost as long as humans have inhabited the earth (Gearheart & Litton, 1979), great public awareness, interest, and even knowledge about it are more recent phenomena. The National Association for Retarded Children (NARC), organized in 1950 and comprised mainly of parents of retarded children, played a prominent role both in stimulating public interest and providing information on mental retardation. Initially, NARC's major purpose was the implementation of model demonstration programs through its own service delivery system. As public schools began to provide more classroom programs specifically for the mildly and moderately retarded, NARC shifted its emphasis to the preschool and severely/profoundly mentally retarded. As services to the mentally retarded expanded and, in some cases, improved, the organization became active in the promotion of legislation (both state and federal) for the purpose of further expanding and improving services for the retarded (Kott, 1971). In 1973, recognizing that the adult retarded also needed an advocate, the organization changed its name to the National Association for Retarded Citizens.

Today, NARC has grown to an organization of some 250,000 members in more than 1,600 local and state chapters. Although it remains largely an organization of parents, professionals in the field of mental retardation and representatives of industry, government, labor, and the entertainment field are included in its membership. The almost missionary zeal of its parent and professional staff members has resulted in NARC's unprecedented success in securing services for retarded citizens in the United States (Gearheart & Litton, 1979).

The decade of the 1960s brought increased public awareness of mental retardation through the leadership of President John F. Kennedy. In 1961, Kennedy appointed a panel of nationally recognized leaders in the field of mental retardation. This panel recommended a national effort to combat the effects of mental retardation (Mayo, 1971). Its specific recommendations involved increasing research efforts, expanding and improving educational programs, increasing public awareness, and improving training programs in the study of all aspects of mental retardation to overcome personnel shortages.

President Lyndon B. Johnson appointed the President's Committee on Mental Retardation by executive order in 1966. The functions of the committee include the provision of advice and assistance regarding mental retardation to the President or Secretary of Health and Human Services. The committee provides specific information in the following areas: (1) the adequacy of the national effort to combat mental retardation; (2) the potential of selected federal programs designed to achieve the President's goals in mental retardation; (3) the provision of adequate liaison between the activities of the federal government and the activities of state and local governments, private foundations, and various private organizations; and (4) the development and dissemination of information regarding the reduction of mental retardation and the amelioration of its effects (*MR 74: A Friend in Washington,* 1975).

The 1960s and 1970s brought a flurry of federal legislation and litigation that affected the mentally retarded, (see Chapter 4, Rights and Responsibilities of Families of Young Handicapped Children). Important concepts such as normalization (Wolfensberger, 1972) and the least restrictive environment have made the general public much more aware of the mentally retarded, their needs, and, of course, their rights.

WHAT IS MENTAL RETARDATION?

Numerous authors (Gearheart & Litton, 1979; Hutt & Gibby, 1979; MacMillan, 1982; Robinson & Robinson, 1976) have noted the difficulty in arriving at a universally acceptable definition of mental retardation. As a concept, mental retardation has eluded precise definition essentially because it is a highly relative and complex sociocultural phenomenon (Scheerenberger, 1971). Gearheart and Litton (1979) suggested four factors that have combined to prevent the development of a single, universally acceptable definition of mental retardation:

1. Mental retardation, regardless of form or cause, is determined primarily on the basis of the sociocultural standards of a given society. These standards are often in a state of constant fluctuation.
2. Many disciplines are involved in providing services to the retarded (e.g., medicine, law, education, social work). Each discipline has developed a definition to suit its professional area of concern.

3. Mental retardation is an extremely complex entity, with different causes and different levels of functioning. It is difficult to include such diversity under one rubric.
4. Because Western civilization prizes intellect, it is difficult to arrive at a definition of mental retardation that does not have negative connotations and is socially acceptable.

A review of a number of definitions of mental retardation reveals that various approaches have been employed in efforts to define the concept. MacMillan (1982) in discussing definitions utilized biological, social, psychosocial, and psychometric in combination with adaptive behavior functioning as categories.

Since physicians were among the first professionals to work with the retarded, it is not surprising to find that early definitions place a heavy emphasis on the biological aspects of the condition (MacMillan, 1982). Ireland (1900), for example, paid special attention to the organic origins of the problem. Ireland (1900) defined mental retardation as

mental deficiency, or extreme stupidity, depending upon malnutrition or disease of the nervous centers, occurring either before birth or before the evolution of mental faculties in childhood. The word imbecility is generally used to denote a less decided degree of mental incapacity. (p. 1)

Some eight years later, Tredgold (1908) proposed a biological definition of retardation that included a social adequacy emphasis. Tredgold defined retardation as

a state of mental defect from birth, or from an early age due to incomplete cerebral development, in consequence of which the person affected is unable to perform his duties as a member of society in the position of life to which he is born. (p. 2)

Professionals who view mental retardation as a social phenomenon have proposed a number of definitions that take into account the individual's ability to function socially in the environment. Since the determinants of adequate social functioning are related to culturally imposed criteria, social definitions of retardation must take into account the relative nature of the condition.

Doll (1941) defined retardation from a psychosocial viewpoint, with emphasis on the social competence of the individual. He stated,

Six criteria by statement or implication have been generally considered essential to an adequate definition and concept. These are (1) social incompetence, (2) due to mental subnormality, (3) which has been developmentally arrested, (4) which obtains at maturity, (5) is of constitutional origin and (6) is essentially incurable. (p. 45)

Kanner (1949) recognized the importance of cultural determinants of retardation by balancing the intellectual deficit with the demands imposed by the particular society. He suggested that certain types of retardates had limitations that were largely related to their cultural milieu.

The popularization of the Stanford-Binet Intelligence Scale, with its ease of administration, objectivity, and well-defined normative comparison groups, led to definitions of retardation that are based on the IQ score. A score of 70 on an IQ test is often used as a cutoff point. Those who score at 70 or below may be considered retarded. Other cutoff scores may be used, however; some school districts define eligibility for special class placement as a score at or below 75 or 80.

The use of the IQ as the sole criterion for determining retardation has been highly controversial. Critics have suggested that IQ scores are derived from a strictly limited sample of behavior and do not encompass the demands of cultural or subcultural groups. Since different skills and behaviors are required for different age groups in different cultures, retardation must be viewed in relation to environmental demands.

The need for a more widely applicable definition of retardation caused professionals from the American Association on Mental Deficiency (AAMD) to formulate a definition in 1959. This definition, revised in 1961 (Heber, 1961), defined mental retardation as

subaverage general intellectual functioning which originates in the developmental period and is associated with impairment in adaptive behavior. (p. 3)

This definition contained both a psychometric and social criterion, and established an upper age limit during which the condition had to originate. All three criteria had to be present for diagnosis of mental retardation.

Heber (1961) further defined each criterion and included information on the measurement of each. Subaverage intellectual functioning was defined as performance on an individual test of intelligence that was more than one standard deviation below the mean. The developmental period was established with an upper chronological age limit of 16 years. Finally, adaptive behavior was defined as behavior that demonstrated the person's ability to meet the natural and social demands of a particular community or society.

From 1961 to 1973, the field of mental retardation underwent significant changes. There were court cases involving the use of intelligence tests with minority and disadvantaged children and criticism surfaced among professional, parental, and advocate groups.

Shifts in prevailing attitudes involving the use of the term *borderline retardation* were evident in the 1977 AAMD revised definition of retardation. The current definition reads (Grossman, 1977):

> Mental retardation refers to significantly subaverage general intellectual functioning existing concurrently with deficits in adaptive behavior, and manifested during the developmental period. (p. 5)

The 1977 revision stipulated that "significantly subaverage general intellectual functioning" is determined by performance on an individual test of intelligence that is more than two standard deviations below the mean. Thus, instead of a ceiling IQ of 84 or 85, the revised definition employs a ceiling IQ of 68 or 70 (dependent on whether the Wechsler or Stanford-Binet is used). In addition, the developmental period was extended to an upper chronological age limit of 18 years. Furthermore, adaptive behavior was more precisely defined in terms of problem areas and age-relevant criteria.

Under the 1977 AAMD definition of retardation, once the IQ score has been determined, a retarded individual is assigned to a level of retardation ranging from mild to profound. Table 6-1 shows the retardation levels and accompanying IQ scores for each level.

Table 6-1 AAMD Levels of Retardation

Retardation Level	Range in Standard Deviation Values	Range in IQ Scores Stanford-Binet	Range in IQ Scores Wechsler Tests
Mild	−2.01 to −3.00	67 to 52	69 to 55
Moderate	−3.01 to −4.00	51 to 36	54 to 40
Severe	−4.01 to −5.00	35 to 20	39 to 25
Profound	Below −5.00	19 and below	24 and below[a]

[a]*Extrapolated.*

The levels are determined by the extent to which the IQ is below the mean in terms of standard deviation units. For the Wechsler tests, a standard deviation is equal to ± 15 IQ points, while the Stanford-Binet has a standard deviation equal to ± 16 points. Obviously, with more severe levels of retardation that are accompanied by physical impairments and lack of verbal ability, the reliability of individual intelligence tests is highly questionable.

In addition to the generic definition of mental retardation and standard definitions based on the level of retardation (Grossman, 1977), Sontag, Burke, and York (1973) proposed the following descriptive definition for the severely and profoundly handicapped (including the retarded):

> [They] are not toilet trained; aggress toward others; do not attend to even the most pronounced social stimuli; self-mutilate; ruminate; do not walk, speak, hear, or see; manifest durable and intense temper tantrums; are not even under the rudimentary forms of verbal control; do not imitate; manifest minimally controlled seizures; and/or have extremely brittle medical existences. (p. 21)

WHAT ARE THE CHARACTERISTICS OF MENTALLY RETARDED CHILDREN?

Characteristics of the Mildly Retarded Young Child

For the most part, mildly retarded preschool children are not identified as different from their nonretarded peers. They resemble other children in physical, behavioral, and even intellectual development. The gross physical abnormalities, language and learning deficits, and overall developmental delays frequently found in more severely retarded children do not usually occur in this group.

The greatest percentage of the mentally retarded population, some 85 percent, fall into this category of retardation, sometimes referred to as cultural-familial, of nonspecific origin, or of unknown etiology. It appears that certain sociological, economic, cultural, and psychological elements, in interaction with hereditary factors, contribute to the occurrence of mild mental retardation.

Cognitive Characteristics

There is a dearth of research on the cognitive characteristics of young mildly retarded children primarily because they are not usually identified until they enter school and certain "academic" tasks differentiate these children from their nonretarded peers. Some early studies (Kirk, 1958; Skeels & Dye, 1939) have been used by advocates of early intervention programs to substantiate their belief that young retarded children could profit from an early, educative environment. Yet neither of these "pioneer" studies focuses on actual cognitive or learning characteristics.

Authorities who propose a developmental learning model (MacMillan, 1982) agree that differences in cognitive abilities between young retarded and nonretarded children are primarily quantitative rather than qualitative. In other words, although the retarded *may* learn at a slower rate and acquire an overall smaller amount of information, their process of learning is essentially the same. It should be noted, however, that the mentally retarded are inefficient learners.

Because of the aforementioned lack of research on the learning characteristics of preschool retarded children, research with older mentally retarded persons must be used as the basis for certain assumptions about preschool children. The following salient characteristics have been noted in older children:

1. The mildly retarded as a group are deficient in attending to relevant stimuli (Mercer & Snell, 1977; Zeaman & House, 1963, 1979); however, although the retarded subjects take longer to understand the task than do nonretarded subjects, once they do understand it performance differences are minimal (Logan & Rose, 1982).

2. As a group, the mildly retarded are deficient in short-term memory, perhaps because of a lack of adequate rehearsal strategies (Bray, 1979). Rehearsal strategies are mediators, either language or visual images, that facilitate memory, such as repetition, mnemonic devices, or grouping.

3. The mildly retarded as a group appear to be deficient in the use of grouping, organizing, or classifying strategies that permit them to cluster information for ease of learning and retention (Spitz, 1966).

4. The results of long-term memory are mixed. Some studies have shown a long-term memory deficit (Prehm & Mayfield, 1970); others have suggested that, although the retarded may take longer to learn the task initially, once they have mastered it they retain it as well as nonretarded persons (MacMillan, 1982).

5. Transfer of learning—the ability to apply prior learning to a similar but not identical situation—appears not to be impaired significantly in mildly retarded learners (Evans & Bilsky, 1979).

Motor and Health Characteristics

The link between mild mental retardation and socioeconomic factors seems irrefutable. With impoverished living conditions comes inadequate nutrition; potential for injury from accident, neglect, or abuse; inadequate medical care; greater potential for contracting infectious diseases; increased likelihood of contact with toxic substances; and significantly decreased likelihood of innoculation against childhood and other diseases. Certain characteristics of either the child's mother or father may also predispose an unborn child to mental retardation. These contributing factors include inadequate maternal nutrition; lack of proper prenatal care; abuse of tobacco, alcohol, or drugs; and maternal age (e.g., very young). Prematurity or low birth weight, in conjunction with lack of oxygen immediately after birth, may also contribute to mild mental retardation. A possible correlate of this is damage to the central nervous system, a factor that has been linked to mild retardation in some research studies (Birch & Gussow, 1970).

Most of these problems are not visible. Children with mild retardation just do not look "funny" or "different," even though they may be in poor health and poor physical condition.

Personality Characteristics

The personal and social characteristics evidenced by young mildly retarded children must be viewed in the context of their home situation. In spite of the clear link between poverty and mild mental retardation, it must be remembered that the characteristics discussed here are generalizations and thus are not applicable to all lower socioeconomic level families.

In families in which one or both parents have had difficulties in school or suffer from a low self-concept, feelings of inadequacy, frustration, and despair are often coveyed to the children. Furthermore, it may be necessary to apply all available financial resources to basic survival, leaving little or no money for such items as educational books, toys, games, or newspapers. When both parents work, or when only one parent—who works—lives with the children, there is virtually no time, energy, and often, motivation to interact with the children.

Living conditions tend to be crowded and noisy, diminishing the need and opportunity to use language. The language that is used tends to be both concrete and oriented to the present.

Characteristics of the Moderately Retarded Young Child

Less than 10 percent of all mentally retarded persons are moderately retarded. The most common clinical syndrome associated with moderate retardation is Down's syndrome, which accounts for nearly 10 percent of all cases of moderate retardation.

Cognitive Characteristics

Research studies regarding the learning or cognitive characteristics of young moderately retarded subjects are rare. Thus, "it is difficult to discriminate clearly characteristics that are specific to the moderately . . . mentally retarded" (Fink & Cegelka, 1982, p. 236). Some basic learning characteristics of young moderately retarded children can be gleaned from research on learning and cognition in older children, however.

From the perspective of the developmental theorists (Zigler, 1969), the cognitive abilities of the retarded are characterized by a slower rate of development related to the IQ and a lesser quantity of information acquired. Both areas may be termed quantitative (e.g., rate, amount), rather than qualitative (e.g., process, neurological structures, or function) differences.

Research in the areas usually associated with learning—attention, memory, organization of input, and transfer of learning—suggests that the moderately retarded are remarkably similar in cognitive characteristics to the mildly retarded. Again, the time required to master tasks seems to be the crucial variable. Once the moderately retarded child is able to attend to the relevant dimensions of a learning task, the learning rate is nearly identical to that of nonretarded peers. The same can be said for memory, organization, and transfer; when the moderately retarded child is able to recognize the requirements of a task; is provided with some organizational or clustering assistance, as well as practice in rehearsal strategies; and practices to the point of overlearning, short-term memory can be greatly improved and long-term memory seems to be equal to that of nonretarded peers.

In summary, it appears that young moderately retarded persons can learn important social and academic skills, provided the learning conditions are *carefully* structured and orchestrated. The upper limits to what they may learn has been suggested by Inhelder (1968): the "use of symbols, the acquisition of new experiences through imitation of others, and the assimilation of customs" (Fink & Cegelka, 1982, p. 242).

Motor and Health Characteristics

Moderately retarded children often have facial, cranial, or other body deformities. A general rule of thumb is that the more severe the retardation, the greater the probability of noticeable physical signs. Many of the physical characteristics are linked directly to specific syndromes of retardation. Some of the more common are

- Down's syndrome. Skull size is small, and occiput is flat. Eyes tend to slant upward. Ears and mouth tend to be small.
- hydrocephalus. Head circumference is enlarged; visual defects and convulsions may occur.
- microcephalus. Skull circumference and stature are small; visual defects may be present.
- mucopolysaccharidoses. Hurler's syndrome, the prototype of this disorder, is associated with a large malformed head; short stature; corneal clouding; and coarse facial features. Hunter's syndrome is the same, without corneal clouding.
- neurofibromatosis (von Recklinghausen's disease). Large, unsightly tumors grow within the nervous system. Spinal defects may be involved.

Many of the syndromes associated with moderate retardation also cause specific health problems that require ongoing medical treatment. For example, Down's syndrome children frequently have structural defects of the heart, lung abnormalities that result in frequent upper respiratory infections, and problems with their teeth and gums. Children with fetal alcohol syndrome have cardiac deformities and growth deficiencies.

Personality Characteristics

There appears to be a relationship between intelligence and the development of appropriate personal and social skills. Limited problem-solving abilities are likely to result in frustration and overreaction to even minimal stress. Impulsivity and hyperactivity further complicate the acquisition of social skills. The younger moderately retarded child is likely to lack basic self-help skills, such as those required for toileting, dressing, and feeding. Play behaviors, cooperativeness, and other social skills are likely to be delayed, and the lag in skill development is likely to increase with age. Many maladaptive behaviors, including stereotyped acts (e.g., rocking or finger flicking) and temper tantrums, may be present, particularly for youngsters in institutionalized settings.

In some cases, behavior in the sense of temperament is a function of the specific syndrome associated with the retardation. For example, children with Hurler's syndrome are usually friendly and affectionate, while children with Hunter's syndrome tend to be hyperactive and difficult to manage. In the same fashion, children with untreated phenylketonuria (PKU) are often described as hyperactive, irritable, and subject to severe temper tantrums (Robinson & Robinson, 1976).

Characteristics of the Severely and Profoundly Retarded Young Child

Mori and Masters (1980) used the term *severely retarded* to refer to children with both severe and profound retardation. The same thing will be done in this book, even though real heterogeneity exists among severely retarded children.

Cognitive Characteristics

The IQ scores that define the severely retarded are considered to be 35 and below for the Stanford-Binet and 39 and below for the Wechsler tests (Table 6-1). Of course, as Snell (1982) noted, "the reliability of individual intelligence tests is questionable when used with nonverbal individuals, as the . . . severely . . . retarded typically are, [because] these definitive IQ boundaries imply a precision that probably cannot be achieved with current psychometric methods" (p. 291).

Inhelder's (1968) research suggested that the severely retarded adult fixates at the level of intelligence normally achieved during the first two to two and one-half years of a child's life. Mori and Masters (1980) summarized the behaviors associated with the period as follows:

1. reflexive actions such as sucking, grasping, visual tracking
2. arm movements, hand waving, hand regard (repeated frequently)
3. eye hand coordination—often beyond the behavioral repertoire of the profoundly mentally retarded, it still remains a critical skill to be acquired and as such, must be programmed for
4. beginning of certain adaptive behaviors—exploration of new objects, discovery of means differentiated from ends, imitation of motor movements
5. cause and effect and object permanence—the child will attempt to discover new means through experimentation and search for hidden objects
6. simple deductive thinking and simple problem solving through mental operations. (p. 14)

The literature in behavioral programming suggests that the severely retarded can learn useful and productive behaviors (Bigelow & Griffiths, 1977; Levy, Pomerantz, & Gold, 1977), provided the conditions under which learning is to occur are carefully orchestrated. In addition, an analysis of the literature clearly reveals that the severely retarded can be taught skills in specific areas, including

- self-help (Azrin & Foxx, 1971; Azrin, Schaeffer, & Wesolowski, 1976; Luckey & Chandler, 1968)
- communication (Guess, Sailor, & Bear, 1976; Kent, 1974)
- social skills (Peterson, Austin, & Lang, 1979)
- daily living skills (Laus, 1977)

Motor and Health Characteristics

The degree of mental retardation is directly correlated to the degree of physical defect. The more severe the mental retardation, the greater the probability of a physically handicapping condition.

Utley, Holvoet, and Barnes (1977) noted that severely retarded persons with physical handicaps have abnormal posture and movement difficulties associated with too little, too much, or constantly fluctuating levels of muscle tone. Voluntary movement is further limited by the absence or delay of righting and equilibrium reactions. Furthermore, the reflexes of those who are both severely retarded and physically impaired frequently persist long after the normal time of inhibition. When these abnormal reflexes persist, they cause abnormal movements that make more advanced forms of movement impossible.

There appears to be a preponderance of sensory defects among severely mentally retarded children. Chinn, Drew, and Logan (1979) reported that disproportionate percentages of deafness, hearing loss, and defects of visual acuity have been found in populations of moderately, severely, and profoundly mentally retarded children.

In addition to the physical handicaps associated with severe mental retardation, this population has more chronic health problems than either the nonretarded or even the mildly and moderately mentally retarded. These chronic health problems can include

- metabolic disorders
- seizures
- abnormal dermatoglyphics
- congenital heart disease
- respiratory diseases or infections
- gastrointestinal disorders
- diabetes

Personality Characteristics

Professionals in special education agree that the incidence of behavioral disturbances is higher among the retarded population than among nonhandicapped individuals. Research indicates that approximately 40 percent of the retarded population may have an emotional or personality deviation, compared with about 10 percent for the nonretarded population (Chinn, Drew, & Logan, 1979).

An extremely high percentage of children who have an IQ below 25 show bizarre symptoms that are compulsively repetitive or self-mutilative (Menolascino, 1972). These behavioral patterns are usually more prevalent among children living in institutions than among children living in home situations. Forehand and Baumeister (1970) indicated that these bizarre patterns are probably related to tension and to a lack of interesting and active pursuits. They are more common in blind retarded individuals than in sighted ones and in the nonambulatory than in the ambulatory (Guess, 1966). Robinson and Robinson (1976) suggested that self-mutilative behaviors can be a form of occupation when normal stimulation is lacking for too long a time period.

Social skills training has proved to be a difficult area. Such training is provided less often, and the skills are measured less frequently despite the acknowledged critical importance of this area (Whitman & Scibak, 1979). If instruction is appropriately orchestrated, the severely retarded can be taught social play with peers (Peterson et al., 1979), play with toys (Wambold & Baily, 1979), and other purposeful social activity (Quilitch & Gray, 1974).

HOW MANY CHILDREN ARE LIKELY TO BE IDENTIFIED AS MENTALLY RETARDED?

There is some controversy regarding the actual number of mentally retarded persons in our society. Often, the terms *prevalence* and *incidence* are used interchangeably, further confusing the issue. Prevalence is the number of cases of a condition identified in a population at a given point in time. Thus, a prevalence rate is a measure of the total number of cases of a condition. Incidence, on the other hand, is a measure of the number of new cases occurring in a population within a specific period of time, usually a year.

The figure used most commonly as an estimate of the prevalence of mental retardation is 3 percent of the population. This corresponds to the percentage of persons with an IQ below 70 and to some surveys conducted in the United States citing a modal figure of 2 to 3 percent (Robinson &

Robinson, 1976). This figure is based on IQ estimate alone, however, with no regard to the measure of adaptive behavior.

Mercer (1973) and Tarjan, Wright, Eyman, and Keeran (1973) argued that the prevalence of mental retardation is closer to 1 percent. In fact, Tarjan and associates noted that, "though 3 percent of the newborn population will be suspected and even diagnosed as mentally retarded sometime during their life, probably during their school years, it is incorrect to assume that at any given time 3 percent of the population is so identified or is apt to be diagnosed" (p. 370).

Robinson and Robinson (1976) and MacMillan (1982) noted that other factors affect the prevalence of mental retardation. Included among these are age, sex, geographical region, racial and ethnic background, and the community. Higher rates of mental retardation are noted for males, in lower socioeconomic status families, among minorities, and in certain geographical regions of the United States.

In summary, an excellent case can be made for distinguishing between prevalence and incidence. As Maloney and Ward (1979) suggested,

> Given all the issues concerning the occurrence of mental retardation, two conclusions can be made. First, the true incidence of mental retardation is probably around 3 percent. In other words, approximately 3 percent of the population will be classified as mentally retarded at some point in their life. However, for a large portion of these people, this will be a temporary label, acquired during the school years only. Given this fact, some researchers suggest that these cases should be called "educationally handicapped" or "educationally disadvantaged." They would reserve the label "mental retardation" for persons with more chronic and pervasive adaptive impairments. The second conclusion follows directly from the first. The true prevalence of mental retardation is probably about 1 percent. Only about 1 percent of the population is classified as mentally retarded at any given point. The 3 percent figure is actually an incidence estimate rather than than a prevalence estimate. (p. 188)

HOW ARE MENTALLY RETARDED CHILDREN IDENTIFIED?

From a practical standpoint, mildly retarded children undergo a much different identification process than do those who are moderately and severely mentally retarded. In most cases, moderate or severe retardation is diagnosed at birth or during the first year of life. The diagnosis is almost always made by a physician (or some medical support professional) and remains with the child into the school years and beyond.

In contrast, the mildly retarded (approximately 80 to 85 percent of the retarded population) are identified by professionals in education, such as teachers and psychologists. The diagnosis of mild retardation is made largely because the child is unable to cope with academic tasks, although the child may excel in some nonacademic areas, such as art, music, or sports.

Often, these youngsters leave the formal public school system and enter society as semiskilled or unskilled workers. Whether the mildly retarded "melt" into society as productive members is a subject laced with controversy. MacMillan (1982), in summarizing the results of adjustment studies, noted that "former EMRs [Educable Mentally Retarded—mildly retarded] appear at the lowest points on scales of social and occupational adjustment. . . . [They do not] compare favorably to the nonretarded person coming from the same social class" (p. 350).

Diagnosis of Mild Mental Retardation

The child who experiences pervasive and severe academic difficulties in school is often referred to the school psychologist for testing. While the diagnostic process varies from state to state and from school district to school district, its goal is to determine whether the child fits the definition of mental retardation, usually a variation of the 1977 AAMD definition. Within this definition are the three criteria for classifying a child as mentally retarded: (1) significant subaverage general functioning, (2) exists concurrently with adaptive behavior deficits, and (3) manifested during the developmental period. *All three* criteria must be satisfied before mild retardation can be diagnosed. This is a rigid requirement to prevent children from being classified as retarded solely on the basis of a single IQ score.

Several authors (MacMillan & Borthwick, 1980; Meyen & Morgan, 1979) have noted a definite trend against diagnosing and placing children in classes for the mildly retarded. Causes for this trend may be (1) fear of litigation, particularly for minority children, in cases of mislabeling and (2) the realization by regular class teachers that, even if they refer the child, they are still likely to have to educate the child because of the least restrictive environment principle of Public Law 94-142 (MacMillan & Borthwick, 1980; Meyen & Morgan, 1979).

Significant Subaverage General Intellectual Functioning

Performance on an individually administered intelligence test that is more than two standard deviations below the mean (usually 100) of the test indicates significant subaverage general intellectual functioning. On the two most frequently used scales, this is represented by an IQ of 67 or below (Stanford-Binet) or 69 or below (Wechsler tests).

The Stanford-Binet is based on mental age. It begins at age 2 and extends through the superior adult range with over 100 separate tests. Both Valett (1964) and Sattler (1965) have proposed schemes for grouping Stanford-Binet items into performance categories. The categories proposed by Sattler are as follows:

- Language. This includes tests related to maturity of vocabulary (in relation to the prekindergarten level), extent of vocabulary (referring to the number of words the child can define), quality of vocabulary (measured by such tests as abstract words, rhymes, word naming, and definitions), and comprehension of verbal relations.

- Memory. This category contains meaningful, nonmeaningful, and visual memory tests. The tests are considered to reflect rote auditory memory, ideational memory, and attention span.

- Conceptual thinking. This category, while closely associated with language ability, is primarily concerned with abstract thinking. Such functions as generalization, assuming an "as if" attitude, conceptual thinking, and using a categorical attitude are subsumed.

- Reasoning. This category contains verbal and nonverbal reasoning tests. The verbal absurdity tests are the prototype for verbal reasoning tests. The pictorial and orientation problems represent a mode for the nonverbal reasoning tests. Reasoning includes the perception of logical relations, discrimination ability, and analysis and synthesis. Spatial reasoning may also be measured by the orientation tests.

- Numerical reasoning. This category includes tests involving arithmetic reasoning problems. The content is closely related to school learning. Numerical reasoning involves concentration and the ability to generalize from numerical data.

- Visual-motor. This category contains tests concerned with manual dexterity, eye hand coordination, and perception of spatial relations. Constructive visual imagery may be involved in the paper folding test. Nonverbal reasoning ability may be involved in some of the visual-motor tests.

- Social intelligence. This category strongly overlaps with the reasoning category so that consideration should be given to the tests classified in the latter as also reflecting social comprehension. Social intelligence includes social maturity and social judgment. The comprehension and reasons-finding tests are seen to reflect social judgment, whereas obeying simple commands, response to pictures, and comparison tests likely reflect social maturity.*

The Wechsler tests are divided into three age ranges. The Wechsler Pre-School and Primary Scale of Intelligence (WPPSI) is used for children from 4 to 6-½ years old. The Wechsler Intelligence Scale for Children— Revised (WISC-R) covers the ages 6 to 16, and the Wechsler Adult Intelligence Scale—Revised (WAIS-R) covers ages beyond 16. One of the major advantages of the Wechsler scales is that they yield a profile type of analysis. The profile can be used to determine relative strengths and weaknesses in cognitive, perceptual, and motor areas.

The WPPSI and WISC-R consist of basic subtests divided into verbal and performance areas (Table 6-2). Both of these tests yield three IQ scores: verbal IQ, performance IQ, and full scale IQ.

A brief description of the WISC-R subtests is provided in Table 6-3. Other tests used to determine the IQ of various populations of young children are described in Table 6-4.

Exists Concurrently with Adaptive Behavior Deficits

Grossman (1977) described adaptive behavior as the effectiveness or degree with which an individual meets the standards of personal independence and social responsibility expected for his or her age and cultural group. Contained within these aspects of adaptive behavior is the concept of social maturity, which takes into account the specific skills or behaviors that are considered appropriate for specific chronological ages. This concept encompasses the general areas of motor development, language development, social skills, and cognitive skills. In an evaluation of adaptive behavior, observations are compared with an established set of age standards for that specific culture.

For the domain of motor development, observations are compared with expected developmental milestones for individuals of the same chronological age. In order to make such a comparison, the evaluator must understand "normal" child development. For example, the motor development of a preschool youngster can be assessed with relative ease if the evaluator

---

*From *Assessment of children's intelligence and special abilities* (2nd ed.), by J. M. Sattler, p. 136, copyright 1982. Reprinted by permission of Allyn & Bacon, Boston, Massachusetts.

Table 6-2 Subtests on the WPPSI and WISC-R

	WPPSI	WISC-R	
Verbal Subtests			
Information	X	X	
Comprehension	X	X	
Similarities	X	X	
Arithmetic	X	X	
Vocabulary	X	X	
Digit span		X	
Sentences	X		
Performance Subtests			
Picture completion	X	X	
Picture arrangement		X	
Block design	X	X	
Object assembly		X	
Coding		X	
Animal house	X		
Mazes	X	X	(Supplementary)
Geometric design	X		
(Animal house retest)	X		

knows that a child should possess specific reflexes, sit alone at approximately seven months, stand by nine months, and walk at one year (Frankenburg, Dodds, & Fandal, 1970). Delayed motor development may be an accompanying characteristic of mild retardation; however, this is not usually the case. Impaired motor development can also occur in such conditions as cerebral palsy and hypotonia, where mental functioning is unaffected, making the determination of intellectual functioning more difficult.

Language development must also receive attention when a child's adaptive behavior is evaluated. Delayed speech due to articulation, fluency, and other expressive problems may indicate retardation (Kirk, 1964; Spradlin, 1963). In addition, receptive and organizational problems involving language suggest retardation. Communication levels can be easily assessed through the use of established developmental milestones for normal speech, language skill areas (reading, vocabulary, spelling, and writing), and social conversation.

Cognitive skills are the most direct measure of general intelligence. According to Piaget, the level of intellectual development in the retarded person is fixated at a specific level. Adaptive behavior is a combination of several aspects of behavior and a function of a wide range of specific abilities and disabilities (Grossman, 1977), and cognitive skills give the

Table 6-3 Factors Assessed by WISC-R Subtests

Subtest	Factor(s) Assessed
Information	Range of information picked up through the years, memory (cultural milieu inferred), verbal comprehension
Comprehension	Verbal comprehension, judgment, understanding
Arithmetic	Arithmetic reasoning, concentration, memory, numerical fluency
Similarities	Concept formation, abstract vs. functional and concrete thinking, verbal comprehension
Vocabulary	Vocabulary, word meaning (cultural milieu inferred), verbal comprehension
Digit span	Memory—attention (automatic factor)
Picture completion	Discrimination between essential and nonessential detail, memory
Picture arrangement	Social alertness, common sense, planning and anticipating, sequencing, ability to synthesize
Block design	Perception, analysis, synthesis, reproduction of abstract designs (logic and reasoning applied to space relationships)
Object assembly	Perception, visual-motor coordination, visual imagery, synthesis of concrete forms, flexibility of working toward a goal, spatial relationships
Coding	Psychomotor speed, eye-hand coordination, pencil manipulation
Mazes	Ability to plan in a new situation (problem solving), ability to delay action, visual-motor coordination

Source: Adapted from *Diagnosing learning problems* (3rd ed.), by W. J. Bush and K. W. Waugh, pp. 167-168, copyright 1982. Reprinted by permission of Charles E. Merrill. Columbus. Ohio.

individual the opportunity to master language, understand the world, and control much of the environment.

Also related to adaptive behavior are social skills. Personality factors such as feelings of adequacy or success, emotional stability, and self-valuation are collectively influenced by the quality of the individual's interpersonal relationships with family, school, and the community. Adaptive behavior is a complex and dynamic attribute that continually changes with maturation and experience. Of course, others' view of an individual's behavior is governed by a number of cultural and societal factors. Although a particular group within a given society may view an individual's skills and behaviors as appropriate, different cultural or societal groups may consider them unacceptable.

It is extremely difficult to assess adaptive behavior by means of norm-referenced tests. Grossman (1977) believed the reason for this to be the difficulty of obtaining information on what a person does routinely, which is essentially the information needed for an adaptive behavior evaluation. Adaptive behavior cannot be measured by instruments given in offices or laboratories; it must be determined by a series of observations in many places over periods of time. The behaviors sampled by current intelligence tests contribute to total adaptation, however, and the level of function on measured intelligence correlates with the level of adaptive behavior (Grossman, 1977).

Like retarded intellectual development, adaptive behavior is categorized into levels of impairment (Grossman, 1977). These levels are scaled from

Table 6-4 Intelligence Tests for Use with Young Children

Test	Description
Columbia Mental Maturity Scale (CMMS; Burgemeister, Blum, & Lorge, 1972)	The CMMS is a pictorial classification test for use with children from three and one-half to nine years, 11 months of age. It requires no verbal and minimal motor response.
Leiter International Performance Scale (LIPS; Leiter, 1948)	The LIPS is a nonverbal performance scale used for measuring intelligence for persons 2 to 18 years of age. The entire test is given without verbal instructions and is useful with children who have limited verbal skills.
McCarthy Scales of Children's Abilities (MSCA; McCarthy, 1972)	The MCSA is designed to evaluate the general intellectual level as well as strengths and weaknesses of children two and one-half to eight and one-half years of age. It covers verbal, perceptual, performance, quantitative, memory, motor, and general cognitive skills.
Minnesota Preschool Scale (Goodenough, Maurer, & Wagenen, 1971)	This test yields both a verbal and nonverbal IQ for children from one and one-half to six years of age. Areas assessed include response to pictures, comprehension, absurdities, vocabulary, speech, and opposites.
Pictorial Test of Intelligence (French, 1964)	This is a nonverbal instrument designed to assess the general intellectual level of children from three to eight years of age. The six subtests are Picture Vocabulary, Form Discrimination, Information and Comprehension, Similarities, Size and Number, and Immediate Recall.

mild (but apparent and significant) deviation from the population norms to an almost complete lack of adaptive behavior at the lower extremes (profound). For example, adults at the severe and profound levels of impairment are quite likely to have central nervous system damage that restricts social behavioral responses. These individuals need training in communication skills and self-care skills and do not profit from academic instruction. Systematic and supervised practice over a long period of time is required before they can dress and feed themselves or find their way around the neighborhood. Little independent behavior is observed (Robinson & Robinson, 1976).

The tentative nature of adaptive behavior levels makes it necessary to examine individuals at fairly frequent intervals. Because adaptive behavior may change as a result of environmental shifts or training emphasis, consideration of these factors is often extremely helpful in evaluating adaptive behavior levels (Grossman, 1977).

As individuals grow older, they must cope with an ever expanding social environment. In measurement terms, there are two competing priorities. First, the developmental orientation suggests that test items be arranged by age level and selected to sample socially adaptive responses common to children of that particular age (Robinson & Robinson, 1976). Robinson and Robinson noted that this is a scale of the Binet type—a few representative items, selected to present a statistically balanced series and to correlate highly with scores on the total scale. This approach is based on normal development and measures an individual's adaptive behavior against age norms. In contrast, the approach based on adaptive behavior, as broadly inclusive of skills and responsibilities in a number of areas, demands the inventory type of scale with subscales (Robinson & Robinson, 1976).

The inventory approach appears to be more popular than the developmental approach because of the ease with which important target behaviors can be included and standards can be established. The majority of inventory scales were standardized on institutionalized mentally retarded populations, which facilitates the standardization process but limits interpretive possibilities.

Robinson and Robinson (1976) described a number of scales that have been designed to measure adaptive behavior or social competence:

- AAMD Adaptive Behavior Scales (Nihira, Foster, Shellhaas, & Leland, 1974)
- Adaptation for Profoundly Retarded (Congdon, 1973)
- 1972 Revision—School Form (Lambert, Wilcox, & Gleason, 1974)
- Alpern-Boll Developmental Profile (Alpern & Boll, 1972)

- Balthazar Scales of Adaptive Behavior (Balthazar, 1971; Balthazar, Roseen, & English, 1968)
- Bristol Social Adjustment Guides (Stott, 1963)
- Cain-Levine Social Competency Scale (Cain, Levine, & Elzey, 1963)
- Fairview Behavior Evaluation Battery for the Mentally Retarded (R. T. Ross, Boroskin, & Giampiccolo, 1970-1974)
- Gardner Behavior Chart (Dayan & McLean, 1963; Wilcox, 1942)
- Hospital Adjustment Scale (McReynolds, Ferguson, & Ballachey, 1963)
- Newman-Doby Measure of Social Competence (Newman & Doby, 1973)
- Preschool Educational Attainment Record (Doll, 1966)
- Progress Assessment Chart of Social Development (Gunzburg, 1968)
- Social Competence Rating (Banham, 1960)
- Vineland Social Maturity Scale (Doll, 1964)

The Alpern-Boll Developmental Profile, the Bristol Social Adjustment Guides, and the Vineland Social Maturity Scale are the only ones of this group originally standardized on normal populations, although one form of the AAMD Adaptive Behavior Scales has now been standardized on both nonretarded children in public school and handicapped children in special classes (Lambert et al., 1974).

These particular scales attempt to isolate the factors usually associated with adaptive behavior. In particular, 12 major areas of adaptive behavior are commonly assessed in the scale (Robinson & Robinson, 1976):

1. self-help skills, e.g., dressing, grooming, toileting
2. communication skills
3. socialization or interpersonal skills
4. locomotion
5. self-direction, e.g., initiative, attending
6. occupational skills
7. economic activity
8. neuromotor development
9. personal responsibility
10. social responsibility, e.g., taking care of others' property
11. emotional adjustment
12. health

Deficits in these major areas of adaptive behavior, as defined by the AAMD, are manifested according to age and cultural group:

1. During infancy and early childhood in the following:
   a. sensorimotor skills development
   b. communication skills (including speech and language)
   c. self-help skills
   d. socialization (development of ability to interact with others)
2. During childhood and early adolescence in the following:
   a. application of basic academic skills in daily activities
   b. application of appropriate reasoning and judgment in mastery of the environment
   c. social skills (participation in group activities and interpersonal relationships)
3. During late adolescence and adult life in the following:
   a. vocational and social responsibilities and performances (Grossman, 1977, p. 13)

Despite the problems with and criticisms of norm-referenced tests, many school districts mandate the use of these tests both for placement and educational program decision making.

Manifested during the Developmental Period

In order to ensure that mental retardation is recognized as a developmental disability and in order to distinguish it from other conditions that may result in impaired intellectual capacity and deficits in adaptive behavior, the AAMD definition of mental retardation requires that the condition be manifested during the developmental period. This encompasses the period from birth to 18 years, presumably when intelligence is developing.

Diagnosis of Moderate and Severe Mental Retardation

Most often, moderate and severe mental retardation are diagnosed during infancy or the first two years of life. Many of the more than 250 conditions known to cause retardation are associated with recognizable physical characteristics that alert the physician attending the birth or the pediatrician attending the neonate to an existing problem. In the absence of gross physical abnormalities, pediatricians may, during the first year, detect neurological problems or delays in motor development. Seizures in this period are often a signal that a child has mental and physical abnormalities.

For those children who do not manifest obvious physical symptoms or gross development delays, mental retardation may not be diagnosed until after two years of age. Parents or the pediatrician may detect a delay in language development, toileting skills, or motor skills; or a lack of social skills (i.e., shyness or inability to play with peers). At this point, the pediatrician may conduct a thorough evaluation, including a developmental and medical history in addition to a physical examination. Further referral may be made for psychological and social evaluations, particularly if the pediatrician is enlightened to the needs of special children and their parents.

WHAT IS THE IMPACT OF MENTAL RETARDATION ON FAMILIES?

Wolfensberger (1967) identified three crises, related to the child's age, that may be experienced by parents of severely retarded children. These stages may be experienced separately or simultaneously:

1. novelty shock crisis. At the time of diagnosis, parents react with shock because the child's actual characteristics are in opposition to the parents' expectations for the child.
2. value crisis. It may be difficult or impossible for parents to accept mental retardation (or its manifestations) because it is in opposition to the parents' system of values. For example, in a family with a value system that emphasizes academic excellence and higher education, the presence of a mentally retarded child unable to excel in these areas may cause great suffering for the parents. The value crisis frequently results in some form of parental rejection, ranging from the mildest form (overprotection) to the most extreme form (immediate institutionalization and denial of the child's existence).
3. reality crisis. The third crisis usually occurs later in the life of the retarded person when the retarded adult may be viewed as dangerous. It also occurs when parents realize the extent of the care the child needs or when necessary professional services are unavailable in the parents' home community.

Wolfensberger (1967) suggested that parents in these various crisis situations require different kinds of professional assistance. Thus, the professional *must* be aware of the crisis the parent is experiencing. The parent in novelty shock needs information and emotional support. Families experiencing the value crisis frequently need ongoing, intensive counseling, while those experiencing the reality crisis require practical assistance to solve day-to-day problems (Wolfensberger, 1967; see also Chapter 3, Helping Families Deal with Practical Problems).

While parents of the mildly retarded child may experience these crises, they are likely to encounter them later, when the child enters the public education system. As discussed earlier, professionals in education become the first to identify the child as retarded. When parents reach the reality crisis, they often ask questions of school personnel such as (Marion, 1981)

- What academic skills will the child be capable of mastering?
- Will the child be able to be self-supporting?
- What kind of occupational choices will be available for the child?
- Will the child be able to live a normal adult life?

Parents may be both apprehensive and ambivalent about their child's school program. They may resist placing their child in special education; if they allow the child to be placed in such a program, they may resist becoming involved in it. Teachers must be aware of the parents' level of readiness for involvement (see Chapter 3, Helping Families Deal with Practical Problems) and must attempt to build the rapport necessary to establish a parent-professional partnership. In order to do this, they must recognize parents are undergoing stress and need help to work through their feelings and emotions and reach a level of acceptance of the child.

WHAT IS THE IMPACT OF MENTAL RETARDATION ON THE FUTURE LIVES OF CHILDREN?

Of course, the future development and adjustment of mentally retarded children are directly related to the severity of the condition. In some cases, the syndrome causing the retardation may result in early mortality, e.g., Tay-Sachs disease, or it may significantly shorten the life span, e.g., the mucopolysaccharide disorders.

For the mildly retarded child, early school experiences should be directed at a "normalizing" curriculum that emphasizes activities essential for school success, such as academic readiness skills and personal-social skills. As the child matures, the educational program should focus on functional skills and preparation for a satisfying personal, social, and vocational existence. Brolin and Kokaska (1979) have identified 22 major competency areas in their life-centered career education curriculum designed to promote adequate adult adjustment for the mentally retarded. Adult adjustment for the mildly retarded may be problematic, however, although appropriate programming can produce a more optimistic prognosis.

Sellin (1979) has produced a summary statement regarding the highest levels of representative adaptive behaviors that mildly retarded persons might develop (Table 6-5). These are representative behaviors suggesting optimal development and may not apply in all cases to all mildly retarded persons.

Few follow-up studies have been conducted on "graduates" of programs for the trainable mentally retarded (moderate retardation). The one major extensive study was conducted by Saenger (1957); it involved 520 adult graduates of trainable mentally retarded classes in New York City. Saenger's results may be summarized as follows:

- Nearly 66 percent of the graduates were living in the community.
- Some 26 percent were in institutions.
- Approximately 73 percent of the graduates were not working, and there was significant variation in the extent of their participation in home-related tasks.
- Nearly 50 percent of the graduates living in the community reported being happy and content.
- In general, most of the parents were satisfied with their child's adjustment.
- Few of the graduates had achieved economic self-sufficiency.

Since much of the educational focus for the moderately retarded is on basic self-help, independent living skills, and personal-social skills, the school program must be designed to develop these skills and to help graduates achieve a level of independence commensurate with their potential and capabilities. Table 6-6 illustrates the highest levels of adaptive behavior the moderately retarded may assume, provided that they receive appropriate educational opportunities.

For the severely mentally retarded, the teaching of daily living skills that increase the individual's level of independence should be given top priority. Early and ongoing intervention can lead to the acquisition of many useful self-care, social, and vocational skills (Mori & Masters, 1980). Tables 6-7 and 6-8 show the highest levels of adaptive behavior that might be possible for severely and profoundly retarded persons.

WHAT INTERVENTION STRATEGIES CAN BE USED FOR MENTALLY RETARDED CHILDREN?

Begab (1974) identified four major dimensions concerning the prevention of mental retardation:

1. genetic factors
2. prematurity
3. nutrition
4. social environmental factors

For the genetic errors known to cause mental retardation, current emphasis is on prenatal diagnosis (often amniocentesis) and subsequent abortion. In some cases, high-risk potential mothers may be given information regarding their probabilities of bearing a retarded child to reduce the incidence of mental retardation. Abortion is fraught with religious, moral, ethical, and even legal implications. A pregnant woman whose expected child is known to be retarded must make an informed choice as to the use of abortion.

Prematurity and low birth weight are related to poverty and the lack of adequate medical and prenatal care in low-income families. With these socioeconomic conditions comes malnutrition and its consequences. It is well-known that pregnant women have certain nutritional requirements, but social action in some form is necessary to employ this knowledge to prevent mental retardation.

Early and ongoing intervention can reduce the impact of social environmental factors on children who are particularly likely to be affected by them. Intervention projects, including those of Kirk (1958), Bereiter and Englemann (1966), and Heber, Garber, Harrington, Hoffman, and Falender (1972), have demonstrated promising results in mitigating the effects of poverty on cognitive functioning of environmentally at-risk children.

While there is evidence that prevention efforts can be effective, Begab (1974) cited eight obstacles to prevention efforts to date:

1. lack of a concentrated and cooperative effort
2. limitations of present knowledge
3. negative attitudinal and economic factors related to intense social programs, particularly in nutrition
4. negative attitudinal and economic factors regarding government spending on preschool intervention programs
5. difficulties in locating and involving at-risk families
6. failure to disseminate and use information regarding birth control, prenatal care, and family planning
7. lack of funding to support ongoing research efforts in genetics, nutrition, and family interventions
8. failure to provide examination for antenatal detection and abortion, as well as information, for high-risk mothers

Table 6-5 Representative Adaptive Behaviors Illustrating Highest Levels for the Mildly Mentally Retarded

Independent Functioning	Physical Development	Communication	Social Development	Economic Development	Occupation	Self-Direction
Self-care and grooming adequate	Move about freely in hometown	Telephone	Rapid, complex or involved, preplanned activities may not be as enjoyed as simple recreation	Some guidance for money management	Can engage in unskilled or semiskilled job	Conscientious and responsible for work, but may require guidance in complex situations
Help in purchasing of clothes	Help in out-of-town travel	Simple letter writing	Seeks group membership	Accurate in change, but does not necessarily use banking facilities	Everyday household chores	May require guidance in care of others
Help and reminders in obtaining health and personal care	Use of complex equipment	Complex conversations	Involved in local recreation and church membership	Errands to several stores for several items without notes	Cook and prepare simple meals	Attending to tasks for more than 15-20 minutes
		Emphasis upon concrete personal experiences; may be restricted in abstractions				

Source: From *Mental retardation: Nature, needs, and advocacy* by D. F. Sellin, p. 13, copyright 1979. Reprinted by permission of Allyn & Bacon, Boston, Massachusetts.

Table 6-6 Representative Adaptive Behaviors Illustrating Highest Levels for the Moderately Mentally Retarded

Independent Functioning	Physical Development	Communication	Social Development	Economic Development	Occupation	Self-Direction
Adequate self-care	Good body control	Read simple prose and sign with comprehension	Cooperative and competitive activities	Errand without notes	Do simple household tasks	Indicate own directions
Select daily clothing	Good gross and fine motor coordination	Use of complex sentences		Two- to four-item purchases without notes	Prepare simple foods which require mixing	Attending to tasks for more than 15-20 minutes
Iron and store clothes						
Care of hair						Conscientious

Source: From *Mental retardation: Nature, needs, and advocacy* by D. F. Sellin, p. 13, copyright 1979. Reprinted by permission of Allyn & Bacon, Boston, Massachusetts.

Table 6-7 Representative Adaptive Behaviors Illustrating Highest Levels for the Severely Mentally Retarded

Independent Functioning	Physical Development	Communication	Social Development	Economic Development	Occupation	Self-Direction
Adequate self-feeding	Throw ball and hit target	Complex sentences	Friendship choices over months	Simple errands and purchases with a note	Can assist with simple household tasks, empty cleaning, carrying	Ask if there is "work"
Can put on clothes (including buttons and zippers)	Run, hop, skip, etc.	Two- or three-step directions	Simple competitive games (i.e., tag)	Knows money has value, but not the values of money	Clear and set table	Attending to task for 10 minutes
Bath with supervision	Sled and skate	Understand but and because	Self-initiated group activities		Prepare sandwich	Makes effort to be dependable and responsible
Wash hands without help		Recognizes signs and reading without comprehension				

Source: From *Mental retardation: Nature, needs, and advocacy,* by D. F. Sellin, p. 15, copyright 1979. Reprinted by permission of Allyn & Bacon, Boston, Massachusetts.

Table 6-8 Representative Adaptive Behaviors Illustrating Highest Levels for the Profoundly Mentally Retarded

Independent Functioning	Physical Development	Communication	Social Development
Feed self with spoon and fork	Hop and skip	300-word vocabulary	Simple games and group activities (house, store, etc.)
Partially toilet trained	Climb stairs with alternating feet	Many gestures	Expressive art and dance
Assistance with clothing	Ride bike or tricycle	Follow one-step directions	
Assistance with bathing	Play dance games	Recognize simple signs and advertising (STOP, EXIT, etc.)	
	Climb trees and jungle gym		
	Throw ball and hit target	Relate experiences in simple language	

Source: From *Mental retardation: Nature, needs, and advocacy,* by D. F. Sellin, pp. 15-16, copyright 1979. Reprinted by permission of Allyn & Bacon, Boston, Massachusetts.

The results of the Perry Preschool Project (Schweinhart & Weikart, 1980) have broad implications for early intervention. The Perry Project began in Ypsilanti, Michigan in 1962 as a longitudinal project to examine the effects of early intervention on disadvantaged children in a daily preschool program with weekly home visits; a control group received no intervention program. The findings of the Perry Project from its beginning until subjects were 15 years old are significant in two major areas:

1. preschool effects on school performance and experience

      Improvement in the cognitive ability at school entry of children who attended preschool is indicated by the increased IQs during kindergarten and first grade. Greater commitment to schooling is evidenced by more highly rated elementary school motivation, by a higher value placed on schooling by teenagers, and by several other aspects of school commitment. Improved school achievement for these children is shown by generally higher achievement test scores during elementary school and distinctly higher scores at eighth grade (age 14) than scores for control group children. Reinforcement of the student role is indicated by more highly rated social development in elementary school, fewer years spent in special education, and greater satisfaction and higher aspirations expressed by parents with respect to the schooling of their children. (p. 31)

2. preschool effects on deviance and social patterns

The Perry Preschool study through age 15 provides the following evidence in these domains. Decreased deviant behavior at school by children who had attended preschool is indicated by more favorably rated classroom conduct and personal behavior during elementary school and by teenagers' reports of being kept after school less often. Decreased delinquent behavior is shown by lower scores for total self-reported delinquent behavior and serious behavior, specifically in the serious categories of taking something from a person by force and damaging institutional property. A possible trend towards future employment success is shown by the fact that 29 percent of teenagers who had attended preschool currently had a job, compared with only 16 percent of teenagers in the control group. (p. 51)

The costs and benefits of the Perry Preschool Project were calculated by marginal benefit-cost analysis, i.e., the differences in expense between the experimental group and the control group. Schweinhart and Weikart reported that the benefits of preschool outweighed the costs:

The undiscounted benefits of two years of preschool education in 1979 dollars were $14,819 per child against a two-year program cost of $5,984 per child ($2,992 per year)—a 248 percent return on the original investment. The internal rate of return on the investment was calculated to be 3.7 percent; the internal rate of return is a discount rate which indicates the average earning power of the investment in the project. In other words, the analysis showed that investment in preschool education was equivalent to an investment receiving 3.7 percent interest over several decades. (The internal rate of return for one year of preschool was calculated to be 9.5 percent.) There are reasons to believe that this is a conservative estimate. (p. 69)

In addition to the great amount of attention given to intervention programs for mildly retarded or at-risk children, several exemplary programs have demonstrated the effectiveness of preschool intervention strategies with moderately and severely retarded children.

The University of Washington's preschool project (Hayden & Haring, 1976) is designed to provide training in cognitive, self-help, and motor areas to Down's syndrome children from diverse backgrounds. Children in the project screened at age one and again at age five on developmental tests demonstrated sustained gains. Further assessments of the children's IQs revealed a mean IQ of 83 for the group, substantially above the usual expected for this group of children.

Bricker and Bricker (1976) reported that, in their intervention project, infants, toddlers, and preschool children made gains in sensorimotor, language, cognitive, and "school readiness" skills.

Chapter 7

Families of Emotionally Disturbed Children

Children who are variously labeled emotionally disturbed, emotionally handicapped, behaviorally disordered, psychotic, or autistic may represent the greatest challenge for early childhood special educators. As Kauffman (1979) noted, disturbed children are not pleasant to be around. Their behavior is often so deviant that it repulses those who must interact with them.

Mental illness has existed since humans first inhabited the earth. Early writings on mental illness stressed that it was caused by demonic possession. Both Hippocrates and Plato advocated humane treatment, but this was forgotten during the Middle Ages when the mentally ill were routinely flogged, starved, and otherwise tortured for allowing evil demons to possess their bodies. In the late nineteenth century and into the twentieth century, awareness of emotional disturbance in children and the need to provide educational programs was increased.

WHAT IS EMOTIONAL DISTURBANCE?

Bryan and Bryan (1979) noted that "no area of exceptionality . . . [is] . . . more difficult to define and assess than emotional and behavioral disorders" (p. 182). Shea (1978) observed that there are probably as many definitions of emotional disturbance as there are people to write them. Frequently, the professional background of the authors (e.g., medicine, psychology, or education), as well as their theoretical predisposition (e.g., behavioral or psychodynamic) shapes the direction of their definitions.

Gearheart (1980) stated that there is no universal definition of emotional disturbance because of the lack of agreement on the following three areas:

1. agreed upon terminology or even descriptive phrases that mean the same thing to all people;

2. the degree of maladjustment needed to "qualify" one as emotionally disturbed; and
3. the number of inappropriate behaviors required to merit the label "emotionally disturbed." (p. 291)

Hallahan and Kauffman (1982) cited seven additional reasons for the lack of consensus regarding the definition of emotional disturbance:

1. inadequate definition of mental health
2. different theoretical models of emotional disturbance
3. difficulties in assessing emotions and behavior
4. variability of children's (both normal and disturbed) behavior and emotions
5. interrelatedness of emotional disturbance and other handicapping conditions
6. functional differences of socializing agents who label and serve children
7. different social and cultural expectations regarding behavior

Clarizio and McCoy (1976), in their review of the literature on problems of defining emotional disturbance, proposed the Bower (1961) definition as the one most widely quoted and often accepted. Bower (1961) suggested that an emotionally disturbed child has one or more of the following characteristics:

1. an unexplained inability to learn that cannot be attributed primarily to intellectual deficits, specific learning disabilities, or differences in cultural or ethnic background. Frequently, this is observed as a significant discrepancy between measured intelligence and actual academic performance.
2. an inability to develop satisfactory social relationships with peers or adults.
3. an inability to perform at an appropriate developmental level; that is, the child behaves immaturely in terms of behavior or interests in comparison with same age peers.
4. an inability to exhibit self-confidence or to overcome feelings of sadness or depression.
5. an inability to cope with stressful situations in school without developing headaches or other psychosomatic reactions.

A sampling of other definitions of emotional disturbance that have been proposed by various authorities in the field documents the diversity among these many definitions:

- Kirk (1972) defined emotional disturbance as a "deviation from age-appropriate behavior which significantly interferes with (1) the child's own growth and development and/or (2) the lives of others" (p. 389).
- Reinert (1976) noted that "children in conflict . . . describes the children being served in school programs. These children are in conflict (nothing more or less) with their environment" (p. 6).
- Kauffman (1977) defined children who were behavior-disordered as "those who chronically and markedly respond to their environment in socially unacceptable and/or personally unsatisfying ways" (p. 23).

As can be noted, the terminology used in these definitions varies considerably. Yet there are some common themes in the definitions of emotional disturbance. Authorities generally agree that the disturbed behavior is (1) extremely deviant, (2) pervasive and persistent, and (3) culturally or socially unacceptable. All children may exhibit such behavior at some point in their lives without being considered disturbed; true emotional disturbance involves behaviors that are marked and chronic over a prolonged period of time. Clarizio and McCoy (1976) noted that the frequency, intensity, and duration of the behaviors must be considered in determining if a child has an emotional handicap.

The definition used in Public Law 94-142 is modeled closely after the Bower definition (1961, 1969), although it makes specific reference to serious emotional disturbance and to autistic and schizophrenic children. As Kauffman (1979) suggested, however, it is necessary to be aware of developmental norms and parental expectations when considering preschool children. For example, the infant who fails to develop appropriate eating or sleeping routines or who fails to "cuddle" may be evidencing early signs of emotional disturbance. Failure to achieve developmental milestones (whether they are cognitive or affective) is also a sign of possible emotional problems. Furthermore, it is important to remember that "disturbed children's behavior upsets others and handicaps the children themselves because it is *developmentally inappropriate and persistent*" (Kauffman, 1979, p. 451).

WHAT ARE THE CHARACTERISTICS OF EMOTIONALLY DISTURBED CHILDREN?

Gearheart (1980) compiled an extensive list of characteristics drawn from various state guidelines for placement of children in programs for the emotionally disturbed. Included among the characteristics noted by Gearheart were the following:

- avoidance of contact with others
- avoidance of eye contact
- ritualistic behavior
- chronic disobedience
- hostility
- temper tantrums
- sleeping or eating disorders
- emotional isolation
- bizarre mannerisms
- low frustration level
- hyperactivity
- out of touch with reality
- preoccupation with objects
- physical aggression
- rapid and severe mood shifts
- verbal aggression and disruptive behavior
- attention disorders
- self-stimulation
- self-mutilation

Intellectual/Cognitive Characteristics

Kauffman (1981) reviewed the research on the intelligence of disturbed children and concluded that, as a group, they tend to be below average in intelligence. As is the case with mental retardation, the more severe the disturbance, the greater the likelihood of a lower IQ. Children identified as mildly or moderately emotionally disturbed tend to score on intelligence tests in what is called the dull normal range. Compared with the nonhandicapped population, greater numbers of the mildly or moderately disturbed are likely to score in the mildly retarded category (IQ of 55 to 70) on IQ tests. The severely disturbed, many of whom are difficult or impossible to test, frequently fall into the moderately retarded category (IQ of 40 to 54). Of course, many behaviors of disturbed children interfere with psychological testing, so it is possible that IQ tests do not accurately reflect their native intelligence.

Since IQ is a good predictor of academic success in school and the lower IQs of the emotionally disturbed correlate with social deficiencies, the disturbed do not generally achieve in school-related academic tasks at a level commensurate with their mental ages. For the severely disturbed, academic and social deficiencies are even more pronounced. These children may not learn to read or write and may lack even the most basic self-care skills.

Frequently, the learning problems of the emotionally disturbed child are the result of inappropriate or interfering behaviors (e.g., inattentiveness or hyperactivity), poor attitude toward school, previous school failure, or low self-esteem. Some severely disturbed children may also have low intelligence because of impaired cognitive processes. Bryan and Bryan (1979) found psychotic children conceptualize in a highly concrete fashion and suffer other deficient cognitive processes.

Personality Characteristics

More than any other characteristic, the personality factors of emotionally disturbed children set them apart from nonhandicapped children. There have been many attempts to classify emotional problems according to specific personality traits. One such approach, dimensional classification, is exemplified by the work of Quay (1979). Employing the behavior ratings of teachers and parents, together with child responses to a questionnaire, Quay identified four categories or clusters of traits:

1. conduct disorders. The most common manifestations of emotional disturbance are conduct disorders, such as fighting and other assaultive behaviors, bullying, abusive language, destructiveness to property, and severe temper tantrums. Essentially, these behaviors cluster around an inability to control aggression.
2. anxiety-withdrawal. The problem of anxiety-withdrawal is central to the severe disorders of childhood (e.g., autism). Behaviors include a retreat from reality, depression, feelings of inferiority, and aloofness. Often, this cluster is particularly debilitating for children, and the prognosis for normal adult functioning is poor.
3. immaturity. While all children behave immaturely on occasion, the behavioral pattern of truly disturbed children is remarkably infantile. Immature children have short attention spans, appear preoccupied, show a preference for younger playmates, and generally display social behaviors that consistently lag behind expectations for their age group.
4. socialized aggression. Behaviors that consistently violate norms and are linked to patterns of juvenile delinquency (e.g., gang membership) are considered socialized aggression.

Motor Characteristics

There is virtually nothing in the literature that suggests particular motor deviations among the emotionally disturbed, except for Quay's (1979) description of the immature child as clumsy. It is safe to assume that no specific motor problems have been identified as part of emotional disturbances. It seems that motor problems are as evenly distributed as they are in the so-called normal population.

Special Characteristics of the Severely Disturbed

There is disagreement in the field (see, e.g., Neel, 1979) regarding whether specific problems such as autism or childhood schizophrenia should be separated from a broader concept of severe emotional disturbance. Because the childhood psychoses affect a number of developmental areas, such as cognitive, perceptual, language, affective, and psychomotor, it is often more productive to view deviant behaviors rather than confusing labels. Nonetheless, the terms are widely used.

Autism

Since autism was first described in the pioneer work of Kanner (1943), a great deal of research on the condition has resulted in a refinement of the original definition. For example, Rutter's (1978) definition is more descriptive, includes observable behaviors, and provides a clustering of four special criteria that must all be present before the label autism can be applied. According to Rutter, the four criteria are

1. a profound and general failure to develop social relationships
2. language retardation, including inability to comprehend spoken language, echolalic speech, and the use of meaningless gibberish
3. ritualistic or compulsive behavior
4. the age of onset limited to two and one-half years or before

Childhood Schizophrenia

The term *childhood schizophrenia* is used to describe a childhood psychosis that develops during the first five years of life after a period of normal development. While the cluster of symptomatic characteristics may vary, the central feature of this disorder remains a lack of contact with reality; these children develop their own world. Other secondary characteristics identified by Kaufman, Herrick, Willer, Frank, and Heims (1959) include

- bizarre movements of the body, such as robotlike walking
- stereotyped behaviors, such as arm flapping
- exhibition of a nonhuman identity by barking like a dog
- speech and language disturbances, such as use of word or sentence fragments, parroting
- inappropriate affect, ranging from a flat affect to explosive characteristics
- distorted time orientation with a blending of past, present, and future

HOW MANY CHILDREN ARE EMOTIONALLY DISTURBED?

The prevalence of emotional disturbance is difficult to estimate because of the different definitions and identification procedures used by various agencies. Kirk and Gallagher (1979) reported estimates of prevalence ranging from 8 to 22 percent, while Grosenick and Huntze (1980) found that the total percentage of behavior-disordered (their term) children and youth identified ranges from 0.5 to 3.2 percent of the school population. Although the U.S. Office of Education used an estimate of 2 to 3 percent for serious disturbance for nearly a decade, less than 1 percent of school-aged children are being identified as emotionally disturbed and served in special education classes. Bower (1969) conducted a comprehensive study of public school children in California and reported that at least three youngsters in the average classroom (10 percent) are sufficiently disordered to warrant the label emotionally handicapped. The Bower estimate is corroborated by Kauffman (1981), who suggested a 6 to 10 percent figure, and Glidewell and Swallow (1968), who argued that 2 to 3 percent of the population are definitely disturbed while another 7 to 8 percent of the school population probably require some less intensive professional services.

HOW ARE EMOTIONALLY DISTURBED CHILDREN
IDENTIFIED?

Unlike many other handicapping conditions, emotional disturbance is not clearly reflected by a particular test score or by an observable impairment. Instead, someone, usually a parent, a babysitter, or a teacher, recognizes certain behaviors that "just don't seem normal." While some problems (e.g., withdrawal) do not call attention to themselves, others (e.g., conduct disorders and immaturity) are not difficult to recognize. Therefore, few public school systems use formal screening procedures; they rely on teacher judgment or formal teacher ratings to identify candidates for assessment. Nelson (1971) noted that teacher ratings of children's behaviors as disturbed are both accurate and reliable.

Once a child has been referred for possible emotional problems, it is necessary to conduct a careful evaluation of the behavior or behaviors that led to the referral. Assessment has several purposes:

1. to determine the exact nature of the child's problem(s)
2. to obtain sufficient information to plan an intervention strategy
3. to provide for a statement of the child's prognosis or ability to reach the therapeutic goals detailed in the intervention plan

As Kauffman (1979) noted "traditional psychiatric and psychological 'diagnosis' is important or useful only insofar as it contributes to one or more of the . . . purposes of assessment" (p. 455). Labels in themselves are essentially valueless from an educational intervention perspective. Instead, it is critical to focus on maladaptive behaviors and appropriate treatment methodologies to reduce the impact of the child's problems. It is important to remember that the purpose of assessment is treatment and not the identification of a clinical syndrome.

The steps involved in the identification process include parental interview, administration of standardized tests, and observation of the child's behavior.

Parental Interview

Most authorities (Kauffman, 1979; A. O. Ross, 1980) agree that parental interviews are essential to the identification/assessment process. The purpose of this interview is to determine (1) the parents' perception of the problem, (2) a developmental chronology of the problem, (3) the events that precede and the consequences that follow manifestations of the problem, (4) the setting or settings in which the problem is most likely to occur, and (5) attempts, if any, at solving the problem. Because parents do not usually describe behavior in terms of observable or measurable events, the interviewer must elicit descriptions of behavior in terms of frequency, duration, or intensity. For example, parents may say the problem is aggression; the interviewer must help parents think in terms of exact descriptions of behavior, such as hitting or kicking.

The skilled interviewer also notes parent behaviors (e.g., discomfort or hesitation) that may be indicative of the family's interaction patterns. Lobitz and Johnson (1975) stress the importance of going beyond the parent's description of the child's problem to an investigation of the family's perceptions, labeling, and attributions.

A. O. Ross (1980) advocates child interviews as a source of data. The usefulness of this approach is dependent on the child's language, functional level in terms of the severity of the disturbance, and overall cooperativeness, however.

Standardized Tests

Several problems are encountered in testing young children who are emotionally disturbed, especially those who are seriously disturbed (Clarizio & McCoy, 1976):

1. limited language. Many tests require the child to make a verbal response or rely heavily on the child's comprehension of spoken language for directions. Since many disturbed children also have language handicaps, they do not always understand what is asked or expected of them.
2. limited experiences. Many disturbed children have never been asked to report their feelings. Therefore, when asked to respond on a self-reporting questionnaire, "What is your favorite activity?" these children may not be able to respond because they never thought about that before.
3. sex differences. There are definite differences between boys and girls not only in maturation but also in social expectations. With regard to social expectations, for example, boys may be more aggressive because it is expected. Few scales used with the disturbed have different normative data by sex.
4. relative instability of personality. Early childhood is a period of rapid maturation and change. The examiner must be careful to note any maturationally induced changes in social-emotional behaviors.
5. negativism. Many disturbed children simply refuse to comply with an examiner's request to complete a task.
6. shyness. Children may withdraw, be unwilling or afraid to participate, or fail to put forth a reasonable effort on test tasks.
7. hyperactivity. If a child is walking around the room, climbing under the desk, or playing with items in the test kit, it is impossible to determine their typical performance.

Even if these children could be tested by means of standard procedures, there are very few tests available for the preschool child.

Since intelligence and conceptual skills are affected by social-emotional functioning, an IQ test is essential to the assessment process. The IQ score in isolation is relatively insignificant, however; the examiner must also obtain information on the child's learning style, perceptual skills (on Wechsler tests), and reasoning and thinking skills.

Achievement tests, often used in the assessment process for school-aged children, are far less useful for the preschool child. The relationship between performance on preschool tests of preacademic skills and later school performance is too low for such preschool tests to have useful predictive reliability.

Often the assessment phase includes the completion of rating scales or checklists, such as the Child Behavior Rating Scale (Cassell, 1972) or the Preschool Behavior Questionnaire (Behar & Stringfield, 1974). These scales have limitations, however. Items chosen for these scales may not be representative of the behaviors the examiner is attempting to determine, for example. Reliability can be a problem, especially if the items require the examiner to make subjective judgments about the child's behavior.

Projective tests are still used as part of the assessment process despite serious concerns regarding their validity, reliability, and usefulness to educational planning (Jackson & Pavnonen, 1980). Some projective tests require the presentation of ambiguous stimuli, such as pictures of inkblots, that the child is to describe. Other projective techniques include interpretations of drawings, sentence completion, drawing objects, or choosing pictures to fit moods. With the movement toward the documentation and analysis of measurable or observable behaviors, there has been a decline in the popularity of assessing "motives, drives, and traits that supposedly cause behavior" (Salvia & Ysseldyke, 1978, p. 377).

Observation

The single best strategy for determining the parameters of problem behavior is observation, either informal or formal. When using informal observation, the observer records behaviors considered significant. Formal observation involves recording the extent to which prespecified behaviors are exhibited (Ysseldyke, 1978).

Ysseldyke described several formal observation techniques:

- narrative data. The observer gathers all possible information about an event or sequence of events. Data may be in the form of audio or video tapes, photographs, films, logs, or diaries.
- rating scales. The observer records the frequency of prespecified behaviors on prepared scales.
- formal behavior recording. The observer records the extent of occurrence of specific predetermined behaviors.

Mori and Masters (1980) discussed the following eight methods of formally recording a child's behavior:

1. narrative recording. Derived from ecological psychology, this method involves a written record of all child behaviors. The narrative includes the observer's starting and ending times, client behaviors, environmental situations, and the behaviors of others present.

2. event recording. The observer uses a tally sheet to record every instance of a previously identified problem behavior. Event recording is another term for a frequency count.

3. documentation of or evidence of behaviors. Certain behaviors need not be directly observed because they produce a product that proves the behavior has occurred. When the product is discovered, it is entered in an observation log. For example, a wet sheet is the product that shows bed-wetting has occurred. If a child steals money from a purse, the evidence is money missing from the purse.

4. duration recording. In order to measure how long a particular behavior occurs, the observer sets a timer at the beginning of the behavior and turns it off when the behavior stops. The length of time transpired is then recorded in an observation log. One behavior particularly amenable to duration recording is a temper tantrum.

5. interval recording. In interval recording, the period during which the observation is to occur is divided into equal units of time. When the behavior (or behaviors) occurs, it is marked in the appropriate time interval. For reasons of recorder reliability, five seconds is usually the shortest suggested interval, several minutes the longest.

6. time sampling. A method often used in conjunction with interval recording is time sampling. Observations are taken after a predetermined length of time has elapsed. Often, a timer is set for five or ten minutes; when that time has elapsed, the observer records the behavior the child displays at that time.

7. test method. In order to measure the quality of a behavior, specified behaviors are observed and recorded in terms of how well they are performed. This method is used for observing "positive" behaviors.

8. automatic recording. Advances in technology have made it possible to monitor heart rate, body movement, perspiration, and a multitude of other human body functions. In addition, electronic devices can be used to measure rocking, striking, verbalization, head hanging, hyperactive movements, body tension, and other behaviors.

WHAT IS THE IMPACT OF EMOTIONAL DISTURBANCE ON THE FAMILY?

Emotionally disturbed children may exhibit particularly irritating behaviors, such as constant crying, irregular sleeping patterns, eating disturbances, intense or negative reactions to stimulation, and failure to respond in a fashion that is "rewarding" to parents or caregivers. The social stigma of having a disturbed child can produce negative side-effects on the family.

Parental Reactions

Marion (1981) cited five problems parents of disturbed children may exhibit:

1. isolation from family and friends
2. despair caused by living in an environment of hostile behavior, physical violence, and humiliation
3. anger caused by a refusal of social service agencies to meet the child's needs
4. frustration caused by going from agency to agency seeking assistance
5. low self-esteem

Isolation

Parents of all handicapped children feel isolated from family and friends to some extent. For the parent of the disturbed child, the problem is intensified. The behaviors displayed by their children are repulsive to and may even frighten some adults.

Rather than face rejection or loss of face, the parents of disturbed children often withdraw from their circle of family and friends. Their refusal to interact socially can be viewed as a protective reaction. They are protecting themselves from ridicule and humiliation. Family and friends may feel uncomfortable around the child; because the parents sense this discomfort, they grow inward in a psychological "circling of the wagons." Parents also want to protect the child from stigmatization. If they do not take the child anywhere, the child cannot do anything that will cause embarrassment.

As indicated earlier, isolation can be particularly devastating to the family of the disturbed child. It can cause them to become a "handicapped family," unable to cope with the internal as well as the external stresses of daily life.

Despair

Unless a person lives under the constant, oppressive tension caused by a seriously disturbed child in the home, it is difficult to understand the despair experienced by parents of emotionally disturbed children. The seriously conduct-disordered child often commits seemingly senseless acts of violence against siblings, objects in the home, and even the parents themselves. These acts of violence may include frightening behaviors, such as setting fires or torturing animals. Parents often feel that they are living their lives under a threatening cloud. This kind of tension produces a great deal of stress. In turn, parents may attempt to reduce the stress in counterproductive ways, for example, through drugs or alcohol.

Another byproduct of despair may be child abuse. The child's deviant behaviors may elicit negative, abusive behavior from parents (Yussen & Santrock, 1982). Frodi (1981) and Kempe and Helfer (1972) presented correlational data that suggested seriously involved infants and young children were at risk for abuse because of the extreme stress involved in caring for them as well as the constellation of aversive (to the parent) behaviors exhibited by such children.

Anger

Parents of emotionally disturbed children have a right to be angry. Despite generally accepted estimates of a prevalence rate of 2 to 3 percent, data released by the U.S. Department of Education subsequent to the passage of Public Law 94-142 indicate that only 0.5 percent of school children are identified as seriously disturbed. Sabatino (1979) suggested that the severely disturbed as a group have been traditionally underserved by the public schools.

Frustration

In many communities, especially those in states where preschool services are not mandated, parents of emotionally disturbed children become frustrated by the treadmill game of agency roulette. Parents attempting to secure some type of assistance are frequently sent from one mental health agency to the next. Only the most persistent fail to become casualties of this bureaucratic shuffle.

Low Self-Esteem

Parents of emotionally disturbed children may devalue themselves and suffer substantial loss of self-esteem. This may be manifested by negative statements about themselves, a loss of pride, a lack of interest in what they do or how they look, and a generally pervasive mood of unhappiness.

Coletta (1977) discussed the needs of parents in terms of Maslow's (1962) hierarchy of needs. For example, a preoccupation with the basic survival needs may prevent family members from investing their full energies in a child's program. Other anxieties may affect the parents and their ability to become involved in the child's program.

As Alexander, Kroth, Simpson, and Poppelreiter (1982) noted, the parents of emotionally disturbed children are a heterogeneous group. They come from all social strata, yet they face many of the same problems. Some parents may experience guilt because they cannot balance their personal needs, the needs of their spouse and other children, and the needs of the emotionally disturbed child. They may feel guilty when they feel a strong need for respite from their disturbed child. As Alexander and associates noted, well-meaning but insensitive professionals can view this as a lack of concern or commitment rather than a legitimate need.

Aside from the problems already elaborated, an emotionally disturbed child in the family can be a source of marital discord. Lobitz and Johnson (1975) identified marital distress among parents, low parental tolerance, and other interpersonal difficulties as symptomatic of a family in conflict.

Parental Contributions to Therapy

Regardless of the problems encountered by parents of emotionally disturbed children, their potential contribution to the therapeutic process is undeniable. The studies that have used parents trained to modify the behavior of their own children have produced uniformly positive results (Johnson & Katz, 1973). Parents as change agents represent an inexpensive, ongoing source of treatment to supplement other therapeutic regimens.

Much of the recent research on family interventions with emotionally disturbed children has focused on teaching behavior management skills to parents. Walker (1979) reported the results of several studies that developed comprehensive parent training programs. By using lectures, assigned readings, and instruction in how to pinpoint, observe, and record child behavior, and by simulating the application of behavioral procedures, professionals have taught parents to use

- self-recording of attention to appropriate behavior
- feedback and a point system with response cost
- differential attention and timeout procedures

- contracting procedures
- extinction and reinforcement of incompatible behaviors.

Other treatment methodologies for parents, including family therapy (Minuchin, 1974), have also been used with success to treat all the members of the family with an emotionally disturbed child.

WHAT IS THE IMPACT OF EMOTIONAL DISTURBANCE ON THE FUTURE LIVES OF CHILDREN?

The overall prognosis for seriously disturbed children, particularly those labeled psychotic (autistic or schizophrenic) or conduct-disordered, is grim. Hallahan and Kauffman (1982) noted that many severely disturbed children become adults who have serious adjustment problems and are unable to lead independent and productive lives. It is not unusual for these adults eventually to be placed in institutional settings (Rutter & Bartak, 1973). While a small number may make a successful adjustment in the community, even achieving success in competitive employment, the vast majority of disturbed adults will never be rid of the deviant characteristics identified in childhood (Kanner, 1971; Kanner, Rodriguez, & Ashenden, 1972).

An examination of follow-up studies on the stability of deviant behavior reveals an equally gloomy picture. In one of the best known follow-up studies, Robins (1966) studied some 500 children referred to a St. Louis mental health clinic between 1924 and 1929. Thirty years later, the adult psychiatric and social status of these subjects were compared with that of a control group. As adults, 34 percent of former child guidance patients were characterized by disabling emotional disturbances. In general, the findings of this study imply that former child patients, particularly those who engage in seriously antisocial behavior, make up a disproportionate percentage of adults with mental disorders.

Zax and Cowen (1972) reported that first-grade students who had been identified as maladjusted continued to manifest problems in personal-social functioning in follow-up studies at the third- and seventh-grade levels. Other investigators have studied the persistence of school adjustment problems. Stringer and Glidewell (1967) reported that 87 percent of the students identified as significantly deficient in both mental health and academic achievement during the early grades maintained the same status throughout the elementary school years. Stennet's (1966) research corroborated the finding that school maladjustment does not improve with the passage of time.

On the basis of their evaluation of adjustment studies, Clarizio and McCoy (1976) concluded that about 30 percent of disturbed children continue to have moderate to severe problems as adults. This is especially true for those children who were labeled psychotic.

The impact of mild and even moderate emotional disturbance on children is much less negative in the long run. It was concluded in several studies reviewed by Clarizio and McCoy (1976) that a significant number of mildly and moderately disturbed children mature and display adult behavior within normal limits. Other studies reviewed by Clarizio and McCoy showed that 66 to 75 percent of mildly or moderately disturbed children were considered well or significantly improved in behavior one or two years after the initial diagnosis.

The extensive research review of Clarizio and McCoy also indicated that shyness and withdrawn behavior tend to diminish and even disappear in later years. Even when they persist, they are less problematic to the person and certainly less disruptive than the behaviors of conduct-disordered persons. There is little evidence to suggest that extreme shyness is predictive of later adult schizophrenia. Furthermore, neurotic symptoms in children (e.g., fears or facial tics) are not valuable predictors of adult neurotic symptoms. Childhood neurotic disorders have a very good long-term prognosis.

Emotional disorders have other negative impacts on children. Because of the similarities between their behaviors and those of learning-disabled children, emotionally disturbed children may evoke many of the same negative reactions from parents, teachers, and peers that the learning-disabled child evokes (see Chapter 5, Families of Children with Sensory, Physical, and Learning Disorders).

The employment future of young adult emotionally disturbed persons is bleak. Brolin and Kokaska (1979) noted that there are still many employment barriers to persons who are disturbed. Sarbin and Mancuso (1970) found that the public was not generally sympathetic to persons labeled disturbed or mentally ill. "They look upon such persons with disrespect and are willing to relegate them to a childlike, non-person role. An exemplar of the general public would place a sizable social distance between himself and those persons labeled mentally ill" (p. 167). Brolin and Kokaska (1979) concluded that the emotionally disturbed have a stigma that is "in many ways more debilitating than other handicapped persons" (p. 80).

WHAT INTERVENTION STRATEGIES CAN BE USED FOR EMOTIONALLY DISTURBED CHILDREN?

The intervention strategies used with emotionally disturbed children are tied very closely to various theoretical models that attempt to account for the formation of personality constructs. These models, and their therapeutic derivatives, are the source of much conflict in the field of intervention with young disturbed children. Rhodes and Tracy (1972 a,b) provided a detailed analysis of the conceptual models and intervention strategies derived from the models used to treat or educate disturbed children.

Biological Approach

Proponents of the biological approach hold the view that disturbed behavior is caused by genetic, neurological, and biochemical factors (Bender, 1968; Gottesman & Shields, 1972; Mandell, Segal, Kuczenski, & Knapp, 1972). The treatment plan associated with this approach involves the medical model or disease-entity approach, i.e., a physical intervention is attempted. The most frequent course of treatment today is psychoactive drug therapy.

Tranquilizers and antidepressants are used to treat schizophrenic children, while stimulants are used to treat hyperactive children. The results of studies of central nervous system stimulants on hyperactive children suggest that activity level may be reduced, motor performance may become more controlled, and the ability to sustain attention may be increased. Most of these improvements occur only in highly structured situations and on repetitive, mechanical tasks, however (Sroufe, 1975). Furthermore, there is no evidence to suggest that central nervous system stimulants improve a child's ability to learn (A. O. Ross, 1980). Thus, it can be said that the ability to concentrate on a task is necessary, but not sufficient, to permit mastery of complex learning activities.

The many disadvantages of psychoactive drugs far outweigh their advantages. Drug therapy should be the treatment regimen of last recourse, used only after all else has failed to change a child's behavior. Even then, drug therapy should be part of a total treatment plan that includes other appropriate interventions (e.g., behavior modification procedures and family counseling). Drugs teach the child nothing. While the child on drug therapy may be more amenable to education, there is no guarantee that the child will learn unless learning is individually tailored to the child's needs.

Ecological Approach

Proponents of the ecological approach (Hobbs, 1974; Swap, 1978) believe that disturbed behavior is a byproduct of the child's inability to interact with the components of the environment. Using terminology borrowed from biological ecology, these theorists speak of ecosystems that involve the complex interactions of groups of people, such as the family, the class, or the play group.

Safford (1978) pointed out that many factors in the ecosystem (e.g., size of the room, temperature, time of day, range of activity) influence the child's behavior. Therefore, the entire system must be modified if the child's deviant behavior is to be controlled. The goal of this approach is to create an environment in the home, the school, and the community that first modifies inappropriate behavior and then maintains desirable behavior once it has been achieved.

The teacher is the manager of the ecosystem in the classroom. The teacher can maintain classroom structure by preplanning the use of time and space, and by carefully designing a reward system with clearly defined expectations and consequences.

The efficacy of this type of approach was the focus of a study conducted by Cruickshank, Bentzen, Ratzeburg, and Tannhauser (1961). This highly structured approach produced modest gains in some areas and served as a prototype for self-contained classes for emotionally disturbed and learning-disabled children during the 1960s and early 1970s.

Psychoanalytic Approach

Some authorities believe that emotional disturbance can be defined by the traditional terminology of psychoanalysis. They view the problem as a pathological disequilibrium among the ego states—the id, the ego, and the superego. Using the clinical approach of psychiatrists and psychologists, they attempt to create a therapeutic milieu (Redl, 1959) that helps the child uncover underlying mental pathology and develop healthy psychological functioning. This approach most often utilizes individual therapy sessions (Bettelheim, 1950, 1967), group therapy sessions (Speers & Lansing, 1964), or parental therapy sessions (Mahler, 1965) to help parents and children resolve basic developmental conflicts (Erikson, 1968) in a positive and healthy manner.

The psychoanalytic approach is a particularly slow and painstaking process with disturbed children. Because of their severe personality disorders, many disturbed children are unable to develop the necessary close attachment with their therapist. Progress may be so slow and in such small increments that it is overshadowed by the enormous investment of patience, effort, time, and money. Finally, "nearly all studies and reviews of psychoanalytically oriented therapy emphasize the lack of positive results" (Clarizio & McCoy, 1976, p. 359).

Psychoeducational Approach

Advocates of the psychoeducational approach (Long, Morse, & Newman, 1980) have attempted to merge relevant principles of psychiatry with educational concerns. Hollister and Goldstein (1969) listed the following components of the psychoeducational process:

1. relationship-building process. The success of the educational program depends on the teacher's ability to create with the student a climate of trust, understanding, and empathy. The procedures involved in this process include (1) steps to prepare the children for relationships before they enter the class, (2) patterns of introducing new children into the class, (3) methods to increase psychological safety, (4) methods to establish expected behaviors, (5) elements of the grouping process, (6) direct emotional support by the teacher, (7) diagnosis and reinforcement of personality strengths, (8) use of reinforcements, and (9) group cohesion-building patterns.
2. perceptual retraining process. Perceptual deficits are diagnosed and methods designed to eliminate them.
3. classroom behavior management process. These procedures include structuring expected behaviors, using peer pressure and group guidance techniques, controlling group misbehavior, and developing strategies for dealing with poor individual behavior.
4. behavior re-education process. Emotionally disturbed children must unlearn maladaptive behaviors and learn new behavior repertoires that enhance personal well-being and acceptance. Procedures used in this process include anticipatory guidance education, planned corrective learning experiences, and general education on personal-social behavior.
5. academic education process. Using a detailed educational diagnosis, the teacher develops an individualized plan for each child. The procedures used include tutoring, remedial methods, and other special methods and materials.
6. process of rehabilitation to the regular class. This is a transition process designed to return the disturbed child to the regular class.
7. supportive operations. These combined liaison processes (clinician-educator liaison and school-home liaison) use techniques such as (1)

consultation, (2) therapeutic opportunities for teachers, (3) case reviews, (4) in-service seminars, (5) parent group activities, and (6) provision of parent counseling, therapy, casework or nursing services. The goal of these procedures is to provide support for educators, foster a multidisciplinary responsibility, and extend special services to the parents to complement and extend the impact of the school program.

Humanistic Approach

Hallahan and Kauffman (1982) noted that the humanistic approach to treating emotionally disturbed children originated in humanistic psychology (Maslow, 1962; Rogers, 1969). The basic attitudes of humanism were summarized by McCandless and Evans (1973):

1. The focus is on each child's uniqueness.
2. To understand the child, it is necessary to grasp the child's global self.
3. The focus is on the child's capacity for constructive growth and creative potential at optimal levels of functioning.
4. Values, attitudes, and beliefs are more important than the specific interchange of social behaviors in different situations.

Educational practices in the humanistic approach are designed to help children live more satisfying lives, have more effective interpersonal relationships, and develop their capacity for self-direction and self-evaluation. The teacher is seen as a catalyst for learning rather than a manager of learning activities.

Behavioral Approach

The principles of operant conditioning are the basis of the behavioral approach. Proponents of this approach believe that all behavior, including inappropriate behavior, is learned and that behavior can be modified by manipulating the environment and the consequences of the behavior.

The behavioral approach includes several distinct steps:

1. observation of behavior.
2. visual presentation of observational data. Data gathered during the first process is displayed on a graph so that the teacher can see the behavior in terms of actual frequency and duration. To be useful, data must also be gathered on antecedents and consequences.

3. identification of effective reinforcers. Before a behavior can be modified, the reinforcers that maintain it must be identified. These reinforcers must be presented to accelerate new or desirable behaviors or withdrawn to decelerate or extinguish inappropriate ones. Reinforcers are not universal; they tend to be unique for each individual.
4. application of a reinforcement schedule. This is the consideration of how and when reinforcement will be delivered.
5. analysis of behavior change. The intervention approach must be measured for effectiveness in changing child behavior.

For a more complete description of the behavioral approach with emotionally disturbed children, the reader is referred to A. O. Ross (1980).

The behavioral approach has produced some impressive results in modifying single severe behavior problems (e.g., aggressive behaviors such as hitting or kicking, self-abusive behaviors such as biting), but, as Leff (1968) noted, behavioral treatment approaches have not made schizophrenic children suddenly normal. Although the successes of this approach may seem to overshadow those of the other approaches, behavior modification has not dramatically reduced clusters or patterns of disturbed behavior.

Other Treatment Approaches

Several interesting derivatives of the major approaches that have been discussed are also being used with disturbed children:

- **diet therapy** (Feingold, 1975). Therapy consists of dietary control to eliminate food additives that are presumed to cause hyperactivity and learning problems. Research has not supported the efficacy of this method, although individual parents report dramatic results.
- **Dreikurs family council** (Dreikurs & Grey, 1970). Family members meet to arrive at solutions to family problems democratically. There is little research regarding the effectiveness of this approach, although it may work well for reasonably adjusted parents who believe in it.
- **family therapy** (Minuchin, 1974). Based on an analysis of subsystems (e.g., marital, parental, and sibling) or how individuals in the family organize themselves in relationship to one another, this method has involved parents as therapists for their own children.
- **play therapy** (Axline, 1947). On the theory that play is a child's most natural mode of self-expression, play therapy gives the child the opportunity to formulate feelings and problems and work these out in the play situation.

- **reality therapy** (Glasser, 1969). The focus of reality therapy is on behavior in the real world and responsibility. Class meetings are used to solve behavioral and educational problems.

A Promising New Approach: Developmental Therapy

One final approach warrants brief consideration. The developmental therapy approach (Wood, 1979; Wood, Swan, & Newman, 1982) blends psychodynamic and behavioral principles into a curriculum that is sequentially arranged in developmental growth patterns. It was formulated at the Rutland Center and the University of Georgia and has been used successfully in preschool programs, day care centers, Head Start, and institutions.

The developmental therapy curriculum is divided into specific sequential tasks in four areas: (1) behavior, (2) communication, (3) socialization, and (4) preacademics or academics. In each of the four curriculum areas, there are specific hierarchical task sequences. These sequences are divided into approximately 170 objectives that delineate normal developmental milestones for social and emotional development from birth to 16 years of age.

The theoretical foundations for the developmental therapy approach are varied. They include the work of Ausubel (1952) and Freud (1973) on elements of ego development; Kohlberg (1969) and Piaget (1954) on moral development; and Bandura (1976) and Erikson (1972) on social-interpersonal development. In addition, Erikson's (1963) psychosocial themes are included in the curriculum as broad categories for motivational development. There are seven themes in the Erikson scheme (Wood et al., 1982):

1. pleasure-pain (trust)
2. dependence-independence (autonomy and power)
3. secondary-narcissism (imitation and identification)
4. fears and expectations (initiative)
5. self-esteem (identification, industry, and activity)
6. conscience (guilt and conflict)
7. independence-dependence (identify formation and values)
   (p. 290)

Finally, cognitive development is guided by the principles of Piaget (1977) and his associates.

The developmental therapy model has been validated as an effective program by the U.S. Office of Education, Joint Dissemination Review Panel. According to Wood and associates (1982):

The effectiveness of the . . . model . . . has been documented: The evidence is valid and reliable; the effect is of educational importance in that problems are significantly reduced and are not evident two years later; and the results have been reproduced by others in various settings. (p. 297)

Conclusion

The number of intervention approaches that can be used with emotionally disturbed children bewilders even the most experienced teacher. Most professionals working with disturbed young children seem to be eclectic in approach, borrowing concepts and elements from different theoretical approaches and applying them in a therapeutic fashion. Regardless of which approach the teacher-therapist adopts, certain important principles apply (Safford, 1978):

1. The needs of young emotionally disturbed children are unique and often do not relate to specific psychiatric categories.
2. Children live in a social system, influencing and being influenced by parents, teachers, and peers.
3. Children must be actively involved in learning specific skills and behaviors in order to experience a sense of competence (White, 1959).
4. Cognitive and affective development are inseparably related.
5. Disturbed children need to be loved and valued by significant adults in their world.

Chapter 8

Families of Gifted and Talented Children

The passage of Public Law 94-142, the Education for All Handicapped Children Act, initiated a massive effort to provide better access to the public education system for all handicapped children in the United States. Unfortunately, the gifted and talented remain outside the protection of this mandate for a free, appropriate education.

Gifted persons frequently go unrecognized. This occurs for many reasons. The family may not value the child's "gifts"; the child may not be given the opportunity for training that may develop the "gifts," this being the case for many poor or minority group children; and frequent swings in public attitudes and policy may create fear and mistrust of our best minds—the so-called eggheads.

WHAT IS GIFTEDNESS?

Many definitions of giftedness have been proposed, but there seems to be little agreement on the meaning of the term *gifted*. Compounding the definition problem is the fact that many different terms are used to describe individuals who are superior in some way, e.g., genius, creative, talented, precocious.

Among the frequently cited definitions is the U.S. Office of Education definition (Marland, 1972):

> Gifted and talented are those identified by professionally qualified persons who by virtue of outstanding abilities, are capable of high performance. These are children who require differentiated educational programs and/or services beyond those normally provided by the regular school program in order to realize their contribution to self and society.

181

Children capable of high performance include those with demonstrated achievement and/or potential ability in any of the following areas, singly or in combination:

1. general intellectual ability
2. specific academic aptitude
3. creative or productive thinking
4. leadership ability
5. visual and performing arts
6. psychomotor ability (p. 2)

A more recent federal definition was used in Public Law 95-561, the Gifted and Talented Children's Act of 1978:

"Gifted and talented" means children and, where applicable, youth who are identified at the preschool, elementary, or secondary level as (1) possessing demonstrated or potential abilities that give evidence of high performance capability in areas such as intellectual, creative, specific academic, or leadership ability or in the performing and visual arts; and (2) needing differentiated education or services (beyond those being provided by the regular school system to the average student) in order to realize these potentialities. *(Federal Register,* May 6, 1976, p. 18666)

Both these definitions grew out of federal efforts to develop programs for persons with special gifts, and they were developed with the input of educators of the gifted from many parts of the United States. Nonetheless, the definitions are not without critics. Gallagher (1979) noted that it is very difficult to measure characteristics such as leadership ability or to recognize "potential" abilities. Renzulli (1978) argued that some school personnel may interpret the definition as a list of independent areas of gifted performance, when in fact types of giftedness are interrelated.

In this book, the terms *gifted* and *talented* will be used to describe those children whose special attributes are on the academic-intellectual and the performing arts-creative continuums. Nonetheless, as Gallagher (1975) noted, "The ability to manipulate internally learned symbol systems is perhaps the *sine qua non* of giftedness" (pp. 10-11). The symbol systems can be oral words (language), written or printed words, numbers, signs and terms. Additional visual symbol systems are used in sculpture, painting, dance, and the theater. One single quality, the ability to manipulate such symbolic systems, links the notions of gifted and talented (Reynolds & Birch, 1977).

WHAT ARE THE CHARACTERISTICS OF GIFTED AND TALENTED CHILDREN?

Much of our knowledge about the characteristics of gifted and talented children is derived from a pioneer study conducted by Terman (1925). Terman conducted a longitudinal study of 1,500 California children whose IQs were 140 and above. His volumes of data on these children not only dispelled many stereotypes on the gifted, but added immensely to our current notion of giftedness.

Terman found that the gifted were above average in physical size, personal health, and health habits. The group grew taller, heavier, and stronger than their peers. Sexual development came earlier in the gifted population and physical development was correlated with intellectual development and giftedness. A significant number of the sample were first-born children.

The myth that giftedness brings with it many undesirable characteristics, such as physical weakness, social ineptness, and emotional instability, has been shattered. In fact, Terman's data suggest that gifted children tend to be *superior* in every way—intelligence, physique, social attractiveness, and emotional stability. The danger is that a new myth—the gifted child is superhuman—will arise. Thus, it is necessary to recognize that (1) although it is true that the gifted as a group are superior in almost every characteristic, individual gifted and talented children deviate from the mean for the group (Hallahan & Kauffman, 1982); (2) many handicapped children are gifted, but may be neglected because it is difficult for some to accept the fact that handicapped persons are superior in any way (Maker, 1977); and (3) the gifted as a group have special characteristics but show the same variation around the mean as the variation shown by any other group around its mean (Hallahan & Kauffman, 1982).

Cognitive Characteristics

Clark (1979) presented an interesting compilation of the cognitive characteristics of gifted and talented children. Included in this category were the following:

- extraordinary quantity of information
- unusual retentiveness
- advanced comprehension
- unusually varied interests and curiosity
- high level of language development

- high level of verbal ability
- unusual capacity for processing information
- accelerated pace of thought processes
- flexible thought processes
- comprehensive synthesis
- heightened capacity for seeing unusual and diverse relationships
- ability to generate original ideas and solutions
- early differential patterns for thought processing
- early ability to use and form conceptual frameworks
- an evaluative approach to themselves and others
- persistent, goal-directed behavior (pp. 23-25)

The Clark conceptualization of giftedness moves away from a simple high IQ or academic talent notion to a more sophisticated examination of cognitive factors. That is, the child who is gifted exhibits not only more knowledge and greater memory, but also advanced capacity, flexibility, and synthesis skills.

Personality Characteristics

In general, the social-emotional development of gifted and talented children proceeds better than that of the typical child. The review of the literature revealed that the gifted and talented

- tend to be happy and well liked by peers, who prefer them as companions (Coleman, 1962; Tannenbaum, 1962).
- are often social leaders during the school years. In fact, their concern for universal problems and the welfare of others begins earlier in development than that of the average child (Martinson, 1961).
- tend to be (1) more independent and less conforming to peer opinions, (2) more dominant, and (3) more competitive (Lucito, 1964).
- tend to be emotionally stable and less prone to neurotic and psychotic disorders than the average child (Ramaseshan, 1957).

The subjects from the Terman study exhibited significant superiority in moral attitudes as measured by tests of character. Their moral judgment developed earlier than that of the average population. Later data (Terman & Oden, 1947) showed that this population, as adults, suffered less from social problems such as divorce, suicide, and alcoholism than the average population. The Terman group also had less ill health, insanity, and a lower mortality rate than the average population.

The gifted and talented are not immune to emotional and social problems, however. Gifted and talented children can suffer from self-doubt, especially if they are faced with the unrealistic expectations of others or themselves. A lack of recognition by parents or teachers, who come to expect superior performance, can also cause problems. Furthermore, in a society that does not always value intellectual precocity, the gifted and talented must often learn to value their own gifts and overcome conflicting parental and peer values. When they do so, social acceptance accelerates, and they can move toward greater intellectual development.

Motor Characteristics

The early Terman finding regarding the superior physical status of the gifted has been substantiated frequently by subsequent research. As a group, gifted children are indeed taller, heavier, stronger, more energetic, and healthier than peers of average intelligence (Martinson, 1961). Lucito (1963) reported that gifted and talented youngsters tend to be superior in "measure of strength of grip, leg strength, push and pull, pumping, running, and other motor activities involving either the whole body or parts of it" (pp. 194-195). The original Terman group was followed into middle age and was found to be maintaining physical superiority (Terman & Oden, 1959).

HOW MANY CHILDREN ARE LIKELY TO BE IDENTIFIED AS GIFTED AND TALENTED?

It is obvious that the data on the incidence and prevalence of giftedness are affected by both the definition chosen and the identification methods employed. In the Terman study, an IQ of 140 was the sole criterion of giftedness. This produces an estimate of 2 to 3 percent of the population as gifted, but strict IQ definitions tend to produce low estimates (approximately 3 percent). Children in this group are likely to come from high socioeconomic status homes, have fewer siblings, and have better educated parents (Fisch, Bilek, Horrobin, & Chang, 1976).

According to Stephens and Wolf (1978), incidence studies of giftedness are rarely found in the literature. Incidence figures vary widely and are sensitive to the socioeconomic conditions of the school.

Estimates of prevalence also vary widely. Marland (1972) estimated the prevalence range as 3 (if only those students with high intellectual ability are included) to 5 percent (if those with special talents who do not fit the high IQ criterion are included).

While the U.S. Department of Education does not publish an official prevalence estimate for giftedness (Hallahan & Kauffman, 1982), Sisk (1981) noted that it has been assumed in federal reports and legislation that 3 to 5 percent of the school population could be considered gifted or talented.

HOW ARE GIFTED AND TALENTED CHILDREN IDENTIFIED?

A variety of identification procedures have been proposed (Clark, 1979; Gearheart, 1980; Sisk, 1979). Most procedures include teacher nominations, standardized tests, and behavioral checklists. The problem is, however, to identify these children early enough in life to create a responsive, cognitive growth-producing environment for them (Clark, 1979). As Reynolds and Birch (1977) noted, the terms *gifted* and *talented* are future-oriented. Educators work with children who have *potential* for gifted and talented performance, in other words, children for whom unusual or extraordinary contributions have been *predicted*.

Scores on individual IQ tests such as the Stanford-Binet or Wechsler tests are often used as one criterion for entrance to a program for the gifted. Often the cutoff score is two standard deviations above the mean (an IQ of approximately 130 or above). As has been noted, IQ tests for children two and below are not very reliable predictors of future performance. By age three, and certainly by age five, however, many potentially gifted and talented children could be identified by trained examiners (Reynolds & Birch, 1977). Although "the individually administered intelligence test remains the most reliable, defensible single means of identifying the gifted" (Hallahan & Kauffman, 1982, p. 387), it is very expensive and is not practical as a general screening tool. The problem remains one of identifying children early enough to capitalize on critical periods (Bloom, 1964) for form perception and language (Clark, 1979).

Parents can be helpful in identifying children with the potential for outstanding performance. In the Terman study (1925), for example, parents noted the following early indications of superior ability—in order of frequency from highest to lowest:

1. quick grasp and understanding of new ideas
2. desire for knowledge
3. retentive memory
4. intelligent conversation
5. rapid progress in school
6. keen general interests
7. range of general information

8. reasoning ability
9. early speech
10. asking of intelligent questions
11. ability in accomplishing difficult tasks
12. keen observation
13. unusual vocabulary
14. originality

A form such as the one shown in Exhibit 8-1 could be used with the parents of young children (15 months to 5 years) to help identify potentially gifted children for further evaluation by professionals.

Gearheart (1980) proposed a three-step process for identifying gifted and talented children of school age. With modification, this process could be employed as a follow-up to the Parental Screening Inventory (Exhibit 8-1) for younger children.

Step 1: Nomination by Teachers or School Counselors

Nominations must be based on a wide range of observations. The gifted child may excel in academic pursuits; the talented child, in music or art. However, as many as half of the gifted and talented population can be missed by the nomination process (Pegnato & Birch, 1959). As Gallagher (1966b) noted, teacher observation can miss the underachieving child, the culturally different child, or the child with motivational or attitudinal problems regarding school. Therefore, nominations can also be made by parents who complete the screening inventory.

Beyond superior academic ability, teachers need to be aware of other clues to possible giftedness or creativity. Among these are

- unusual curiosity
- unusual persistence at any given task
- restlessness, inattentiveness, or even aggressiveness, when given repetitive or superficial tasks
- originality
- imagination (Gearheart, 1980)

Step 2: Evaluation

The child's past records, attitudes, motivation, and health history must be thoroughly evaluated. Specific tests, including individual IQ tests, are appropriate to this step. The tests used in this step may be administered in two stages: screening and individual assessment.

Exhibit 8-1 Parent Screening Inventory

The following items are presented as behavior descriptions that may or may not describe your child. Check the items from 1 (Little) to 5 (Much) as best describes your child as you see him or her.

	Little		*Moderate*		*Much*
	1	*2*	*3*	*4*	*5*
1. INTELLECTUAL CURIOSITY Pursues interests to satisfy curiosity; questions the unusual; wants to know how and why; will interact nonverbally with objects to "see how they work."					
2. OBSERVATION Is alert and observant beyond his or her years; aware of many stimuli.					
3. FLEXIBILITY Able to approach problems or ideas from a number of perspectives; able to find alternate ways of solving problems.					
4. FLUENCY Able to produce large number of ideas or products, often very quickly.					
5. LANGUAGE Has a large vocabulary; developed speech early; comfortable using speech to solve problems; asks questions.					
6. PERSISTENCE Ability to follow through on tasks or problems.					
7. ORIGINALITY Often use original methods to solve problems; able to combine ideas in a number of ways.					

8. IMAGINATION May "play" with ideas; can respond freely to stimuli with production of mental images.					
9. INDEPENDENCE IN THOUGHT Inclined to follow own organization and ideas rather than structuring of others.					
10. INDEPENDENCE IN ACTION Able to plan and organize activities, direct action, evaluate results.					
11. PHYSICAL ABILITY Coordinated beyond years; seems particularly agile and limber.					
12. SOCIAL MATURITY Able and willing to "work" and play with others; shows consideration; can abide by rules.					
13. HAPPY QUALITIES Seems happy and comfortable in most situations; seems cheerful.					
14. MEMORY Able to remember ideas, events; extraordinary recall.					
15. DOMINANCE Asserts self with influence in group situations.					
16. EMOTIONAL STABILITY AND CONTROL Able to cope with frustration; adjusts to change with minimum stress; expresses and displays emotions properly.					

In this stage, professionals use group intelligence tests (e.g., Otis-Lennon Mental Ability Test) and group achievement tests (e.g., California Achievement Test). Both are useful for identifying nominees for further intensive, individual testing. Children who score above an established cutoff score automatically move to the second substage of this process. Group tests may not identify children with reading problems, emotional or motivational problems, disadvantaged children, or underachieving gifted children, however (Gallagher, 1966b).

Children who have scored above screening cutoffs are assessed by a certified psychologist. They are given an individual test of intelligence, such as the Stanford-Binet or the Wechsler tests, or a test of creativity, such as the Torrance Tests of Creative Thinking. If the area of concern involves a special talent, such as art, dance, or music, then experts in these areas should analyze the child's potential talent.

Even in this step, culturally different and handicapped gifted children may be overlooked because of the bias of certain standardized tests. The culturally different gifted child differs in many respects from the gifted child in the cultural mainstream; however, certain mental traits are shared, including the ability to

- manipulate meaningfully some symbol system of value in the particular cultural group
- think logically, given appropriate data
- use stored knowledge to solve problems in a creative fashion
- reason by analogy
- extend knowledge to new situations or unique applications (Gallagher & Kinney, 1974)

Step 3: Committee Deliberation Process

The identification process for programs for gifted and talented students culminates in a committee deliberation process. All data gathered in the first two steps are analyzed, program options considered, and a recommendation made. Gearheart (1980) observed four possible recommendations:

1. The student is recommended for placement.
2. The student is placed on stand-by until a space is available.
3. Further evaluation is recommended.
4. The student is not recommended.

WHAT IS THE IMPACT OF GIFTEDNESS ON FAMILIES?

It might be expected that the recognition of a child with special gifts or talents would be a cause for joyous celebration by the family. Unfortunately, this is not always the case. Some families, indeed some cultures, do not value creative thinking and, instead, promote conformity. Other families may apply excessive pressure on the child to achieve, thereby producing tension and frustration. Regardless of the reaction, labeling students as gifted or talented changes parental expectations and attitudes (not to mention the child's self-concept). It should also be noted that gifted children often have gifted parents who exhibit many of the same characteristics.

Because it is necessary to create an intellectually stimulating environment in the home, particularly for the young gifted child, Clark (1979) recommended the provision of family in-service programs. These programs must be designed to help families better understand both the needs and problems of the child. They should focus on the strategies that can be used to build the child's self-concept and areas of functioning, e.g., cognitive, affective, or psychomotor. Furthermore, training can help families understand the agency's program and create an environment of open communication with the agency professional so that problem-solving strategies can be devised.

Clark (1979) recommended at least five formal training sessions to present content on giftedness. If her suggestions are adapted and content on special talents is added, the sessions have the following content:

1. Understanding Giftedness and Special Talents
   - Who are the gifted and talented?
   - How are giftedness and talents nurtured?
2. Emotional and Social Development of the Gifted and Talented
   - How is self-esteem developed?
   - How can you present values?
   - How do you foster creativity?
   - How do you encourage special talents?
3. Meeting the Needs of the Gifted and Talented
   - What kinds of program alternatives are available?
   - What special curriculums are used?
   - What are the learning abilities of the gifted or talented child?
   - How can integrated learning in all domains be fostered?

4. Effective "Teachers" at Home
   - How can the home environment be made more nurturing for special gifts and talents?
   - How can families improve communication among members? With the service agency?
5. Effective Teachers in School
   - How can families work in the home to support the efforts of teachers?
   - How can family members support teachers' efforts by direct involvement in the classroom?
6. What Can We Do Now?
   - How can families plan with the school or agency?
   - What is the best way to maximize child-family-teacher interaction?
   - What advocacy measures, particularly with regard to legislatures, can be taken?
   - How can families become active in their communities for gifted and talented education?

Like the parents of handicapped children, the parents of gifted and talented children face many challenges. There are frustrations, shattered expectations, joys, and sorrow. Families of gifted and talented children need support, and they must be supportive of their children. These special children need time when their families listen to them, when they are allowed to "free wheel" their creative ideas in bursts of energy without being judged as daydreamers or inhabitants of a fantasy world.

Families also must treat their gifted and talented children as individuals—not as geniuses, high IQs, or great musicians. The gifted or talented child is still a child, a complex organism who is more than a high IQ. Siblings are also individuals and should *never* be compared to the gifted or talented child. Each child in a family, whether handicapped or gifted, has special "gifts" and should be loved and valued for these "gifts."

Gifted or talented children frequently feel isolated because their special gifts make them stand out when they desire to conform; this is of particular significance with adolescents. Families must be extra supportive and provide comfort to the child who finds being different a problem. Families may need professional assistance to help the gifted or talented child learn to accept being different.

Families need to be realistic in their expectations of their gifted and talented children and to help these children be realistic in their expectations of themselves. Families often demand perfection of their gifted children;

even if they do not, the children may demand it of themselves. Families need to be models that occasional failures and mistakes are acceptable. This is really a part of learning, the part that makes it easier to do something new or difficult the next time. Families can help gifted children establish realistic, attainable goals and then provide the support necessary to accomplish the goals.

Finally, families need to understand the gifted child's excitement and seemingly endless energy. Divergence of thought and failure to complete projects are common. Gifted and talented children need direction so that priorities can be established and growth can be nurtured. Exploration is to be rewarded and guided, even at the expense of a few unfinished projects. Not only families, but also the gifted child must develop tolerance. This extraordinary child must be tolerant of siblings and peers who do not process new information as quickly or remember as much. In doing so, the child will learn to value each person's individuality and uniqueness.

WHAT IS THE IMPACT OF GIFTEDNESS AND SPECIAL TALENTS ON THE FUTURE LIVES OF CHILDREN?

The results of the Terman study show that the children in his sample population grew into extremely successful adults. As a group, their record of accomplishment is substantial. They excelled in subsequent education, in the arts and sciences, the professions, the business world, and, perhaps most importantly, in their personal and family lives (Terman & Oden, 1959). This marvelous record should not be interpreted to mean that the gifted can fend for themselves, however. Torrance (1980) and Guilford (1975) have pointed out that being gifted is not a guarantee of future success. As Guilford (1975) argued:

> Of all the children who become the responsibility of educators, the "gifted" ones have the most probable potential for becoming effective problem solvers. The general picture, unfortunately, is that only a few of them actually fulfill such promise, either for lack of immediate need, motivation, or development of skills in creative thinking. We can educate those children either with or without the cultivation of such talents; they will ordinarily not blossom to full extent on their own. (p. 107)

The gifted and talented child faces two major problem areas: (1) coping with special gifts in a society that does not appreciate and may in fact be hostile to intellectuals, and (2) dealing with emotional problems that may occur regarding the optimal use of the gifts or talents.

In some ways, special gifts can be burdensome to children. Gifted or talented children with a great need for success and recognition may become discouraged and frustrated when they fail to meet self-imposed high standards. Being different can lead to nonconformist behavior that increases isolation and feelings of rejection. When perceived differences are viewed as a negative attribute, gifted or talented children may devalue themselves, further eroding their self-concept.

When the gifted child enters a school program that does not react sensitively to the child's cognitive needs, boredom and impatience may result. Divergent thinking and creative solutions may be viewed as a challenge to the authority of the teacher. This, in turn, may lead to alienation and perception of the child as a disruptive troublemaker. Real frustration regarding the inability of peers (and often teachers) to understand creative insights can lead to social conflict; for example, peers may view the gifted child as conceited.

Some gifted children never really use their gifts to their own or society's benefit. Clark (1979) used the term *underachieving gifted child* to refer to "someone who has shown exceptional performance on a measure of intelligence and who, nevertheless, does not perform as well as expected for students of the same age on school related tasks" (p. 279). Underachievement may be related to poor teaching (Bricklin & Bricklin, 1967) or family situations that do not nurture and develop the gifts (Bricklin & Bricklin, 1967; Daniel, 1960). Characteristics of the family of the underachieving gifted child include

- dependence of the child on the mother
- negative relationship between the father and the child
- unrealistic goals set by parents
- failure of parents to reward achievement
- social and emotional problems in the family
- failure of parents to show affection, trust, or approval
- restrictive and severe punishments

In the final analysis, it seems that children with special gifts or talents can develop these gifts to the maximum when parents and teachers are receptive to diversity. Early educational experiences in the home, the preschool, and the elementary school are crucial in determining whether the children will use their special gifts or talents and how well they will use them. Early experiences that encourage exploration and curiosity, challenge children to determine solutions to problems in creative ways, introduce escalating levels of complexity in the learning environment, and provide appropriate emotional support and social interaction promote these gifts and talents and help these children realize their potential for personal fulfillment and social contributions.

WHAT INTERVENTION STRATEGIES CAN BE USED FOR GIFTED AND TALENTED CHILDREN?

Marland (1972) noted that

> the relatively few gifted students who have had the advantage of special programs have shown remarkable improvements in self-understanding and in ability to relate well to others, as well as in improved academic and creative performance. The programs have not produced arrogant, selfish snobs; special programs have extended a sense of reality, wholesome humility, self-respect and respect for others. A good program for the gifted increases their involvement and interest in learning through the reduction of the irrelevant and redundant. (p. 23)

Despite the massive professional support for special education for the gifted and talented (Gearheart, 1980; Hallahan & Kauffman, 1982; Reynolds & Birch, 1977; Safford, 1978), there is a clear lack of empirical evidence to support the efficacy of educational programs for this population. Although common sense and logic point out the value of special programs, it has not been scientifically documented that gifted children become gifted adults who contribute to the social welfare or are personally fulfilled because of special education. While this lack of evidence has certainly not helped secure adequate funding or legislation to support special education for these youngsters, it has not deterred school districts and service agencies from providing specialized intervention.

Organization of School Programs for the Gifted

Getzels and Dillon (1973) identified more than 20 specific programs and practices for providing education to the gifted and talented. The three most common types are acceleration, enrichment, and special ability grouping.

Acceleration

Methods of acceleration include: early entry into kindergarten, grade skipping, advanced placement, and the compression of time spent studying a subject or primary area. The research done on this approach is uniformly positive (Braga, 1969; Gallagher, 1966b; Lucito, 1964); there is no research evidence that acceleration is harmful to the children involved. Some of the advantages of acceleration are that it

- can be used in any school
- allows capable students to complete school earlier and thus enter their careers sooner
- results in a savings of educational costs
- reduces boredom and frustration for bright students

Despite the preponderance of evidence in support of acceleration, "it is probably the least used administrative arrangement for providing services for the gifted" (Sisk, 1979, p. 375). It is highly favored by parents (and later by children when asked), but often resisted by teachers and administrators who fear mislabeling, adhere to traditional movement through the grades for convenience sake, ignore research, or still cling to the erroneous notion that acceleration leads to social maladjustment (Clark, 1979; Sisk, 1979). As Sisk (1979) argued, successful acceleration for the gifted "demands administrators who are thoroughly aware of the individual student's ability, achievement, social and emotional maturity, as well as totally sympathetic receiving teachers, administrators, and parents" (p. 376).

Enrichment

Sisk (1979) maintained that any provision of service for the gifted involves enrichment in some form. The problem is that, while enrichment is embraced by administrators (who see it as the least expensive means of providing service), there is little agreement among education professionals as to the meaning or the value of the practice. Stanley (1976) argued that enrichment as a practice cannot stand alone and must be offered in conjunction with acceleration of subject matter or grade placement.

Clark (1979) defined enrichment as the addition of areas of learning not found in traditional curriculums. Most programs that use enrichment adhere to this definition, providing somewhat unrelated experiences or a variety of exploratory activities without acceleration. Many education professionals (e.g., Stanley, 1976; Sisk, 1979) prefer to interpret enrichment as indepth learning, at an accelerated pace, of a variety of experiences that are integrated with the regular program.

In order for enrichment to be successful, it must be carefully planned, thoroughly integrated with the regular curriculum, conducted by teachers able to orchestrate the learning environment to bring about desired results, and buttressed by a wide range of supportive activities and services. Gallagher (1964) suggested using activities that develop the gifted child's ability to

- associate and interrelate concepts
- evaluate facts and arguments critically
- create new ideas and originate new lines of thought
- reason through complex problems
- understand other situations, other times, and other people; to be less bound by one's own peculiar environmental surroundings (p. 80)

Renzulli (1977) proposed a model of enrichment with three types of activities, two of which are appropriate for all children and one particularly suited to the needs of gifted and talented youngsters. Type I activities (general exploratory) provide all children with access to media, materials, and in-class activities so that they may identify individual topics of interest. Type II activities (group training) employ games and simulations to increase creativity, emotional awareness, and problem-solving methods of all children. Type III activities (individual and small group investigations of real problems) are especially useful with gifted and talented children. Children investigate real life problems by actually assuming such roles as scientists or journalists. A problem is defined, a suitable method of inquiry is used, and results are provided to consumers.

Special Ability Grouping

The method called special ability grouping may involve special classes or schools, before or after school programs, "pullout" programs (gifted children are segregated for a time and then return to the regular class), or summer institutes. This particular method and its derivatives have received considerable criticism from those who advocate mainstreaming. Nonetheless, few educators of the gifted and talented would deny that these students need to spend some measure of time with other gifted and talented youngsters for the intellectual challenges offered. Obvious advantages of this arrangement include the following:

- Students can learn at their own accelerated pace.
- Interaction among gifted students stimulates and motivates them.
- Extra subject matter can be presented.

Principles for Teaching the Gifted and Talented

Regardless of the administrative arrangement chosen to educate the gifted child, certain principles of teaching apply to all subjects, skills, and age levels. Bryan and Bryan (1979) summarized specific suggestions and research drawn from various authors with regard to classroom activities and learning needs of gifted and talented children. Included among their recommendations are the following:

- Isolated facts should not be taught; rather, the focus should be on the basic structure or theory underlying the content to be learned.
- When possible, activities should be structured so as to promote the discovery of unusual or unique solutions.
- Methods of obtaining information should be stressed, rather than the facts themselves.
- In areas of little teacher expertise, outside experts should be used whenever possible.
- Independent activities, with children progressing at their own rates, are highly desirable.
- Teachers should provide an atmosphere in which children feel free to experiment without fear of failure. The stimulation of highly creative ideas through processes such as brainstorming should be encouraged.
- Competition should be encouraged, as it tends to be both motivating and enjoyable.
- The use of typical positive reinforcements should be avoided, since gifted children are often intrinsically motivated (and thus reinforced) to master the tasks given to them. However, gifted children should be rewarded creatively for their efforts.

Special Techniques for Early Intervention

Giftedness does not appear to be detectable at birth or even during the first year of life. Research (Fisch et al., 1976; Willerman & Fiedler, 1974) indicates that tests of motor or cognitive ability administered in the first year of life are not reliable predictors of later special abilities in these areas. This presents a dilemma. Early intervention is desirable, but difficult because of our inability to identify the target population.

Clark (1979) presented a cogent argument for providing an optimal interactive environment for infants to enhance cognitive development. The more responsive and stimulating the environment, the greater the likelihood that visual, motor, and cognitive systems can be used in concert and at peak efficiency.

The first four years of life are critical to the development of cognitive and personality skills. Among others, Piaget (1954) described the importance of the first two years, and White (1975) noted the crucial nature of the first three years of life, documenting the child's need for early, meaningful, and active interactions with the environment. The first four years can be subdivided into three particularly critical phases: birth to 3 months, 10 to 24 months, and two to four years.

Birth to 3 Months

Clark (1979) stated that the period from birth to 3 months is a crucial developmental period for infants because visual complexity is best learned during this time. Infants are not mobile participants in interactions, so families and caregivers must provide an environment that is responsive to them. Table 8-1 provides specific suggestions to families for activities most appropriate to this age group (Mori & Olive, 1980). If basic needs are met and caregivers attend to the infant's cues of distress, children develop basic trust, learn that they are loved, and, most importantly, recognize they can influence their environment.

Ten to Twenty-Four Months

White (1975) maintained that the period from 10 to 24 months is the most crucial for intellectual development. He suggested that balanced development during this period requires exploration of the world and involves motor, language, intellectual, and social development.

This period is one of mobility and active exploration of the environment. Families need to provide a safe world where the child can examine toys, household objects, and, of course, the outdoors. During this phase, active physical exploration and the opportunity to manipulate objects (e.g., blocks and pegboards) are essential.

Language is also developing during this period. Families can help their child develop language by talking a great deal to the child and reinforcing the child's efforts to use language. Playing naming games (Mori & Olive, 1980) further stimulates this crucial skill. Table 8-2 provides specific suggestions to families for activities most appropriate to this age period (Mori & Olive, 1980).

Two to Four Years

The final preschool phase is a period of rapid cognitive and language development. The toddler's vocabulary expands from approximately 200

Table 8-1 Suggested Activities for Infants Birth to 3 Months

Activity	Skill Developed
Move the location of crib Use bed sheets with different colors and patterns Hang mobiles on the crib Play flashing light games at night with the light switch when the room is dark	Visual
Place a wind chime near an air source in infant's room Talk, coo, laugh, sing, and play soft music on radio or tape recorder	Auditory (prelanguage)
Hold and cuddle infant's bare skin Lightly brush infant's skin with soft materials and fabrics, tickle, soothe, give little pinches or backrubs. When infant indicates hand regard, put little bells on elastic for the wrist Texture blanket Rock infant (vestibular stimulation)	Haptic (tactile and kinesthetic)
Devise "smell bottles" or let infant smell perfume bottles, spice bottles, etc. Rub the infant with various oils and powders after bath	Olfactory
Construct or purchase crib mobiles that the infant can bat and play with Texture blanket	Cognitive
Respond to infant's distress cues Respond to infant's movements and activities	Affective (including trust)

words at age two to approximately 900 to 1,000 words at age three. Also during this period, toddlers begin to string together two- and three-word sentences. Although largely telegraphic, these sentences contain pronouns or nouns and verbs; therefore, they are functionally complete sentences. By the third year of life, children are quite capable of understanding much of the language used by adults for ordinary conversation. From this point on, language emerges rapidly so that, by age four, most children have mastered the basic syntax of their language. From a cognitive standpoint, children in this period do not always need to manipulate things physically; objects and events now possess labels acquired from a rapidly developing language.

Table 8-2 Suggested Activities for Toddlers 10 to 24 Months

Activity	Skill developed
Continue to use and expand the visual, auditory, haptic, and olfactory experiences in Table 8-1	Sensory
Provide toys and objects, e.g. blocks, puzzles, nesting cubes, pegboards and formboards, tops, beads (large wooden or plastic) to string Play games, e.g., peek-a-boo, hide and seek, finger plays, matching and sorting games	Concept development, cognitive
Name objects Read books to child Talk to child Reinforce language usage	Language
Practice walking Dance with child to music Play mini-obstacle course games	Motor

Parents may begin to recognize precocity during this period. They should continue to expand on the previously presented activities. The key to development for the potentially gifted or talented child is freedom and encouragement to explore and satisfy natural curiosity. "Teaching" exchanges with parents should be fun and guided by the idea that activities and trips are times to explore, ask questions, solve problems, suggest creative solutions, and receive reassurance from the family so that the child's potential can be actualized. Specific activities for this period may be drawn from sources such as Beck (1967), Clark (1979), and Engelmann and Englemann (1966).

Intervention for the Prekindergarten and Early School Years

Safford (1978) has suggested a series of activities for use with prekindergarten and young gifted and talented children. His areas of emphasis include

- supporting intrinsic motivation
- encouraging discovery learning
- encouraging and supporting creativity
- encouraging expression through nonverbal activity

- emphasizing the "fantasy and feeling" dimension of children's literature
- fostering social awareness and interpersonal relations

Active pursuit of these areas of emphasis challenges the child's curiosity, and learning itself becomes part of an internal reward system. Children develop a love for learning when the learning environment is rich with activities and problems to be solved. The discovery method values the process, the means of solving the problems rather than the solution itself.

Creativity is encouraged and supported by a classroom environment that supports diversity. Games, simulations, sociodrama, and brainstorming are just a few of the many activities that foster creativity. Guilford (1959) identifies flexibility as an important dimension of creativity. In this case, flexibility is needed in using both time and space.

Nonverbal activity offers a different avenue for creative expression. Children need the opportunity to participate in play and creative dramatics, art, music, and movement, including dance and gymnastics.

Finally, children should be taught to understand their feelings (Safford, 1978) and their values. Special programs (Bessell & Palomares, 1970; Dinkmeyer, 1969) can be used effectively to help children understand not only their own feelings, but also the feelings of others and how the two relate to healthy personal-social growth.

Clearly, there are many awesome challenges in educating gifted and talented children. Failure to educate them appropriately may result not only in the loss of our "most precious resource—human minds," but also in the loss of many potentially important contributions to the betterment of society. Unfortunately, the plight of gifted children has not improved greatly since Mead (1954) noted that

> if they learn easily, they are penalized for being bored when they have nothing to do; if they excel in some outstanding way, they are penalized as being conspicuously better than the peer group. . . . The culture tries to make the child with a gift into a one-sided person, to penalize him at every turn, to cause him trouble in making friends and to create conditions conducive to the development of a neurosis. Neither teachers, the parents of other children, nor the child's peers will tolerate a wunderkind. (p. 213)

Part III

Models for Developing Family Education Programs

Chapter 9, the only chapter in this section, is divided into three major parts. The first part of the chapter addresses four basic models for delivering services to young children with special needs and their families: (1) home-based, (2) center-based, (3) home/center-based, and (4) parent-operated programs. The second major part of the chapter focuses on programs for developing skills and attitudes in parents involved in intervention programs. In the final section, methods of evaluating the effectiveness of family intervention programs are discussed.

Chapter 9

Developing Programs for Families of Young Children with Special Needs

Parent involvement has become an accepted, even fundamental, aspect of programming in special education. The passage of Public Law 90-538, the Handicapped Children's Early Education Assistance Act (HCEEAA) and the creation of the Handicapped Children's Early Education Program (HCEEP); the research reports on the effectiveness of preschool intervention and parental participation in that process (Bronfenbrenner, 1974); and the passage of Public Law 94-142, the Education for All Handicapped Children Act of 1975, have unalterably set the course of parent involvement in the education of young handicapped children.

Turnbull, Turnbull, and Wheat (1982) wrote that current federal law mandating parental involvement is based on three major assumptions:

1. Parents should make decisions about their child's education.
2. Parent participation ensures the rights of the child under Public Law 94-142.
3. Parents are capable of teaching and already function as their children's teachers.

It is implicit in the law that parents will be provided with the necessary training to fulfill their role in early intervention programs. In fact, Shearer and Shearer (1977) note that "it thus becomes mandatory that projects [those funded by HCEEP] develop training programs for parents with the objective of teaching parents to be effective in working with and teaching their own child" (p. 213).

Because of the legal mandate and the recognition of the vital contribution that well-trained parents can make, professionals in early intervention have designed several models to facilitate parent training.

205

MODELS FOR OPERATING PARENT PROGRAMS

There are typically four basic service delivery models for providing intervention to preschool handicapped children and involving their parents in the program. The models are home-based, center-based, home/center-based, and parent-operated.

Home-Based Programs

The home-based system relies heavily on the parent as the child's primary teacher. Staff-family interaction in which parents receive instruction and support occurs in the home. The target of intervention is usually the parent-child dyad with the involvement of the father considered equally important as that of the mother. The handicapped child receives individual attention and is not usually grouped with other children for instructional activities.

Programs that follow this model are usually based on certain assumptions regarding parental participation. First, parents are considered the most effective teachers of their children, provided that they receive ongoing instruction and support. Projects or agencies using this model believe that parents know their children better than professionals do and that parent involvement can greatly accelerate the acquisition of new skills. Fredericks, Baldwin, and Grove (1974) demonstrated that parents involved as teachers of their children can reduce the time required for a child to acquire a skill by 50 percent.

Second, parents in the home-based model are working with children in their natural environment. Because parents are naturally reinforcing agents, they can be taught to use methods that facilitate behavior acquisition of functional skills. The child's behavior occurs in a natural setting and therefore does not have to be transferred from the school setting.

Third, when intervention is occurring in the home, the involvement of the father and the rest of the family (e.g., siblings) is a more realistic, attainable goal. Family members have more direct access to the child and thus have greater opportunities for meaningful teaching-learning interactions.

The success of this model depends on the establishment of the parent-professional partnership. The agency assigns a home visitor to work with the family. The home visitor usually visits the family at least once per week to provide training in

- using the program curriculum or training materials
- teaching skills

- using reinforcement strategies
- observing and recording child behavior
- documenting child progress toward goal attainment

During the sessions, the home visitor and the parent jointly select pertinent training objectives for the child and plan how best to achieve them. The home visitor may demonstrate the teaching of the skill to the parents, gradually becoming less directive and turning over the responsibility to the parent.

The home-based model has been used successfully in large geographical areas where the cost of transporting children is prohibitive; areas where there are few but diversely handicapped children, precluding the establishment of a center-based program; and areas where parental involvement would be minimized because of geographical or psychological distance between the home and the school (Shearer, 1976).

Center-Based Programs

In the center-based intervention program, children (and parents) are brought to a central location for services. Since the program usually operates for only two or three hours per day, parental involvement in follow-up activities in the home is considered vital to program success. Children may be grouped with similarly handicapped children (e.g., in a program for blind preschoolers), or they may be served in noncategorical and even integrated (with nonhandicapped children) classrooms.

Program developers using this approach make certain assumptions regarding parental participation. First, they believe that programs providing services to children must also provide support to families. The center-based program brings parents together with other parents of exceptional children. During the training activities, workshops, or daily school routines, parents interact with one another and provide mutual support.

Second, the complex problems of young handicapped children require early intensive intervention in an interdisciplinary program. Children receive intensive instruction from professionals in areas such as self-help skills or language while parents have the opportunity to observe, participate, and acquire enough skills to carry the programming into the home. Since children often enter programs at different times throughout the year, training programs for parents must be flexible, ongoing, and individualized.

Third, parents of the severely handicapped are often investing a great deal of time with the child in the home. The center-based program offers them a brief respite from the intensive parent-child interaction pattern while still allowing them to contribute to the child's program.

Fourth, the center-based program makes it possible to offer training to parents in areas common to all programs or for all children (e.g., child development and behavior management techniques). Center staff may work with parents through conferences, group meetings, workshops, and individual or group instruction activities.

While center-based programs vary greatly, they have certain features in common. In programs for older preschoolers (i.e., two to five years), children may attend classes at the center for two or three hours per day for four or five days per week. Parents may observe the activities and are often invited to participate as classroom helpers at least one day per week. This experience supplements the formal training opportunities in that parents learn teaching and other skills via demonstration and practice. Parents have direct access to instructional or liaison staff and are provided with information and advice to facilitate related activities in the home.

The center-based model is frequently used in urban areas with good mass transportation. These larger population centers often have greater concentrations of handicapped children, even in the low incidence areas, which makes centralized programming more feasible.

Home/Center-Based Programs

The center-based and the home-based models may be combined. In such a home/center-based program, children (and parents) receive services in a centralized program, but home visitors provide support and ensure continuity between the center's intervention activities and the follow-up training in the home. In this type of program, the parents provide instruction in the home that either is supplemental to that provided in the center or is not covered by the center program.

Certain assumptions underlie the home/center-based program. First, since parents often become discouraged by a lack of child progress, program developers believe that parents may become more willing participants in a structured home program if they observe child success in the center program. Their eagerness to participate can be cultivated if home visitors are available as resource persons.

Second, the home/center-based model allows for parent-to-parent interaction in an interdisciplinary setting, but it still permits individualized attention in each child's natural setting. In addition, children derive the benefit of social interaction with peers at the center while receiving individual attention from parents and professionals in the home setting.

Third, many professionals believe that child progress is greatest in a combined home-center program. Fredericks, Baldwin, and Grove (1976) suggested that if a parent will conduct for ten minutes to a half hour a day a training program at home in conjunction with the same training program being conducted at the school, the child will acquire the taught skill in a significantly quicker time. In fact, the data show that the systematic program involving the parent in conjunction with the school program will almost double the rate of acquisition of the skill. (pp. 108-109)

The operation of a quality home/center-based program combines the best elements of the two models. Children attend regular sessions at the center and receive instruction in key developmental areas. Parents become both observers of intervention and participants in the instructional process. They receive individual and group instruction in various skill areas. Home visitors also make regular visits to the home to ensure continuity of programming. Parents receive further instruction and feedback on teaching performance.

The combined program approach seems best suited for urban areas with concentrated populations and minimal travel distances.

Parent-Operated Programs

Although not as common as the three that have been discussed, the parent-operated model is nonetheless a viable means of providing early intervention services to young exceptional children and their families. In this model, all essential program services, including intake, direct service, parent training, liaison, and ancillary services, are planned, implemented, and evaluated by parents. Professionals are utilized essentially as consultants to train parents in

- child development
- observation skills
- data recording
- teaching skills
- reinforcement strategies
- methods of recording child progress

Consultants then continue to work with trained parents who, in turn, train and work with "new" parents in program services.

According to Wiegerink and Parrish (1976) the use of the parent-operated model is based on six assumptions:

1. Parents know their child better than anyone else does, and this knowledge can be a valuable resource to all who work with the child.
2. Parents usually spend more time with their child than anyone else does, and the time can be used to provide training consistent with the program's philosophy and goals.
3. Parents can have a significant impact on one another by sharing similar problems and providing emotional support.
4. Parents can provide ongoing child progress data ensuring program accountability and facilitating program decision making.
5. Parent-provided child behavioral data are useful in monitoring intervention effectiveness.
6. Parents provide personnel not readily available from other sources.

In areas where there are few professionals trained in early intervention or communities are not willing to commit the kind and amount of resources necessary to provide even minimal intervention programs for young exceptional children, parent-operated programs may fill a serious void in service delivery. Parents are a vast, largely untapped reservoir of human resources. In the parent-operated model, it is assumed that parents can be prepared to take the major responsibility for teaching their children and to use more effective methods of child rearing.

PROGRAMS FOR DEVELOPING SKILLS AND ATTITUDE CHANGES IN FAMILIES OF YOUNG HANDICAPPED CHILDREN

Much has been written about the need to train parents so that children with special needs will become more effective adults. Several authors (Lillie, 1978; Scheinfeld, 1969; Skolnick, 1978) have raised serious questions and concerns regarding the impact of parents on children's development, however, particularly when training programs focus on the parent-child relationship in isolation from the total parental experience.

Lillie (1978) urged program providers to focus also on the needs of the parents as individuals and members of a family unit. If parent training is to have a maximum effect, it must be integrated into the family environment. As Lillie (1978) noted

> When we approach the individual parent as an entity removed from the environment of the family, we approach that parent on a one-dimensional plane for a specific training purpose. If, on the other hand, we approach the parent with the assumption that he/ she fits into a family environment that includes other members

and other needs, we may have much more impact. The needs of . . . [the] . . . parent . . . are multi-faceted. (pp. 97-98)

If the training of parents to assume new or more involved roles as teachers of their children is to be successful, it must assist them in meeting their basic needs as individuals, as well as their needs as parents. Parents whose own basic needs are met will certainly be in a better position to meet the new needs or challenges that arise in being the parent of a handicapped child. Thus, as Lillie (1978) advocated, the trainers of parents must first recognize them as adult members of a dynamic ecological construct. Furthermore, these professionals must be aware of parents' needs for self-esteem and self-actualization.

As noted in Chapter 3, Helping Families Deal with Practical Problems, the agency professional must treat the parent as an equal, worthy of trust and respect. The professional must show a respect for the parent's strengths and a desire for the parent's participation in the intervention program in a meaningful fashion.

Needs of Families and Parents of Young Handicapped Children

Both professional experience (Mori & Olive, 1980) and a review of the literature (Bromwich, 1981; Foster et al., 1981; Hanson, 1981; Karnes & Zehrbach, 1975) reveal that families and parents of young handicapped children have several clear-cut needs.

Need for Self-Esteem

It is not at all unusual for the parents to suffer a great loss of self-esteem when a handicapped child is born. Parents may blame themselves or each other and begin to regard themselves in a negative fashion. This problem is further complicated by professionals who "talk down" to parents, thus conveying a lack of respect, or judge parents according to a personal value system that conflicts with that of the family. Professionals must show respect for the parents, as well as confidence in their ability to establish a positive relationship with their child. Frequently, the intervention program, with its focus on parental support, counseling, and training, can address this need.

Need to Achieve Self-Confidence in Parenting Skills

Parents face many dilemmas in raising a handicapped child. Parents often express concern over their helplessness in meeting the child's needs or in doing the "right" thing. Often, the child's behavioral excesses or lack of an expected behavior is a source of embarrassment for the parents.

Parents must recognize the accomplishments of their handicapped child even when these accomplishments occur long after the time they normally occur in other children. Parents must also deal with the attitudes of friends and family who may view parental demands on the handicapped child as "cruel or excessive," although the parents know that such demands are necessary and appropriate to prevent the child's disability from becoming a true handicap or an excuse.

Parents need to understand that effective parenting can be learned but that there is no one correct way to be a "good parent." It is also helpful for parents of young handicapped children to know that other parents are experiencing the same problems.

Need to Overcome Feelings of Isolation, Depression, and Ambivalence toward the Child

Parents of handicapped children frequently feel isolated, depressed, or lonely because they withdraw socially from their circle of friends or because they are afraid to leave the child with a babysitter. Lack of contact with other adults leads to despair and feelings of rejection. Compounding this problem is the fact that parents often have ambivalent feelings toward their handicapped child. This ambivalence, ranging from rejection on the one hand to "smothering" on the other hand, causes guilt in parents or families. Parents often express a feeling of inadequacy because they do not love their child all the time or because they are not capable of positive feelings about the child.

When parents have these needs, professionals must encourage them to go out by themselves both to participate in social activities and to pursue their own personal and individual interests. Babysitting services for the handicapped may be available and should be identified by agency staff. Professionals should also reassure the parents that ambivalence toward the child is a feeling common among many parents. Guilt regarding this feeling should be lessened through discussion with staff and other parents.

Need to Attend to Their Own Needs and the Needs of Other Family Members

The mother often devotes much time and energy to the handicapped child in a misguided attempt to "make the child get better." This strains the relationship between the husband and wife, as well as the relationship between the siblings, if present, and the parents. When the wife refuses to go out socially and complains that her husband does not understand the child or appreciate her efforts to help the child, the husband-wife relationship deteriorates, adding special stresses to those already existing. Furthermore, if the parents believe that the normal siblings can take care of themselves or that their negative reaction to being deprived of their mother's time is somehow selfish, the family is in turmoil.

Families must become aware of the need to build internal family acceptance of the situation and to provide emotional support for each other and the siblings. The importance of husband-wife "alone time," away from the handicapped child, the siblings, and the house, cannot be overemphasized.

Need for the Working Mother to Overcome Guilt

Since Rawlings (1978) reported that nearly 50 percent of all married women with children under age 18 are now working, more and more mothers of handicapped children are faced with the need to overcome guilt. Mothers often report feelings of guilt because they are away from their child and because they are not able to work full-time and still have sufficient energy to attend to their child's special needs.

The agency professional must help the mother who must work understand that (1) the quality of the time spent is more critical than the quantity; (2) interaction during such times as feeding, dressing, and bathing can be important times for learning and building a positive relationship; (3) involving the child, especially toddlers and beyond, in the housekeeping activity (e.g., giving the child a rag to "help dust") is extremely meaningful and enjoyable for the child; and (4) setting aside "special time blocks" to give each child individual attention can bring much more positive relationships.

Need to Know What to Expect from the Child, the Program of Intervention, and the Future

One of the most critical and debilitating aspects of having a handicapped child is the uncertainty—the lack of information about the future. Programs that fail to give parents vital, honest information about the child, the program, and the future cannot meet the family's needs. Unless these needs are met, parents cannot be expected to become meaningfully involved in the program.

Changing Parental Attitudes Through Family Systems Theory

As mentioned earlier, the prevailing method of providing parent intervention tends to focus either on the individual parent (usually the mother) or on the mother-child dyad. When the focus is on the individual mother, the effort involves some form of parental counseling, either group or individual, that attempts to resolve the crises (Wolfensberger, 1967) being experienced by the mother. An alternative to the individual counseling approach is the parent-initiated behavior management approach, which provides specific training to the mother with the intention of changing mother-child relationships and solving typical problems of child rearing.

As early intervention programs have matured over the past several years, professionals have recognized the need to examine the family unit and its multifaceted interrelationships. Professionals now realize that family members interact in a fashion that facilitates the satisfaction of individual and group needs. Family members must complete certain tasks and fulfill certain roles in order for the unit as a whole to grow and mature. Recent literature (Foster & Berger, 1979; Foster et al., 1981) has stressed the need for a theoretical approach that accounts for the multiple interactive relationships within a family.

The structural approach (Minuchin, 1974) and the strategic approach (Haley, 1976) to family systems theory operate from a base that suggests behavior is affected by the context. Therefore, problems are best understood as endemic to the interactions between people in the system—a system that is dysfunctional, at least in regard to the particular problem being studied.

When the structural approach is applied, the professional examines both the subinteractions (e.g., husband-wife, parent-sibling) and the patterns, roles, and functions of the various family members. When the family structure is functional, there are clear boundaries around the interactions and between the generations, with distinct roles and functions for each family member. In the dysfunctional family, the boundaries may be transgressed or at least unclear so that an identifiable structure does not emerge.

The early childhood practitioner should recognize that problems in a family in intervention almost always go beyond the individual parent (mother) or the mother-child dyad. It is essential to examine the problem in the context of the family constellation and to involve the entire family in the intervention program. A child's problems are not the child's alone, nor can the child solve these problems alone. The problems affect all those who live with the child. The adult reactions, in turn, affect the progress of the child in matters of eventual adjustment to the problem; social, mental, and emotional growth; and, subsequently, the degree of participation the child may achieve in society. Therefore, it is most desirable to encourage families to participate actively in their child's intervention program.

Several purposes are served by involving families in their child's intervention program. The family-child relationship can be greatly improved.

Intervention is far more effective when families understand and meet the child's and their own needs. Parents benefit from the exchange of information with professioals and others who have had similar experiences. Finally, the program itself may benefit because families may become advocates in the community for stronger programs.

Parents have taken many active roles in numerous intervention programs throughout the United States. They have worked as administrators and participated on advisory councils; they have disseminated information and advocated the cause of such programs through public relations activities and legislative activities. They have served as volunteers to programs and as models for other parents. In many instances, parents have given much time and support by counseling other parents whose children have similar problems. They have served as the primary teachers of their own children, developing curriculums and original teaching devices. They have learned to gather, record, assess, and evaluate data. Indeed, they have become paraprofessionals in every sense of the word. Many parents have returned to school for further training and have reentered the field as professionals. Their personal experiences and expertise have made their contributions most valuable.

Those who participate in early childhood intervention programs must have a certain sensitivity to the feelings, messages, and needs of others. Initially, programs were designed to focus on the child. In practice, however, the feelings and needs of the family have such an impact on the success of the program that professionals must also be well trained in crisis and family counseling techniques. That training is most effective when it provides practice for those who would counsel others to understand and gain command of their own feelings when under stress. Practitioners need the skills of an educator, a counselor, and general social worker as they work with people who are living through very trying situations.

It may also be useful for professionals to understand the basic principles of "crisis counseling" as suggested by Parad (1975) and Lazarus (1966). A crisis may cause drastic alterations in a family's values, concepts of role, and communication systems. Crisis counseling and intervention involves an intensive six-week period of counseling and problem-solving supports immediately following the event that precipitated the crisis; it can be a most helpful method of providing supportive services for families in distress.

Certain principles of caring for others are part of quality counseling, whether during the period immediately following the crisis or during the long years of programming that may follow. Good counselors must be good listeners. They must listen with acceptance, rather than shock and judgment, and they must ask how the person being counseled feels about a situation. They know that they can effect change only with genuine concern. Counselors become adept at watching "body language" and hearing what is really being said. They are able to accept the fact that stress and disappointment may cause those they serve to turn upon them in anger. Effective counselors try to approach a person's pain with reality. On the other hand, counselors do not flood people suffering denial with reality; they introduce facets of the problem gradually, because human beings adapt one step at a time. Practitioners accept the children and the parent as they are and guide them through programs by means of many immediate and small successes.

Whether functioning as educators or counselors, practitioners sometimes reach a point where they cannot help with all a child's or family's problems. They should recognize their own limitations and refer clients to more highly trained professionals or recommend other programs when necessary. If conflict arises, they may suggest another practitioner, which is not unusual. Good training in available community service is vital in this regard.

Siblings may either help or add to the problems of families in a state of crisis. The number of children in a family, as well as the temperaments of those children, greatly affects the energy and time a parent can expend on a child with special needs. Handicapped children frequently have a great desire to play with and be like their brothers and sisters, however, and this desire can become a highly motivating factor in the child's successful growth and development. In this case, practitioners are well advised to include siblings in the training program and listen to them for helpful suggestions.

Grandparents, aunts, and uncles, as well as family friends, may become important in intervention programs. Their support is invaluable. They frequently provide respite for the parents and may even become involved in the training program itself. They may also become advocates in community efforts to gain legislative funding for special education programs. They may have a tremendous effect on the family's "coping" skills as they influence value systems, role perceptions, and family communication systems.

Just as all individuals react to stress in different ways, families develop different patterns of coping. There are strengths and weaknesses in every family. Crisis may unify one family and cause the collapse of another. Knowing practitioners must become sensitive to the family's emotional climate as they begin the intervention program.

On the first several visits, practitioners should not only assess the child's problems but also become well acquainted with the family's values, patterns of living, and perceptions of roles. They should (1) look for the strengths of the family and the child; (2) learn what family members enjoy, dislike, and feel about their lives; and (3) learn how they feel about the effect of the handicapped child's birth upon their lives. This knowledge will provide a vital foundation for good rapport and a successful ongoing program.

Families participate more enthusiastically in the intervention program if various facets of the child's needs are shown to relate to family interests. It is most important not to bombard the family with intensive training, theory, and group meetings until the initial grief is somewhat ameliorated. Simple exercises and games involving immediate reward can be taught as a part of the daily bathing or feeding routine, however. The program should begin so gradually that all involved quickly come to feel confident and successful.

Practitioners must recognize the parents' value system as a way to interest them in the intervention program. Furthermore, in order to influence another person, it is necessary to use fundamental methods of persuasion. People will not try something new until their resistance is softened, their interest has been captured, and they begin to want what is being offered. Once parents see the value of an intervention program, the practitioner has only to get their commitment to the program. The practitioner may have to give them new information or additional reasons to desire the recommended program. Parents may need many opportunities to reconsider until they decide to participate fully in the intervention program.

Strategies for Maximizing Parent Involvement in Intervention Programs

Frequently, professionals are disappointed in parent participation in formalized groups. Parents may resist participation because they are not yet ready to listen to others' problems, because they feel their needs are already being met by the professional, or because they do not realize the benefits that sharing may afford. Scheduling, vacations, illness, and general reluctance to attend any meetings add to the absenteeism at structured gatherings.

The initial introduction of parents to the intervention program is critical. An effort must be made to avoid overwhelming the parents at first. Parents must be convinced that the program can meet their needs and the needs of their child. When they perceive their first efforts as successful, parents become much more hopeful and open to the work of the program. It is also wise to stress the abilities, rather than the problems, of the child.

Parents are soon able to participate in planning their child's program with the aid of educators and therapists.

Educators are well advised to remember that parents did not originally choose to participate in this field of endeavor. A certain reluctance to fill in endless forms and data sheets is to be expected. Parents chose other professions, and they are rarely dedicated to the cause of educational research. On the other hand, more and more parents are refusing to be intimidated by professionals and hope to participate in all decisions that affect their child. They expect to read all reports and attain copies of their child's files. They want realistic suggestions for managing the child, as their problems are ongoing and there are few pat solutions. Parents resent "final" diagnoses and labeling, although they may find no diagnosis at all equally frustrating. They need to be continually helped to look for the good in their child and their situation.

Programs that meet these needs will be most effective in intervening on behalf of children with problems. Gorham (1975) provided sound advice from a parental perspective for professionals attempting to maximize parental participation in intervention programs. Included among her suggestions are

- Involve the parent every step of the way.
- Devise a realistic management plan as part of the assessment outcome. Provide the family with suggestions for living with the problem on a day-to-day basis, considering child needs, the capacities of the family, and the resources of the community.
- Provide "how to" advice for parents, using the network of community services.
- Provide written materials, including reports, in clear and understandable language.
- Give copies of *all* reports to parents. They must stay informed to stay involved.
- Make sure the parent knows that there is no such thing as a "final" diagnosis.
- Assist the parent in understanding the child's abilities and assets as well as the disabilities and deficiencies. What the child can do is much more important to the child (and the parent) than what the child cannot do.
- Help the family think of life with the special needs child in the same terms as life with other children in the family. Thus, life is viewed as an ongoing, problem-solving process.
- Warn the family of service gaps or inadequacies in the community.

- Help parents think positively, even if some professionals with whom they have contact perceive the child in a negative fashion.

This practical, straightforward advice from a parent may help professionals overcome parental attrition in intervention programs. Attrition remains a serious concern because it reduces the impact of the total program. Factors associated with attrition include the following (Stile, Cole, & Garner, 1979):

- meetings held at inconvenient times or locations
- parent input not solicited
- unwarranted assumptions made regarding prerequisite skills of parents
- ongoing feedback not provided to parents
- parents feel threatened by professionals
- unrealistic expectations for program outcomes
- "burnout" from previous efforts, either in other programs or as advocates
- programs not aimed at social needs of parents in addition to skill needs of child
- reluctance of parents of mildly involved children to associate with parents of severely impaired children

To overcome these problems and those noted by Gorham (1975), Stile and associates (1979) recommended a series of strategies geared to increasing and maximizing the involvement of families (Exhibit 9-1).

Strategies for Teaching Skills to Parents in Intervention Programs

Good trainers make no assumptions regarding what families want or need in the way of training. Thus, it is essential to conduct a needs assessment with the families and parents who are to receive the training. Because parents may be reluctant to express a need if a needs assessment is done verbally and in a nonstructured fashion, it is strongly recommended that a formal, structured, written needs assessment be conducted. This assessment should be brief, clear, and nonthreatening to the parent. A sample form is provided in Exhibit 9-2.

Once the information has been compiled from the needs assessment, the trainer must engage in some preliminary preparation prior to the first formal training session. For example, the information or tasks the parent is expected to master should be analyzed to ensure successful learning by

Exhibit 9-1 Synthesis of Strategies for Maximizing Parental Involvement in Programs for Exceptional Children

Program Design
Pre-Program
1.1   Provide program orientation (suggest parents visit existing programs, talk to current enrollees).
1.2   Provide information regarding planned outcomes; what expectations can be met.
1.3   Provide flexible schedules for instruction.
1.4   Publicize meeting time and location.
1.5   Parent-agency contractual agreement (provide parents with information relative to the extent of their participation).
1.6   Include whole family in programming efforts (i.e., not just mother).
1.7   Assess individual needs of children.
1.8   Assess individual needs of parents.
Program
1.9   Implement individualized program.
1.10   Provide home carry-over activities (i.e., charting behaviors).
1.11   Provide home-to-school feedback.
1.12   Conduct sessions in parents' home.
1.13   Eliminate dominance of one or few participants.
1.14   Substitute technical terminology with nontechnical language.
1.15   Lower reading level in parents' manuals.
1.16   Lend toys and equipment.
Post-Program
1.17   Use of program graduates as "faculty members" in subsequent programs.
1.18   Provide follow-up services.
1.19   Evaluate program effectiveness for revision purposes.
Staff-Parent Interaction
2.1   Ask parents, when possible, to administer programs using professionals as consultants.
2.2   Provide continuous home-school feedback.
2.3   Recognize parents as members of the teaching team.
2.4   Provide contact with home (weekly phone calls, monthly conferences).
Characteristics of Parents and Families
3.1   Provide free babysitting.
3.2   Provide transportation/escort services.
3.3   Provide activities for children during sessions.
3.4   Provide information about family-related support agencies.
3.5   Provide opportunity for make-up of missed sessions.
Mobility
4.1   Construct self-instructional packaged materials.
4.2   Provide follow-up (written/phone) assistance.
4.3   Help establish contact in new location.

Exhibit 9-1 Continued

Other Strategies
5.1   Collect refundable cash deposits.
5.2   Make continued programming contingent on parent involvement.
5.3   Collect fees.

Source: From "Maximizing parental involvement in programs for exceptional children: Strategies for education and related service personnel," by S. Stile, J. Cole, and A. Garner, pp. 78-79, in *Journal of the Division for Early Childhood,* copyright 1979. Reprinted by permission of the Council for Exceptional Children, Division for Early Childhood, Reston, Virginia.

the parent. The task analysis process yields small steps that can be taught one at a time, establishing failure-free learning and building self-confidence in the parent or family members.

It is easiest to teach parents to use a direct, behavioral approach with their child. If the parents are taught the principles of behavior management, they learn the need for consistency in interactions with their child while the child learns the concept of consequences for behaviors or actions. The following steps and suggestions form a sample training program and format that might be used with families of young handicapped children.

I. Introductory Session

During the first session, families should receive instruction on the various record forms used by the agency. Instructions, both verbal and written, should be kept simple and direct. The use of long, detailed forms can lead to family frustration with the program and may contribute significantly to attrition.

II. Prerequisites to Learning

Many handicapped young children exhibit behaviors that interfere with learning. Thus, the second session should be devoted to teaching parents the following prerequisites to learning:

1. methods to achieve and maintain eye contact
2. the use of prompting and cues
3. use of reinforcement and rewards

These procedures should be thoroughly demonstrated with the child. Family members should then practice with the child or with the trainer playing the role of the child. Family members should be encouraged and rewarded not only for their accomplishments, but also for their efforts.

Exhibit 9-2 Sample Needs Assessment

Below are listed ten suggested areas of instruction for parent training in our expanded summer clinic program. Please rate each area on its importance to you as parents. Place a check in the appropriate box.

	Very Important	Important	Not Very Important
1. Assisting in group activities with the children such as creative play, arts and crafts, swimming and snack programs.			
2. Observing your child's therapy sessions.			
3. Participating in group parent counseling sessions.			
4. Learning to assist in your child's therapy.			
5. Participating in individual parent counseling sessions.			
6. Receiving information about all aspects of normal child development.			
7. Receiving information about speech, hearing and language disorders.			
8. Receiving information about normal speech and language development.			
9. Learning to cope with your child's specific problems.			
10. Receiving an explanation of evaluation procedures used for identifying speech, hearing or language disorders.			

Other suggestions for programming will be appreciated. Please be specific.

Name _____

Child's Name _____ Child's Birthdate _____

Mailing Address _____

Telephone _____

Please fill out the information above and return in a self-addressed stamped envelope.
    I am interested in applying for this program for my child and myself.

Source: From *Planning for evaluation: A resource book for programs for preschool handicapped children: Documentation,* by T. Suarez and P. Vandiviere, p. 40, copyright 1978. Reprinted by permission of the Technical Assistance Development System, Chapel Hill, North Carolina.

III. Program or Curriculum

Some agencies use commercial curriculums, and it is essential for parents or family members to receive specific instruction on the use of these materials. This is especially true for home- or home/center-based programs that use the parent in a primary role as teacher. In these approaches, the parent must be completely familiar with the program—its philosophy, methods, materials, and record-keeping procedures.

IV. Teaching Skills in Various Areas

The fourth session is an extension of both Sessions II and III. Parents or family members receive instruction on extending the prerequisites to learning skills with the specific materials to be used. When a commercial curriculum is used, the skills are usually presented as (1) specific target behaviors, with (2) skill sequences in a (3) task analysis format. Since the task analysis may not be broken down enough, particularly for more severely impaired children, the trainer will need to present detailed information on how to prepare a task analysis. The families should also receive further instruction on prompting and the use of shaping strategies.

An essential component of this session is instruction in the use of reinforcement schedules for rewarding appropriate behavior. The families should receive information on the use of continuous reinforcement to establish a behavior with subsequent switching to a variable schedule. The concept of fading, i.e., gradually withdrawing reinforcement, should also be presented. Parents or family members should have the opportunity to observe the trainer working with children and also to practice with the child or the trainer playing the role of the child.

V. Materials and Materials Adaptation

Frequently, commercial materials are not appropriate or are too expensive to purchase for use with handicapped preschoolers. Parents should receive instruction in how to make and adapt materials for use with their child. For example, a crib mobile is a useful toy for teaching various perceptual-motor and cognitive skills, but many mobiles are very expensive and often too fragile for use with the young child who has special needs. Mori and Olive (1980) describe a crib mobile that can be made by parents from materials found in virtually any home (e.g., elastic, yarn, and sponges).

VI. Follow-Up Session(s)

In follow-up sessions, the trainers should:

- evaluate home training sheets (if used) to see if the child made progress
- review and share materials parents have made
- reinforce parent efforts, especially when the child shows real gains

- provide support, encouragement, and any follow-up skill training the parents may request

During this session(s), it is often appropriate and necessary to assess change in parent knowledge, attitude, or behavior. A sample form to document these changes is provided in Exhibit 9-3.

In summary, it is essential for agency personnel responsible for family training to

- make the family members' learning experience as success-guaranteed as possible
- provide parents or family members with cues for performance
- demonstrate all techniques the trainee should learn
- reinforce both effort and accomplishment
- provide the tasks to be learned in a sequential manner
- allow the trainee to practice the skill—gradually "fade out" and let the trainee assume more responsibility
- involve the family members in suggesting procedures for their own child
- encourage questions
- make sure the parent knows the trainer is always available for consultation if the need arises
- be aware of any signs that the trainee is becoming anxious about the demands of the program, child success, or any other problem that can cause attrition

EVALUATING THE EFFECTIVENESS OF FAMILY EDUCATION PROGRAMS

With the reality of shrinking federal support and the possibility of block grant funding for programs for handicapped children, there emerges a growing need for program evaluation data as part of the process of allocating limited funds to competing programs (Takanishi & Feshbach, 1982). Unfortunately, as Huberty and Swan (1977) noted, the evaluation component is one of the most overlooked aspects of intervention programs. While some efforts have been made to evaluate the effectiveness of intervention on children (Bricker & Bricker, 1976; Hayden & Haring, 1976; Kirk, 1958; Schweinhart & Weikart, 1980), little corollary effort has been expended to evaluate the effectiveness of intervention with parents.

Exhibit 9-3 Sample Parent Progress Inventory

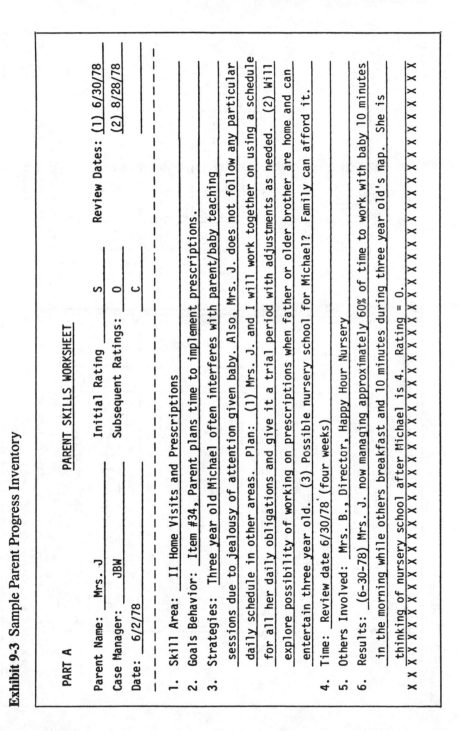

PART A

PARENT SKILLS WORKSHEET

Parent Name:	Mrs. J	Initial Rating	S	Review Dates: (1) 6/30/78
Case Manager:	JBW	Subsequent Ratings:	0	(2) 8/28/78
Date:	6/2/78		C	

1. Skill Area: II Home Visits and Prescriptions

2. Goals Behavior: Item #34, Parent plans time to implement prescriptions.

3. Strategies: Three year old Michael often interferes with parent/baby teaching sessions due to jealousy of attention given baby. Also, Mrs. J. does not follow any particular daily schedule in other areas. Plan: (1) Mrs. J. and I will work together on using a schedule for all her daily obligations and give it a trial period with adjustments as needed.   (2) Will explore possibility of working on prescriptions when father or older brother are home and can entertain three year old.   (3) Possible nursery school for Michael? Family can afford it.

4. Time: Review date 6/30/78 (four weeks)

5. Others Involved: Mrs. B., Director, Happy Hour Nursery

6. Results: (6-30-78) Mrs. J. now managing approximately 60% of time to work with baby 10 minutes in the morning while others breakfast and 10 minutes during three year old's nap. She is thinking of nursery school after Michael is 4. Rating = 0.

Exhibit 9-3 continued

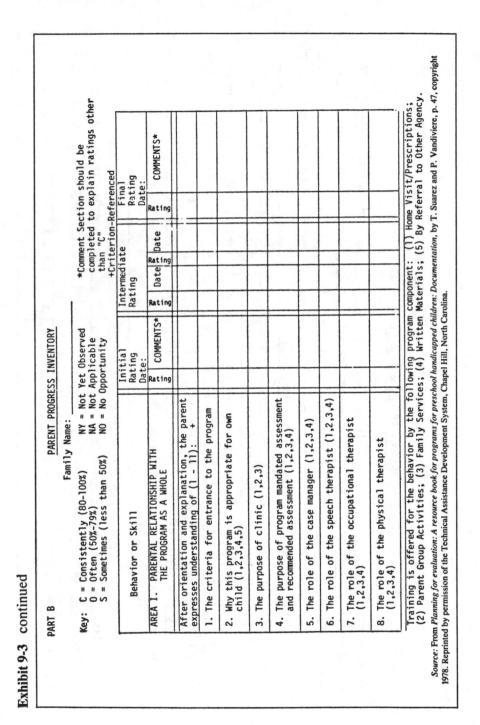

PART B

PARENT PROGRESS INVENTORY

Family Name: _____

Key: C = Consistently (80-100%)   NY = Not Yet Observed
      O = Often (50%-79%)   NA = Not Applicable
      S = Sometimes (less than 50%)   NO = No Opportunity

*Comment Section should be completed to explain ratings other than "C"
+Criterion-Referenced

Behavior or Skill	Initial Rating Date: Rating	COMMENTS*	Intermediate Rating Rating	Date	Rating	Date	Final Rating Date: Rating	COMMENTS*
AREA I. PARENTAL RELATIONSHIP WITH THE PROGRAM AS A WHOLE								
After orientation and explanation, the parent expresses understanding of (1 - 11): +								
1. The criteria for entrance to the program								
2. Why this program is appropriate for own child (1,2,3,4,5)								
3. The purpose of clinic (1,2,3)								
4. The purpose of program mandated assessment and recommended assessment (1,2,3,4)								
5. The role of the case manager (1,2,3,4)								
6. The role of the speech therapist (1,2,3,4)								
7. The role of the occupational therapist (1,2,3,4)								
8. The role of the physical therapist (1,2,3,4)								

Training is offered for the behavior by the following program component: (1) Home Visit/Prescriptions; (2) Parent Group Activities; (3) Family Services; (4) Written Materials; (5) By Referral to Other Agency.

Source: From *Planning for evaluation: A resource book for programs for preschool handicapped children: Documentation,* by T. Suarez and P. Vandiviere, p. 47, copyright 1978. Reprinted by permission of the Technical Assistance Development System, Chapel Hill, North Carolina.

Evaluation may be defined as a process of determining whether program objectives have been accomplished by comparing the objectives with the actual outcomes (Lillie, 1976). Wang and Ellett (1982) use the term *program validation* to describe the process of providing "information about an educational intervention program that can be used to make decisions about its use at a particular time, for a particular purpose, and under particular conditions" (p. 35).

Planning: The Key to Effective Evaluation

Unfortunately, evaluation is frequently an afterthought. It is crucial, however, for the evaluation plan to be developed during the planning stages of the program as part of an ongoing commitment to the validation process. Evaluation must be planned in order to match program needs and resources to program goals and objectives and in order to integrate the entire evaluation component smoothly into the entire program (Huberty & Swan, 1977).

During the planning stage, the evaluator can identify program inputs or the components that go into the actual operation of the program, such as the philosophy and the population to be served (Caldwell, 1977). This is essential in order to ensure that the measures used to assess effectiveness adequately reflect anticipated outcomes (Sheehan, 1981).

The evaluator should also develop a plan for timing the collection (or analysis) of data (Sheehan, 1981), a task that can be greatly facilitated by the development of a work schedule (Huberty & Swan, 1977) that includes the evaluation tasks to be completed and tentative time points to complete them. Once these tasks have been completed, the evaluator is ready to begin the implementation phase.

Implementing the Evaluation Plan

In their discussion of program validation, Wang and Ellett (1982) noted that the types of information needed to implement the evaluation plan can be viewed from two perspectives: program development and refinement, and program adoption/adaptation and dissemination.

Program Development and Refinement

The purposes of evaluation related to program development and refinement are to (1) obtain data-based evidence of the effectiveness of an intervention program and identify aspects of its design or implementation that need modification to derive the intended outcomes and (2) assess the extent to which the intervention program can be employed in service settings to approximate the service provider's idea of the program (Wang & Ellett, 1982).

Service providers in an agency serving young handicapped children and their families must be concerned about the degree to which the components of their intervention program are being implemented and the outcomes they are producing. Evaluation of this nature yields data on (1) which program features are working and which are not, (2) the extent to which program features produce certain intended (and unintended) outcomes, and (3) which program features need improvement to obtain the desired outcomes or objectives.

Program Adoption/Adaptation and Dissemination

Validation related to program adoption/adaptation and dissemination assumes great importance when other service providers are judging whether a program should be implemented in their service setting. According to Wang and Ellett (1982), three types of validations are relevant to this perspective: (1) effectiveness of the program in producing intended outcomes, (2) the extent to which the program is being implemented in accordance with the design and the extent to which adaptations were made, and (3) the degree to which the program can be replicated somewhere else— the "implementability" of the program.

If the service provider is interested in the implementation of this evaluation scheme, an input-process-output model is required (Figure 9-1). This model facilitates the systematic collection of important, but often fragmented, data about intervention programs, their implementation, and their effects. The solid lines represent the sequence of change process from the adoption/adaptation and dissemination perspective; the process is interactive from the development and refinement perspective, as suggested by both solid and dotted lines (Wang & Ellett, 1982).

The use of this model by service providers interested in evaluating their intervention program for parents necessitates the identification of input variables, process variables, and output variables. Examples of each of these types of variables may be found in Exhibit 9-4. The list of input, process, and output variables in Exhibit 9-4 is not intended to be inclusive or exhaustive. These variables are simply examples of the various components that will need to be a part of the model proposed in Figure 9-1.

Before preparing the evaluation report, the evaluator may wish to use a summary instrument to link input, process, and output information. An example summary form is provided in Exhibit 9-5.

Figure 9-1 A Model of Program Validation

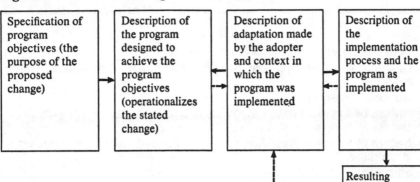

Solid lines indicate change process; broken lines indicate feedback-refinement process.

Source: From "Program validation: The state of the art," by M. D. Wang and C. D. Ellett, *Topics in Early Childhood Special Education*, 1982, *1*, 39. Reprinted by permission of Aspen Systems Corporation, Rockville, Maryland.

Writing the Evaluation Report

The preparation of the evaluation report is an essential stage of the program validation process. Evaluation is often conducted for many audiences, e.g., program administrators; funding sources, such as federal, state, or local government agencies; parents; or professionals. To a great extent, the audience for whom the evaluation report is intended will influence the manner and style of the final report. The evaluator should first determine what kind of information the audience needs in order to avoid overwhelming the audience with more than is needed or causing confusion by including other interesting but not vital information. Other important hints regarding the writing of the report have been recommended by Morris and Fitz-Gibbon (1978):

- Start with the most important information.
- Make the report readable by avoiding jargon, long sentences, "boilerplate," and other deadwood.
- Highlight the important points by using headings, good spacing, and layouts that include boxes, changes in type style, and underlining.

Exhibit 9-4 Examples of Program Inputs, Processes, and Outputs

---

Inputs

- Stated goals and objectives for intervention
- Characteristics of intervention staff (disciplinary orientation, training, etc.)
- Budgetary resources
- Nature of a typical day, i.e., What happens to, for, or with children and families on a given day?
- Nature of a typical staff day, i.e., How do staff spend their time on a given day?
- Staff turnover rates
- Staff role descriptions
- Amount and frequency of interagency cooperation
- Amount and frequency of staff conferences for planning
- Amount, frequency, and type of staff pre- and in-service training
- Goals of the families being served, i.e., Do the goals of the agency match the goals of the families being served?

Processes

- What is the relationship between frequency of contact and parental awareness of agency goals?
- What is the relationship between temporary outcome measures such as the regularity of participation, verbal endorsement of program, expressed satisfaction with program, and utilization of different components of program (such as parent services only, child services only, parent and child services)?
- What is the relationship between frequency of parent contact with program components and diffusion of project ideas to other adults having contact with the target child (e.g., grandparents, baby-sitters, etc.)?
- What is the relationship between child's participation in the intervention program and mother's self-image as reflected in such variables as housekeeping, attention to other children in the family, social interactions with other families, and relations to community agencies?
- What is the relationship between child's participation in the program and parents' ability to serve as a child advocate when the child goes into a public school program?
- Is there a relation between providing transportation, baby-sitting for other children not in the program, and increased family participation in the program?
- If a program does not offer a service necessary for achievement of one or more program objectives, are parents able to use their own ingenuity?

Exhibit 9-4 continued

- What kinds of in-service training knowledge and skills are encountered by staff in relation to their own requests for training? What level of satisfaction do they have with the training that is provided?
- What is the "goodness of fit" between parent and/or child response and staff training?
- What is the frequency of different types of child behavior (crying, on-task behavior, aggression, smiling, singing) in different types of program activities?
- What is the relationship between frequency of participation and rate of change (motor, cognitive, affective) shown by the child?

Outputs

- The number of families served in a given period of time compared to estimated per objectives
- Amount, frequency, and types of intervention administered, i.e., home visits, counseling sessions
- Amount, frequency, and type of appointments missed
- Turnover among client-families
- Amount, frequency, and type of interagency contacts, i.e., consultations, referrals
- Amount, frequency, and type of staff and/or family training offered
- Number of families needing intervention services identified in a given time period
- Number of volunteers and amount, frequency, and type of service provided by them
- Amount, type, and frequency of public relations efforts by agency staff, i.e., speeches to local organizations, media spots, etc.

Source: Adapted from "Evaluating program effectiveness," by B. M. Caldwell, in *Infant education: A guide for helping handicapped children in the first three years,* by B. M. Caldwell and D. J. Stedman (Eds.), pp. 152-157, copyright 1977. Reprinted by permission of the University of North Carolina, Chapel Hill, North Carolina, and Walker and Company, New York, New York.

The following is a sample format for an evaluation report:

I. Face Sheet
   A. Title/name of agency
   B. Evaluator
   C. Audience
   D. Date of report
   E. Period covered by report
II. Evaluation Abstract/Summary
   A. Purpose of evaluation
   B. Major findings and recommendations
   C. Limitations of evaluation

Exhibit 9-5 Sample Summary Chart for Evaluation

Objectives	Measurement Instruments		Data Collection Procedures			Data Analysis Techniques	Evaluator's Report Due
	Name of Instrument	Date to Be Completed	Target Group	Scheduled Date	Person Responsible		

III. Background Information (depends on audience and may be brief or lengthy)
   A. Philosophy of the program
   B. Goals/objectives of the program
   C. Service audience (characteristics)
   D. Nature of program (materials, services, resources)
   E. Professional staff and others involved in the program
IV. Evaluation Design
   A. Purpose
   B. Inputs (with instruments used)
   C. Processes (with instruments used)
   D. Outputs (with instruments used)
   E. Data collection procedures
 V. Results
   A. Presentation of outcomes
   B. Discussion
 VI. Cost and Benefits (optional)
VII. Conclusions and Recommendations
This format may be used as a checklist of contents for an evaluation report.

References

Abeson, A., & Zettel, J. The end of the quiet revolution: The Education for All Handicapped Children Act of 1975. *Exceptional Children,* 1977, *44,* 114-128.

Ainsworth, M. The effects of maternal deprivation: A review of findings and controversy in the context of research strategy. In *Public Health Papers,* 14. Geneva: World Health Organization, 1962.

Ainsworth, M. The development of infant-mother attachment. In B.M. Caldwell & H.H. Riccuiti (Eds.), *Review of child development research* (Vol. 3). Chicago: University of Chicago Press, 1973.

Ainsworth, M. Infant-mother attachment. *American Psychologist,* 1979, *34,* 932-937.

Alexander, R., Kroth, R., Simpson, R., & Poppelreiter, T. The parent role in special education. In R. McDowell, G. Adamson, & F. Wood (Eds.), *Teaching emotionally disturbed children.* Boston: Little, Brown, 1982.

Alpern, G., & Boll, T. *Developmental profile.* Indianapolis: Psychological Development Publication, 1972.

Appell, M., & Tisdall, W. Factors differentiating institutionalized from noninstitutionalized referred retardates. *American Journal of Mental Deficiency,* 1968, *73,* 424-432.

Armentrout, J., & Burger, G. Children's reports of child-rearing behavior at five grade levels. *Developmental Psychology,* 1972, *7,* 44-48.

Ausubel, D. *Ego development and the personality disorders.* New York: Grune & Stratton, 1952.

Axline, V. *Play therapy.* Boston: Houghton Mifflin, 1947.

Azrin, N., & Foxx, R. A rapid method of toilet training the institutionalized retarded. *Journal of Applied Behavior Analysis,* 1971, *4,* 89-99.

Azrin, N., Schaeffer, R., & Wesolowski, M. A rapid method of teaching profoundly retarded persons to dress by a reinforcement guidance method. *Mental Retardation,* 1976, *14,* 29-33.

Bagnato, S.J., & Neisworth, J.T. *Linking developmental assessment and curricula: Prescriptions for early intervention.* Rockville, MD: Aspen Systems Corporation, 1981.

Balthazar, E. *Balthazar Scales of Adaptive Behavior, Section I: The Scales of Functional Independence (BSAB-I).* Champaign, IL: Research Press, 1971.

Balthazar, E., Roseen, D., & English, G. *The Central Wisconsin Colony Scales of Adaptive*

235

Behavior: The Ambulant Battery. Madison, WI: Wisconsin State Department of Administration, 1968.

Bandura, A. The role of modeling processes in personality development. In W.W. Hartup & N.L. Smothergill (Eds.), *The young child.* Washington, DC: National Association for the Education of Young Children, 1967.

Bandura, A. Social learning analysis of aggression. In A. Bandura & E. Ribes-Inesta (Eds.), *Analysis of delinquency and aggression.* New York: John Wiley & Sons, 1976.

Bandura, A., & Huston, A. Identification as a process of incidental learning. *Journal of Abnormal and Social Psychology,* 1961, *63,* 311-318.

Bane, M. *HEW policy toward children, youth, and families.* Discussion paper prepared under Order #SA-8139-77 for the Office of the Assistant Secretary for Planning and Evaluation, Cambridge, MA, 1978.

Banham, K. *A social competence scale for adults.* Durham, NC: Family Life Publications, 1960.

Barraga, N. *Increased visual behavior in low-vision children.* New York: American Foundation for the Blind, 1964.

Barraga, N. *Visual handicaps and learnings: A developmental approach.* Belmont, CA: Wadsworth Publishing Co., 1976.

Barsch, R. *The parent-teacher partnership.* Arlington, VA: Council for Exceptional Children, 1969.

Bateman, B. The modifiability of sighted adults' perceptions of blind children's abilities. *New Outlook for the Blind,* 1964, *58,* 133-135.

Baumrind, D. Child care practices anteceding three patterns of preschool behavior. *Genetic Psychology Monographs,* 1967, *75,* 43-88.

Baumrind, D. Current patterns of parental authority. *Developmental Psychology Monographs,* 1971, 4 (1, Pt. 2).

Beck, J. *How to raise a brighter child.* New York: Trident, 1967.

Beckwith, L. Relationships between infants' social behavior and their mothers' behavior. *Child Development,* 1972, *43,* 397-411.

Begab, M. The major dilemma of mental retardation: Shall we prevent it? (Some social implications of research in mental retardation). *American Journal of Mental Deficiency,* 1974, *78,* 519-529.

Behar, L., & Stringfield, S. *The Preschool Behavior Questionnaire.* Durham, NC: LINC Press, 1974.

Bender, L. Childhood schizophrenia: A review. *International Journal of Psychiatry,* 1968, *5,* 211-230.

Bereiter, C., & Englemann, S. *Teaching disadvantaged children in the preschool.* Englewood Cliffs, NJ: Prentice-Hall, 1966.

Berger, E.H. *Parents as partners in education.* St. Louis: C.V. Mosby, 1981.

Bessell, H., & Palomares, U. *Methods in human development, theory manual* (1970 revision). San Diego: Human Development Training Institute, 1970.

Bettelheim, B. *Love is not enough.* New York: Macmillan, 1950.

Bettelheim, B. *The empty fortress.* New York: Free Press, 1967.

Biehler, R. *Child development: An introduction* (2nd ed.). Boston: Houghton Mifflin, 1981.

Bigelow, G., & Griffiths, R. An intensive teaching unit for severely and profoundly retarded women. In T. Thompson & J. Grabowski (Eds.), *Behavior modification of the mentally retarded* (2nd ed.). New York: Oxford University Press, 1977.

Bigge, J. Self-care. In J.C. Bigge (Ed.), *Teaching individuals with physical and multiple disabilities.* Columbus, OH: Charles E. Merrill, 1976.

Bigner, J. *Parent-child relations: An introduction to parenting.* New York: Macmillan, 1979.

Biklen, D. *Let our children go: An organizing manual for advocates and parents.* Syracuse, NY: Human Policy Press, 1974.

Birch, H.G., & Gussow, J.D. *Disadvantaged children: Health, nutrition, and school failure.* New York: Grune & Stratton, 1970.

Blatt, B. Introduction: The threatened planet. In A.P. Turnbull & H.R. Turnbull (Eds.), *Parents speak out: Views from the other side of the two way mirror.* Columbus, OH: Charles E. Merrill, 1979.

Bloom, B. *Stability and change in human characteristics.* New York: John Wiley & Sons, 1964.

Boatner, E., Stuckless, E., & Moores, D. *Occupational status of the young deaf adults of New England and the need and demand for a regional technical vocational training center.* West Hartford, CT: American School for the Deaf, 1964.

Bower, E. *The education of emotionally handicapped children.* Sacramento: California State Department of Education, 1961.

Bower, E. *Early identification of emotionally handicapped children in school* (2nd ed.). Springfield, IL: Charles C. Thomas, 1969.

Boyce, V. The home eye test program. *Sight Saving Review,* 1973, *43.*

Braga, J. Analysis and evaluation of early admission to school for mentally advanced children. *Journal of Educational Research,* 1969, *63,* 103-106.

Bray, N.W. Strategy production in the retarded. In N.R. Ellis (Ed.), *Handbook of mental deficiency: Psychological theory and research.* Hillsdale, NJ: Lawrence Erlbaum, 1979.

Bray, N., Coleman, J., & Bracken, M. Critical events in parenting handicapped children. *Journal of the Division for Early Childhood,* 1981, *3,* 26-33.

Bricker, W., & Bricker, D. The infant, toddler, and preschool research and intervention project. In T.D. Tjossem (Ed.), *Intervention strategies for high risk infants and young children.* Baltimore: University Park Press, 1976.

Bricklin, B., & Bricklin, P. *Bright child—Poor grades: The psychology of underachievement.* New York: Delacorte, 1967.

Brolin, D., & Kokaska, C. *Career education for handicapped children and youth.* Columbus, OH: Charles E. Merrill, 1979.

Bromwich, R. *Working with parents and infants.* Baltimore: University Park Press, 1981.

Bronfenbrenner, U. The psychological costs of quality and equality in education. *Child Development,* 1967, *38,* 909-925.

Bronfenbrenner, U. *A report on longitudinal evaluations of preschool programs: Is early intervention effective?* (DHEW Publication No. [OHD] 76-30025). Washington, DC: U.S. Government Printing Office, 1974.

Brown, R. *A first language: The early stages.* Cambridge, MA: Harvard University Press, 1973.

Brown v. Board of Education of Topeka, Kansas, 347 U.S. 483 (1954).

Bryan, J., & Bryan, T. *Exceptional children.* Sherman Oaks, CA: Alfred Publishing Company, 1979.

Bryan, T. Peer popularity of learning disabled children. *Journal of Learning Disabilities,*

1974, *7*, 304-309.

Bryan, T., & Bryan, J. *Understanding learning disabilities* (2nd ed.). Sherman Oaks, CA: Alfred Publishing Company, 1978.

Burgemeister, B., Blum, L., & Lorge, I. *Columbia Mental Maturity Scale,* (3rd ed.). New York: Harcourt Brace Jovanovich, 1972.

Cain, L., Levine, S., & Elzey, F. *Manual for the Cain-Levine Social Competency Scale.* Palo Alto, CA: Consulting Psychologists Press, 1963.

Caldwell, B. Evaluating program effectiveness. In B.M. Caldwell & D.J. Stedman (Eds.), *Infant education: A guide for helping handicapped children in the first three years.* New York: Walker and Company, 1977.

Campbell, S. Mother-child interactions in effective, impulsive, and hyperactive children. *Developmental Psychology,* 1973, *8,* 341-349.

Campbell, S. Mother-child interaction: A comparison of hyperactive, learning disabled, and normal boys. *American Journal of Orthopsychiatry,* 1975, *45,* 51-57.

Cansler, D.P., Martin, G.H., & Valand, M.C. *Working with families: A manual for early childhood programs serving the handicapped.* Winston-Salem, NC: Kaplan Press, 1975.

Carr, J. The effect of the severely subnormal on their families. In A.M. Clarke & A.D. Clarke (Eds.), *Mental deficiency.* New York: Free Press, 1974.

Carroll, T.J. *Blindness.* Boston: Little, Brown, 1961.

Cassell, R. *Child Behavior Rating Scale.* Los Angeles, CA: Western Psychological Services, 1972.

Castle, D., & Warchol, B. Rochester's demonstration home program: A comprehensive parent-infant project. *Peabody Journal of Education,* 1974, *51,* 186-191.

Cazden, C. *Child language and education.* New York: Holt, Rinehart & Winston, 1972.

Chinn, P., Drew, C., & Logan, D. *Mental retardation: A life cycle approach* (2nd ed.). St. Louis: C.V. Mosby, 1979.

Chinn, P.C., Winn, J., & Walters, R.H. *Two-way talking with parents of special children: A process of positive communication.* St. Louis: C.V. Mosby, 1978.

Clarizio, H., & McCoy, G. *Behavior disorders in children* (2nd ed.). New York: Crowell, 1976.

Clark, B. *Growing up gifted.* Columbus, OH: Charles E. Merrill, 1979.

Clements, S.D. Minimal brain dysfunction in children. NINDS Monograph No. 3., Public Health Service Bulletin #1415. Washington, DC: U.S. Department of Health, Education and Welfare, 1966.

Cohen, R. Pregnancy stress and maternal perceptions of infant endowment. *Journal of Mental Subnormality,* 1966, *12,* 18-23.

Coleman, J. *The adolescent society.* New York: Free Press of Glencoe, 1962.

Coletta, A. *Working together: A guide to parent involvement.* Atlanta: Humanics Limited, 1977.

Congdon, D. The Adaptive Behavior Scales modified for the profoundly retarded. *Mental Retardation* 1973, *11,* 20-21.

Connor, F.P., Williamson, G., & Siepp, J. *Program guide for infants and toddlers with neuromotor and other developmental disabilities.* New York: Teachers College Press, 1978.

Coopersmith, S. *The antecedents of self-esteem.* San Francisco: W.H. Freeman, 1967.

Cruickshank, W., Bentzen, F., Ratzeburg, F., & Tannhauser, M. *A teaching method for brain-injured and hyperactive children*. Syracuse, NY: Syracuse University Press, 1961.

Daniel, R. Underachievement of superior and talented students. In B. Shertzer (Ed.), *Working with superior students*. Chicago: Scientific Research Associates, 1960.

Dayan, M., & McLean, J. The Gardner Behavior Chart as a measure of adaptive behavior of the mentally retarded. *American Journal of Mental Deficiency*, 1963, *67*, 887-892.

Dembinski, R., & Mauser, A. What parents of the learning disabled really want from professionals. *Journal of Learning Disabilities*, 1977, *10*, 49-55.

Denhoff, E. Medical aspects. In W.M. Cruickshank (Ed.), *Cerebral palsy: A developmental disability* (3rd rev. ed.). Syracuse, NY: Syracuse University Press, 1976.

Deno, E. Special education as developmental capital. *Exceptional Children*, 1970, *37*, 229-237.

Deshler, D. Issues related to the education of learning disabled adolescents. *Learning Disability Quarterly*, 1978, *1*, 2-10.

Dinkmeyer, D. DUSO (developing understanding of self and others—A kit of materials). Circle Pines, MN: American Guidance Service, 1969.

Dinkmeyer, D., & McKay, G.D. *Parent's handbook*. Circle Pines, MN: American Guidance Service, 1976.

Doll, E.A. The essentials of an inclusive concept of mental deficiency. *American Journal of Mental Deficiency*, 1941, *42*, 214-219.

Doll, E.A. *Vineland Social Maturity Scale*. Minneapolis: American Guidance Service, 1964.

Doll, E.A. *Preschool Attainment Record* (Research Ed.). Circle Pines, MN: American Guidance Service, 1966.

Dreikurs, R. *Children: The challenge*. New York: Hawthorne, 1964.

Dreikurs, R., & Grey, L. *A parent's guide to child discipline*. New York: Hawthorne, 1970.

Drotar, D., Baskiewicz, A., Irvin, N., Kennell, J., & Klaus, M. The adaptation of parents to the birth of an infant with a congenital malformation: A hypothetical model. *Pediatrics*, 1975, *56*, 710-717.

DuBose, R. Developmental needs in blind infants. *The New Outlook for the Blind*, 1976, *2*, 49-52.

DuBose, R. Working with seriously impaired children, Part I: Visual impairments. In S.G. Garwood, (Ed.), *Educating young handicapped children: A developmental approach*. Germantown, MD: Aspen Systems Corporation, 1979a.

DuBose, R. Working with seriously impaired children, Part II: Hearing impairments. In S.G. Garwood, (Ed.), *Educating young handicapped children: A developmental approach*. Germantown, MD: Aspen Systems Corporation, 1979b.

Englemann, T., & Englemann, S. *Give your child a superior mind*. New York: Simon & Shuster, 1966.

Enzer, N.B. Parent-child and professional interaction. In D.L. Lillie & P.L. Trohanis (Eds.), *Teaching parents to teach: A guide for working with the special child*. New York: Walker and Company, 1976.

Erikson, E. *Childhood and society* (2nd ed.). New York: Norton, 1963.

Erikson, E. *Identity: Youth and crisis*. New York: Norton, 1968.

Erikson, E. Play and actuality. In M. Piers (Ed.), *Play and development*. New York: Norton, 1972.

Evans, R.A., & Bilsky, L.H. Clustering and categorical list retention in the mentally retarded. In N.R. Ellis (Ed.), *Handbook of mental deficiency: Psychological theory and research*

(2nd ed.). Hillsdale, NJ: Lawrence Erlbaum, 1979.

Farber, B. Effects of a severely mentally retarded child on family integration. *Monographs of the Society for Research on Child Development*, 1959, *24*, Series No. 71.

Farber, B. Family organizations and crisis: Maintenance of integration in families with a severely mentally retarded child. *Monographs of the Society for Research on Child Development*, 1960, *25* (Series No. 75).

Farber, B. *Mental retardation: Its social context and social consequences*. Boston: Houghton Mifflin, 1968.

Feingold, B. *Why your child is hyperactive*. New York: Random House, 1975.

Feiring, C., & Lewis, M. The child as a member of the family system. *Behavioral Science*, 1978, *23*, 225-233.

Field, T. Interaction patterns of primary versus secondary caretaker fathers. *Developmental Psychology*, 1978, *14*, 183-185.

Fink, W., & Cegelka, P.T. Characteristics of the moderately and severely mentally retarded. In P.T. Cegelka & H.J. Prehm (Eds.), *Mental retardation: From categories to people*. Columbus, OH: Charles E. Merrill, 1982.

Finnie, N. *Handling the young cerebral palsied child at home*. New York: Dutton, 1975.

Fisch, R., Bilek, M., Horrobin, J., & Chang, P. Children with superior intelligence at seven years of age. *American Journal of Diseases of Children*, 1976, *130*, 481-487.

Flash-card Vision Test for Children. New York: New York Association for the Blind, 1966.

Folger, J., & Chapman, R. A pragmatic analysis of spontaneous imitations. *Journal of Child Language*, 1978, *5*, 25-38.

Folio, M. Assessing motor development in multiply handicapped children. Paper presented at annual meeting of the Council for Exceptional Children. New York, April 1974.

Forehand, R., & Baumeister, A. Effect of frustration on stereotyped body rocking: Follow-up. *Perceptual and Motor Skills*, 1970, *31*, 894.

Foster, M., & Berger, M. Structural family therapy: Applications in programs for preschool handicapped children. *Journal of the Division for Early Childhood*, 1979, *1*, 52-58.

Foster, M., Berger, M., & McLean, M. Rethinking a good idea: A reassessment of parent involvement. *Topics in Early Childhood Special Education*, 1981, *1*, 55-65.

Fraiberg, S., Smith, M., & Adelson, E. An educational program for blind infants. *Journal of Special Education*, 1969, *3*, 121-139.

Frankenburg, W., Dodds, J., & Fandal, A. *Denver Developmental Screening Test*. Denver: University of Colorado Medical Center, 1967, 1970.

Fredericks, H.D., Baldwin, V., & Grove, D. A home-centered parent training model. In J. Grimm (Ed.), *Training parents to teach: Four models*. Chapel Hill, NC: Technical Assistance Development Systems, 1974.

Fredericks, H.D., Baldwin, V., & Grove, D. A home-center based parent-training model. In D.L. Lillie & P.L. Trohanis (Eds.), *Teaching parents to teach: A guide for working with the special child*. New York: Walker, 1976.

French, J. *Pictorial Test of Intelligence*. Boston: Houghton Mifflin, 1964.

Freud, A. The concept of developmental lines. In S.G. Spair & A.C. Nitsburg (Eds.), *Children with learning problems*. New York: Brunner-Mazel, 1973.

Frodi, A. Contributions of infant characteristics to child abuse. *American Journal of Mental Deficiency*, 1981, *85*, 341-349.

Furrow, D., Nelson, K., & Benedict, H. Mother's speech to children and syntactic development: Some simple relationships. *Journal of Child Language,* 1979, *6*, 423-442.

Furth, H.G. Influence of language on the development of concept formation in deaf children. *Journal of Abnormal Social Psychology,* 1961, *63*, 386-389.

Furth, H.G. *Deafness and learning: A psychosocial approach.* Belmont, CA: Wadsworth, 1973.

Gabel, H., & Kotsch, L. Extended families and young handicapped children. *Topics in Early Childhood Special Education,* 1981, *1*, 29-35.

Gallagher, J. *Teaching the gifted child.* Boston: Allyn & Bacon, 1964.

Gallagher, J. Children with developmental imbalances: A psychoeducational definition. In W.M. Cruickshank (Ed.), *The teacher of brain injured children: A discussion of the bases for competency.* Syracuse, NY: Syracuse University Press, 1966. (a)

Gallagher, J.J. *Research summary on gifted child education.* Springfield, IL: Illinois Department of Education, 1966. (b)

Gallagher, J. *Teaching the gifted child* (2nd ed.). Boston: Allyn & Bacon, 1975.

Gallagher, J.J. Issues in education for the gifted. In A.H. Passow (Ed.), *The 78th yearbook of the National Society for the Study of Education, Part I: The gifted and talented: Their education and development.* Chicago: University of Chicago Press, 1979.

Gallagher, J., Cross, A., & Scharfman, W. Parental adaptation to a young handicapped child: The father's role. *Journal of the Division for Early Childhood,* 1981, *3*, 3-14.

Gallagher, J., & Kinney, L. (Eds.). *Talent delayed—Talent denied, the culturally different gifted child—A conference report.* Reston, VA: The Foundation for Exceptional Children, 1974.

Gardner, H. *Developmental psychology* (2nd ed.). Boston: Little, Brown, 1982.

Garwood, S.G. From the editor. *Topics in Early Childhood Special Education,* 1981, *1*, viii-ix.

Gath, A. Parental reactions to Down's syndrome. *Journal of the Division for Early Childhood,* 1979, *1*, 11-17.

Gayton, W., & Walker, L. Family management of Down's syndrome during the early years. *Family Physician,* 1974, *9*, 160-164.

Gearheart, B.R. *Special education for the '80s.* St. Louis: C.V. Mosby, 1980.

Gearheart, B.R., & Litton, F.W. *The trainable retarded: A foundations approach* (2nd ed.). St. Louis: C.V. Mosby, 1979.

Getzels, J., & Dillon, J. The nature of giftedness and the education of the gifted. In R. Travers (Ed.), *Second handbook of research on teaching.* Chicago: Rand McNally, 1973.

Giacobbe, G.A., Carlton, B.S., Blanton, E.H., Fallen, A.S., & Clarke, B.S. Working with the parents. In N.H. Fallen & J.E. McGovern (Eds.), *Young children with special needs.* Columbus, OH: Charles E. Merrill, 1978.

Glasser, W. *Schools without failure.* New York: Harper & Row, 1969.

Glidewell, J., & Swallow, C. *The prevalence of maladjustment in elementary schools.* Chicago: University of Chicago Press, 1968.

Goodenough, F. Anger in young children. *Institute for Child Welfare Monograph.* Minneapolis: University of Minnesota Press, 1931.

Goodenough, F., Maurer, K., & Wagenen, M. *Minnesota Preschool Scale.* Circle Pines, MN: American Guidance Service, 1971.

Gordon, I. Parenting, teaching, and child development. *Young Children,* 1976, *31*, 134-142.

Gordon, S. *Living fully: A guide for young people with a handicap, their parents, their teachers, and professionals.* New York: John Day, 1975.

Gordon, T. *Parent effectiveness training.* New York: Peter Wyden, 1970.

Gorham, K. A lost generation of parents. *Exceptional Children, 1975, 41,* 521-525.

Gottesman, I., & Shields, J. *Schizophrenia and genetics: A twin study vantage point.* New York: Academic Press, 1972.

Graliker, B., Fishler, K., & Koch, R. Teenage reaction to a mentally retarded sibling. *American Journal of Mental Deficiency, 1962, 66,* 838-843.

Grays, C. At the bedside: The pattern of acceptance in parents of the retarded child. *Tomorrow's Nurse, 1963, 4,* 30-34.

Green, M., & Solnit, A. Reactions to the threatened loss of a child: A vulnerable child syndrome. Pediatric management of the dying child, Part 3. *Pediatrics, 1964, 34,* 58-66.

Grosenick, J., & Huntze, S. *National needs analysis in behavior disorders: Severe behavior disorders.* Columbia, MO: University of Missouri, 1980.

Grossman, H.J. (Ed.). *Manual on terminology and classification in mental retardation.* Washington, DC: American Association on Mental Deficiency, 1977.

Grove, N. Conditions resulting in physical disabilities. In J. Bigge (Ed.), *Teaching individuals with physical and multiple disabilities.* Columbus, OH: Charles E. Merrill, 1976.

Guess, D. The influence of visual and ambulation restriction on stereotyped behavior. *American Journal of Mental Deficiency, 1966, 70,* 542-547.

Guess, D., Sailor, W., & Baer, D. *Functional speech and language training for the severely handicapped.* Lawrence, KS: H. & H. Enterprises, 1976.

Guilford, J.P. Three faces of intellect. *American Psychologist, 1959, 14,* 469-479.

Guilford, J.P. Varieties of creative giftedness, their measurement and development. *Gifted Child Quarterly. 1975, 19,* 107-121.

Gunzburg, H. *Social competence and mental handicap.* London: Baillere, Tindall, & Cassell, 1968.

Guralnick, M.J., Richardson, H.B., & Heiser, K.E. A curriculum in handicapping conditions for pediatric residents. *Exceptional Children, 1982, 48,* 338-346.

Guralnick, M.J., Richardson, H.B., & Kutner, D.R. Pediatric education and the development of exceptional children. In M.J. Guralnick & H.B. Richardson, Jr. (Eds.), *Pediatric education and the needs of exceptional children.* Baltimore: University Park Press, 1980.

Hagen, M. "Burnout"—Teachers and parents. *Views, 1981, 1,* 4-6.

Haley, J. *Problem solving therapy.* San Francisco: Jossey-Bass, 1976.

Hallahan, D., & Kauffman, J. *Introduction to learning disabilities: A psychobehavioral approach.* Englewood Cliffs, NJ: Prentice-Hall, 1976.

Hallahan, D., & Kauffman, J. *Exceptional children* (2nd ed.). Englewood Cliffs, NJ: Prentice-Hall, 1982.

Hammer, E. Families of deaf-blind children: Case studies of stress. Paper presented at the First Regional American Orthopsychiatric Association Conference, Dallas, Texas, November 1972.

Hanson, M.J. A model for early intervention with culturally diverse single and multiparent families. *Topics in Early Childhood Special Education, 1981, 1,* 37-44.

Hart, V. Crippling conditions. In M.S. Lilly (Ed.), *Children with exceptional needs: A survey of special education.* New York: Holt, Rinehart and Winston, 1979.

Hartup, W. The social worlds of childhood. *American Psychologist, 1979, 34,* 944-950.

Harvey, B. Cystic fibrosis. In E. Bleck & D. Nagel (Eds.), *Physically handicapped children:*

A medical atlas for teachers. New York: Grune & Stratton, 1975.

Harvey, J. The enabling legislation: How did it all begin? In J.B. Jordan, A.H. Hayden, M.B. Karnes, & M.M. Wood (Eds.), *Early childhood education for exceptional children: A handbook of ideas and exemplary practices.* Reston, VA: Council for Exceptional Children, 1977.

Hay, W. Mental retardation problems in different age groups. *American Journal of Mental Deficiency,* 1951, *55,* 191-197.

Hayden, A., & Haring, N. Early intervention for high risk infants and young children: Programs for Down's syndrome children. In T.D. Tjossem (Ed.), *Intervention strategies for high risk infants and young children.* Baltimore: University Park Press, 1976.

Heber, R.F. A manual on terminology and classification in mental retardation (Rev. ed.). *American Journal of Mental Deficiency Monograph,* 1961 (Supp. 64).

Heber, R., Garber, H., Harrington, S., Hoffman, C., & Falendar, C. *Rehabilitation of families at risk for mental retardation: Progress report.* Madison, WI: University of Wisconsin, 1972.

Heilbrun, A. Identification with the father and sex-role development of the daughter. *Family Coordinator,* 1976, *25,* 411-416.

Hess, R. Parental behavior and children's school achievement: Implications for Head Start. In E. Grotberg (Ed.), *Critical issues in research related to disadvantaged children.* Princeton, NJ: Educational Testing Service, 1969.

Hetherington, E. Effects of paternal absence on sex typed behavior in Negro and white preadolescent males. *Journal of Personality and Social Psychology,* 1960, *1,* 87-90.

Hetherington, E. The effects of familial variables on sex-typing, on parent-child similarity, and on imitation in children. In J.P. Hill (Ed.), *Minnesota Symposium on Child Psychology* (Vol. 1). Minneapolis: University of Minnesota, 1967.

Hetherington, E. Effects of father absence on personality development in adolescent daughters. *Developmental Psychology,* 1972, *7,* 313-326.

Hewett, F., & Forness, S. *Education of exceptional learners* (2nd ed.). Boston: Allyn & Bacon, 1977.

Hiskey, M. *Hiskey-Nebraska Test of Learning Aptitude.* Lincoln, NE: Union College Press, 1966.

Hobbs, N. Nicholas Hobbs. In J.M. Kauffman & C. Lewis (Eds.), *Teaching children with behavior disorders: Personal perspectives.* Columbus, OH: Charles E. Merrill, 1974.

Hollister, W., & Goldstein, S. Psychoeducational process in classes for emotionally handicapped children. In H. Dupont (Ed.), *Educating emotionally disturbed children.* New York: Holt, Rinehart and Winston, 1969.

Horton, K. Infant intervention and language learning. In R.L. Schiefelbusch & L.L. Lloyd (Eds.), *Language perspectives: Acquisition, retardation, and intervention.* Baltimore: University Park Press, 1974.

Huberty, C., & Swan, W. Evaluation of programs. In J.B. Jordan, A. Hayden, M. Karnes, & M. Wood (Eds.), *Early childhood education for exceptional children: A handbook of ideas and exemplary practices.* Reston, VA: Council for Exceptional Children, 1977.

Humphries, T.W. Parent-child interaction and learning disabilities. *Journal of the Division for Early Childhood,* 1979, *1,* 18-27.

Hutt, M.L., & Gibby, R.G. *The mentally retarded child: Development, training, and education* (4th ed). Boston: Allyn & Bacon, 1979.

Inhelder, B. *The diagnosis of reasoning in the mentally retarded* (2nd ed.). New York: John

Day, 1968.

Ireland, W.W. *The mental afflictions of children: Idiocy, imbecility, and insanity*. Philadelphia: Blakiston, 1900.

Jackson, D., & Pavnonen, J. Personality structure and assessment. In M. Rosenweig & L. Porter (Eds.), *Annual review of psychology*. Palo Alto, CA: Annual Review, 1980.

Jensen, C., & Kogan, K. Parental estimates of the future achievement of children with cerebral palsy. *Journal of Mental Deficiency Research*, 1962, *6*, 56-60.

Johnson, C., & Katz, R. Using parents as change agents for their children: A review. *Journal of Child Psychology and Psychiatry*, 1973, *14*, 181-200.

Johnson, R., & Medinnus, G. *Child psychology: Behavior and development* (3rd ed.). New York: John Wiley & Sons, 1974.

Jourard, S. *Personal adjustment*. New York: Macmillan, 1958.

Kagan, J. The concept of identification. *Psychological Review*, 1958, *65*, 296-305.

Kanner, L. Autistic disturbances of affective contact. *Nervous Child*, 1943, *2*, 217-250.

Kanner, L. Miniature textbook of feeblemindedness. *Child Care Monographs*, 1949, *1*.

Kanner, L. Follow up study of eleven autistic children originally reported in 1943. *Journal of Autism and Childhood Schizophrenia*, 1971, *1*, 119-145.

Kanner, L., Rodriguez, A., & Ashenden, B. How far can autistic children go in matters of social adaptation? *Journal of Autism and Childhood Schizophrenia*, 1972, *2*, 9-33.

Karnes, M.B. *Payoff of early intervention*. Chicago: Council for Children with Learning Disabilities, 1973.

Karnes, M.B., & Lee, R.C. *Early childhood*. Reston, VA: Council for Exceptional Children, 1978.

Karnes, M.B., & Teska, J.A. Toward successful parent involvement in programs for handicapped children. In J.J. Gallagher (Ed.), *New directions for exceptional children: Parents and families of handicapped children*, 1980.

Karnes, M., & Zehrbach, R. Matching families and services. *Exceptional Children*, 1975, *41*, 545-459.

Kauffman, J. *Characteristics of children's behavior*. Columbus, OH: Charles E. Merrill, 1977.

Kauffman, J. Emotional disorders in young children. In S.G. Garwood (Ed.), *Educating young handicapped children: A developmental approach*. Rockville, MD: Aspen Systems Corporation, 1979.

Kauffman, J. *Characteristics of children's behavior* (2nd ed.). Columbus, OH: Charles E. Merrill, 1981.

Kaufman, I., Herrick, J., Willer, L., Frank, T., & Heims, L. Four types of defenses in mothers and fathers of schizophrenic children. *American Journal of Orthopsychiatry*, 1959, *29*, 460-472.

Kelly, E.J. *Parent-teacher interaction: A special educational perspective*. Seattle: Special Child Publications, 1974.

Kempe, C., & Helfer, R. *Helping the battered child and his family*. Philadelphia: J.B. Lippincott, 1972.

Kent, L. *Language acquisition program*. Champaign, IL: Research Press, 1974.

Keogh, B., & Becker, L. Early detection of learning problems: Questions, cautions, and guidelines. *Exceptional Children*, 1973, *40*, 5-11.

Keogh, B., & Donlon, G. Field dependence, impulsivity, and learning disabilities. *Journal of Learning Disabilities,* 1972, *5,* 331-336.

Keogh, B., & Glover, A. Research needs in the study of early identification of children with learning disabilities. *Thalmus, Newsletter of the International Academy for Research in Learning Disabilities,* November 1980.

Keogh, B., Tchir, C., & Windeguth-Behn, A. Teacher's perceptions of educationally high risk children. *Journal of Learning Disabilities,* 1974, *7,* 367-374.

Kirk, S.A. *Early education of the mentally retarded: An experimental study.* Urbana, IL: University of Illinois Press, 1958.

Kirk, S.A. Research in education. In H.A. Stevens & R. Heber (Eds.), *Mental retardation: A review of research.* Chicago: University of Chicago Press, 1964.

Kirk, S.A. *Educating exceptional children.* Boston: Houghton Mifflin, 1972.

Kirk, S., & Gallagher, J.J. *Educating exceptional children* (3rd ed.). Boston: Houghton Mifflin, 1979.

Kirk, S., Karnes, M., Kirk, W. *You and your retarded child: A manual for parents of retarded children.* Palo Alto, CA: Pacific Books, 1968.

Koegler, S. The management of the retarded child in practice. *Canadian Medical Association Journal,* 1963, *89,* 1009-1014.

Kohlberg, L. Stage and sequence: The cognitive developmental approach to socialization. In D.A. Goslin (Ed.), *Handbook of socialization theory and research.* Chicago: Rand McNally, 1969.

Korner, A., & Thoman, E. Visual alertness in neonates as evoked by maternal care. *Journal of Experimental Child Psychology,* 1970, *10,* 67-68.

Kott, M.G. The history of mental retardation. In J.H. Rothstein (Ed.), *Mental retardation: Readings and resources* (2nd ed.). New York: Holt, Rinehart and Winston, 1971.

Kroneberg, H., & Blake, G. *Young deaf adults: An occupational survey.* Hot Springs, AR: Arkansas Rehabilitation Service, 1966.

Kübler-Ross, E. *On death and dying.* New York: Macmillan, 1969.

Lamb, M. The development of mother-infant and father-infant attachments in the second year of life. *Developmental Psychology,* 1977, *13,* 637-648.

Lamb, M., & Lamb, J. The nature and importance of the father-infant relationship. *Family Coordinator,* 1976, *25,* 379-386.

Lambert, N., Wilcox, M., & Gleason, W. *The educationally retarded child.* New York: Grune & Stratton, 1974.

Langhorne, J., & Loney, J. Childhood hyperkinesis: A return to the source. *Journal of Abnormal Psychology,* 1976, *85,* 201-209.

Langley, M.B. Working with young physically impaired children: Part A—The nature of physical handicaps. In S.G. Garwood (Ed.), *Educating young handicapped children: A developmental approach.* Germantown, MD: Aspen Systems Corporation, 1979.

Laus, M.D. *Travel instruction for the handicapped.* Springfield, IL: Charles C. Thomas, 1977.

Lavelle, N. Parents expectations and causal attributions concerning their children's performance on school-related tasks. Unpublished doctoral dissertation, UCLA, 1977.

Lavelle, N., & Keogh, B. Expectations and attributions of parents of handicapped children. In J.J. Gallagher (Ed.), *New direction for exceptional children: Parents and families of handicapped children,* 1980.

LaVor, M., & Krivit, D. The Handicapped Children's Early Education Assistance Act,

Public Law 90-538. *Exceptional Children,* 1969, *35,* 379-383.

Lazar, I., & Darlington, R. *Lasting effects after preschool* (DHEW Publication No. [OHDS] 79-30179). Washington, DC: Department of Health, Education and Welfare, Administration for Children, Youth, and Families, 1979.

Lazarus, R.S. *Psychological stress and the coping process.* New York: McGraw-Hill, 1966.

Leff, R. Behavior modification and the psychoses of childhood: A review. *Psychological Bulletin,* 1968, *69,* 396-409.

Leiter, R. *Leiter International Performance Scale.* Chicago: Stoettling Co., 1948.

LeMasters, E. *Parents in modern America.* Homewood, IL: Dorsey, 1974.

Lennenberg, E.H. *Biological foundations of language.* New York: John Wiley & Sons, 1967.

Lerner, J. *Children with learning disabilities* (2nd ed.). Boston: Houghton Mifflin, 1976.

Lerner, J., Mardell-Czudnowski, C., & Goldenberg, D. *Special education for the early childhood years.* Englewood Cliffs, NJ: Prentice-Hall, 1981.

Levine, M.D. The child with school problems: An analysis of physician participation. *Exceptional Children,* 1982, *48,* 296-304.

Levy, S.M., Pomerantz, D., & Gold, M. Work skill development. In N.G. Haring & L. Brown (Eds.), *Teaching the severely handicapped* (Vol. 2). New York: Grune & Stratton, 1977.

Lillie, D.L. An overview to parent programs. In D.L. Lillie & P.L. Trohanis (Eds.), *Teaching parents to teach: A guide for working with the special child.* New York: Walker and Company, 1976.

Lillie, D.L. An ecological approach to working with parents as adults and family members. In P.L. Trohanis, M. Maddox, & P. Bailey (Eds.), *Points of view: A state implementation grant conference proceedings document.* Chapel Hill, NC, and Seattle, WA: TADS and WESTAR, 1978.

Linde, T.F., & Kopp, T. *Training retarded babies and preschoolers.* Springfield, IL: Charles C. Thomas, 1973.

Lobitz, G., & Johnson, S. Normal versus deviant children: A multimethod comparison. *Journal of Abnormal Child Psychology,* 1975, *3,* 353-374.

Logan, D.R., & Rose, E. Characteristics of the mildly mentally retarded. In P.T. Cegelka & H.J. Prehm (Eds.), *Mental retardation: From categories to people.* Columbus, OH: Charles E. Merrill, 1982.

Lohnes, P. Evaluating the schooling of intelligence. *Educational Researcher,* 1973, *2,* 6-11.

Long, N., Morse, W., & Newman, R. (Eds.). *Conflict in the classroom* (4th ed.). Belmont, CA: Wadsworth, 1980.

Love, H. *The mentally retarded child and his family.* Springfield, IL: Charles C. Thomas, 1973.

Lowenfeld, B. The child who is blind. *Exceptional Children,* 1952, *19,* 96-102.

Lowenfeld, B. *Our blind children: Growing and living with them* (2nd ed.). Springfield, IL: Charles C. Thomas, 1964.

Lucito, L. Gifted children. In L.M. Dunn (Ed.), *Exceptional children in the schools.* New York: Holt, Rinehart and Winston, 1963.

Lucito, L. Independence—Conformity behavior as a function of intellect: Bright and dull children. *Exceptional Children,* 1964, *31,* 5-13.

Luckey, R., & Chandler, P. Demonstrative habilitative and self-care nursing projects for multi-handicapped retardates. *Mental Retardation,* 1968, *6,* 10-14.

MacMillan, D.L. *Mental retardation in school and society* (2nd ed.). Boston: Little, Brown, 1982.

MacMillan, D., & Borthwick, S. The new EMR population: Can they be mainstreamed? *Mental Retardation,* 1980, *18,* 155-158.

Mahler, M. On early infantile psychosis. *Journal of the American Academy of Child Psychiatry,* 1965, *4,* 554-568.

Mahler, M. *Separation—Individuation* (Vol. 2). London: Jason Aronson, 1979.

Maker, J. *Providing programs for the gifted handicapped.* Reston, VA: Council for Exceptional Children, 1977.

Maloney, M.P., & Ward, M.P. *Mental retardation and modern society.* New York: Oxford University Press, 1979.

Mandell, A., Segal, D., Kuczenski, R., & Knapp, S. The search for the schizococcus. *Psychology Today,* 1972, *6,* 68-72.

Marion, R.L. *Educators, parents, and exceptional children.* Rockville, MD: Aspen Systems Corporation, 1981.

Marland, S.P. *Education of the gifted and talented.* Washington, DC: U.S. Office of Education, 1972.

Martinson, R. *Education programs for gifted pupils.* Sacramento: California State Department of Education, 1961.

Maslow, A. *Toward a psychology of being.* New York: Van Nostrand, 1962.

Masters, L.F., Mori, A.A., & Lange, E.K. *Adapted physical education: A practitioners' guide.* Rockville, MD: Aspen Systems Corporation, 1983.

Mayo, L.W. Summary of the report of the President's Panel on Mental Retardation. In J.H. Rothstein (Ed.), *Mental retardation: Readings and resources* (2nd ed.). New York: Holt, Rinehart and Winston, 1971.

McCandless, B., & Evans, E. *Children and Youth: Psychosocial development.* Hinsdale, IL: Dryden Press, 1973.

McCarthy, D. *Manual for the McCarthy Scales of Children's Abilities.* New York: Psychological Corporation, 1972.

McCarthy, J.J., & McCarthy, J.F. *Learning disabilities.* Boston: Allyn & Bacon, 1969.

McReynolds, P., Ferguson, J., & Ballachey, E. *Hospital Adjustment Scale.* Palo Alto, CA: Consulting Psychologists Press, 1963.

Mead, M. The gifted child in the American culture today. *Journal of Teacher Education,* 1954, *5,* 211-214.

Meadow, K. Development of deaf children. In E.M. Hetherington (Ed.), *Review of child development research* (Vol. 5). Chicago: University of Chicago Press, 1975.

Menolascino, F. Primitive, atypical, and abnormal behaviors. In E. Katz (Ed.), *Mental health services for the mentally retarded.* Springfield, IL: Charles C. Thomas, 1972.

Menolascino, F., & Egger, M. *Medical dimensions of mental retardation.* Lincoln, NE: The University of Nebraska Press, 1978.

Mercer, C., Algozzine, R., & Trifiletti, J. Early identification—An analysis of the research. *Learning Disability Quarterly,* 1979, *2,* 12-24.

Mercer, C.D., & Snell, M.E. *Learning theory research in mental retardation.* Columbus, OH: Charles E. Merrill, 1977.

Mercer, J.R. The myth of 3% prevalence. In R.K. Eyman, C.E. Meyers, & G. Tarjan (Eds.), Sociobehavioral studies in mental retardation, *Monographs of the American Association on Mental Deficiency,* 1973, No. 1.

Meyen, E.L., & Morgan, M. A perspective on the unserved mildly handicapped. *Exceptional Children,* 1979, *45,* 526-530.

Michaelis, C.T. Mainstreaming: A mother's perspective. *Topics in Early Childhood Special Education,* 1981, *1,* 11-16.

Mills v. Board of Education of the District of Columbia, 348 F. Supp. 866 (D.D.C. 1972).

Minuchin, S. *Families and family therapy.* Cambridge, MA: Harvard University Press, 1974.

Moore, T. Language and intelligence: A longitudinal study of the first eight years. Part II: Environmental correlates of mental growth. *Human Development,* 1968, *11,* 1-24.

Moores, D. *Education of the deaf: Psychology, principles and practices.* Boston: Houghton Mifflin, 1978.

Moores, D. Hearing impairments. In M.S. Lilly (Ed.), *Children with exceptional needs: A survey of special education.* New York: Holt, Rinehart and Winston, 1979.

Moores, D., Fisher, S., & Harlow, M. *Postsecondary programs for the deaf: Monograph VI: Summary and guidelines.* University of Minnesota Research, Development and Demonstration Center in Education of Handicapped Children, Research Report No. 80, 1974.

Moores, D., Weiss, K., & Goodwin, M. *Recommended policies and procedures: Preschool programs for hearing impaired children.* University of Minnesota Research, Development and Demonstration Center in Education of Handicapped Children: Research Report No. 104, 1976.

Moores, D., Weiss, K., Goodwin, M. Early intervention programs for hearing impaired children: A longitudinal evaluation. *ASHA Monographs,* 1978.

Mori, A. Career education for the learning disabled—Where are we now? *Learning Disability Quarterly,* 1980, *3,* 91-101.

Mori, A., & Masters, L. *Teaching the severely mentally retarded: Adaptive skills training.* Germantown, MD: Aspen Systems Corporation, 1980.

Mori, A. & Olive, J. The blind and visually handicapped mentally retarded: Suggestions for intervention in infancy. *Visual Impairment and Blindness,* 1978, *72,* 273-279.

Mori, A.A., & Olive, J.E. *Handbook of preschool special education.* Rockville, MD: Aspen Systems Corporation, 1980.

Moroney, R. Public social policy: Impact on families with handicapped children. In J.L. Paul (Ed.), *Understanding and working with parents of children with special needs.* New York: Holt, Rinehart and Winston, 1981.

Morris, L.L., & Fitz-Gibbon, C.T. *How to present an evaluation report.* Beverly Hills, CA: Sage Publications, 1978.

Moss, H. Sex, age, and state as determinants of mother-infant interaction. *Merrill Palmer Quarterly,* 1967, *13,* 19-36.

Moss, H., & Robson, K. Maternal influences on early social visual behavior. *Child Development,* 1968, *39,* 401-408.

MR 74: A friend in Washington. Report of the President's Committee on Mental Retardation. DHEW Publication No. (OHD) 7-21010, Washington, DC, 1975.

Myklebust, H., Boshes, B., Olson, D., & Cole, C. *Minimal brain damage in children* (Contract 108-65-142), Final Report. U.S. Public Health Service, 1969.

National Society for the Prevention of Blindness. *Home Eye Test for Preschoolers.* New York: The Society, 1972.

National Society for the Prevention of Blindness. *NSPB fact book: Estimated statistics on blindness and visual problems*. New York: The Society, 1966.

Neel, R.S. Autism: Symptoms in search of a syndrome. In F.H. Wood & K.C. LaKin (Eds.), *Disturbing, disordered or disturbed?: Perspectives on the definition of problem behavior in educational settings*. Minneapolis: Advanced Training Institute for Trainers of Teachers for Seriously Emotionally Disturbed Children and Youth, University of Minnesota, 1979.

Nelson, C. Techniques for screening conduct disturbed children. *Exceptional Children*, 1971, *37*, 501-507.

Nelson, K. Studies in child language and multilingualism. *Annals of the New York Academy of Sciences*, 1980, *345*, 46-67.

Nelson, K. Experimental gambits in the service of language acquisition theory: From the Fiffin Project to operation input swap. In S. Kuczaj (Ed.), *Language development: Syntax and semantics*. Hillsdale, NJ: Lawrence Erlbaum, 1981.

Nelson, K., Denninger, M., & Messe, M. Memory parameters in language acquisition. Paper presented at the Society for Research in Child Development, Boston, MA, April, 1981.

Newcomber, P., & Hammill, D. ITPA and academic achievement: A survey. *The Reading Teacher*, 1975, *28*, 731-741.

Newman, H., & Doby, J. Correlates of social competence among trainable mentally retarded children. *American Journal of Mental Deficiency*, 1973, *77*, 722-732.

Newman, J. Psychological problems of children and youth with chronic medical disorders. In W.M. Cruickshank (Ed.), *Psychology of exceptional children and youth* (4th ed.). Englewood Cliffs, NJ: Prentice-Hall, 1980.

Nihira, K., Foster, R., Shellhaas, M., & Leland, H. *A.A.M.D. Adaptive Behavior Scale* (1974 Revision). Washington, DC: American Association on Mental Deficiency, 1974.

Northcott, W.H., & Fowler, S.A. Developing parent participation. In D.L. Lillie & P.L. Trohanis (Eds.), *Teaching parents to teach: A guide for working with the special child*. New York: Walker and Company, 1976.

Oakland, T., & Matuszek, P. Using tests in nondiscriminatory assessment. In T. Oakland (Ed.), *Non-biased assessment of minority group children*. Lexington, KY: University of Kentucky, Coordinating Office for Regional Resource Centers, no date.

Owen, R., Adams, P., Forrest, T., Stolz, L., & Fisher, S. Learning disorders in children: Siblings studies. *Monographs of the Society for Research in Child Development*, 1971, *36*, No. 144.

Parad, H. Principles of crisis intervention. In H. Parad (Ed.), *Emergency psychiatric care*. Bowie, MD: Charles Press, 1975.

Parke, R., & O'Leary, S. Father-mother-infant interaction in the newborn period: Some findings, some observations, and some unresolved issues. In K. Reigel & J. Meacham (Eds.) *The developing individual in a changing world* (Vol. 2). The Hague: Mouton, 1976.

Parke, R., & Sawin, D. The family in early infancy: Social interactional and attitudinal analyses. In F. Pederson (Ed.), *The father-infant relationship: Observational studies in a family context*. New York: Praeger, 1980.

Parke, R., & Sawin, D. The father's role in infancy: A reevaluation. *Family Coordinator*, 1976, *25*, 365-371.

Pegnato, C., & Birch, J. Locating gifted children in junior high schools: A comparison of methods. *Exceptional Children*, 1959, *25*, 300-304.

Pennsylvania Association for Retarded Children v. Commonwealth of Pennsylvania, F. Supp. 279 (E.D. Pa. 1972).

Perske, R. The dignity of risk. In W. Wolfensberger (Ed.), *The principle of normalization in human services*. Toronto: National Institute on Mental Retardation, 1972.

Peterson, G., Austin, G., & Lang, R. Use of teacher prompts to increase social behavior: Generalization effects with severely and profoundly retarded adolescents. *American Journal of Mental Deficiency,* 1979, *84,* 82-86.

Piaget, J. *The construction of reality in the child.* New York: Basic Books, 1954.

Piaget, J. *The development of thought: Equilibrium of cognitive structures.* New York: Viking Press, 1977.

Piaget, J., & Inhelder, B. *The psychology of the child.* New York: Basic Books, 1969.

Pieper, E. Grandparents can help. *The Exceptional Parent,* 1976, *6,* 7-10.

Prehm, H.J., & Mayfield, S. Paired-associated learning and retention in retarded and nonretarded children. *American Journal of Mental Deficiency,* 1970, *71,* 42-47.

Pringle, N., & Bossio, V. A study of deprived children. *Vita Humana,* 1958, *1,* 65-92.

Quay, H. Classification. In H. Quay & J. Werry (Eds.), *Psychopathological disorders of childhood* (2nd ed.). New York: John Wiley & Sons, 1979.

Quick, A.D., Little, T.L., & Campbell, A.A. *Project MEMPHIS: Enhancing developmental progress in preschool exceptional children.* Belmont, CA: Lear Siegler, Inc./Fearon Publishers, 1974.

Quilitch, H., & Gray, J. Purposeful activity for the PMR: A demonstration project. *Mental Retardation,* 1974, *12,* 28-29.

Ramaseshan, P. The social and emotional adjustment of the gifted. Unpublished doctoral dissertation, University of Nebraska, 1957.

Ramey, C., Beckman-Bell, P., & Gowen, J. Infant characteristics and infant-caregiver interactions. In J.J. Gallagher (Ed.), *New directions for exceptional children: Parents and families of handicapped children,* 1980.

Ranier, J., Altshuler, K., & Kallmann, F. (Eds.). *Family and mental health problems in a deaf population* (2nd ed.). Springfield, IL: Charles C. Thomas, 1969.

Rawlings, S. *Current population reports: Perspectives on American husbands and wives* (Series p-23, No. 77, Bureau of the Census). Washington, DC: U.S. Government Printing Office, 1978.

Redina, I., & Dickerscheid, J. Father involvement with first-born infants. *Family Coordinator,* 1976, *25,* 373-378.

Redl, F. The concept of a therapeutic milieu. *American Journal of Orthopsychiatry,* 1959, *29,* 721-734.

Reed, E., & Reed, S. *Mental retardation: A family study.* Philadelphia: W.B. Saunders, 1965.

Reid, D.K., & Hresko, W. *A cognitive approach to learning disabilities.* New York: McGraw-Hill, 1981.

Reinert, H. *Children in conflict: Educational strategies for the emotionally disturbed and behaviorally disordered.* St. Louis: C.V. Mosby, 1976.

Renzulli, J. *The enrichment triad model: A guide for developing defensible programs for the gifted and talented.* Wethersfield, CT: Creative Learning Press, 1977.

Renzulli, J.S. What makes giftedness? Re-examining a definition. *Phi Delta Kappan,* 1978, *60,* 180-184, 261.

Report of the Ad Hoc Committee to define deaf and hard of hearing. *American Annals of the Deaf,* October 1975, pp. 509-512.

Reynolds, M., & Birch, J. *Teaching exceptional children in all America's schools.* Reston, VA: Council for Exceptional Children, 1977.

Rheingold, H. Independent behavior of the human infant. In A. Pick (Ed.), *Minnesota Symposia on child psychology* (Vol. 7). Minneapolis: University of Minnesota Press, 1973.

Rhodes, W., & Tracy, M. (Eds.). *A study of child variance: Theories* (Vol. 1). Ann Arbor, MI: University of Michigan Press, 1972a.

Rhodes, W., & Tracy, M. (Eds.). *A study of child variance: Interventions* (Vol. 2). Ann Arbor, MI: University of Michigan Press, 1972b.

Richman, N. Behavior problems in preschool children: Family and social factors. *British Journal of Psychiatry,* 1977, *131,* 523-527.

Robins, L. *Deviant children grown up.* Baltimore: Williams & Wilkins, 1966.

Robinson, N.M., & Robinson, H.B. *The mentally retarded child* (2nd ed.). New York: McGraw-Hill, 1976.

Rogers, C. *Freedom to learn.* Columbus, OH: Charles E. Merrill, 1969.

Rogers, C.R. *On becoming a person.* Boston: Houghton Mifflin, 1963.

Roos, P. Parents and families of the mentally retarded. In J.M. Kauffman & J.S. Payne (Eds.), *Mental retardation: Introduction and personal perspectives.* Columbus, OH: Charles E. Merrill, 1975.

Roos, P. Parents of mentally retarded children—Misunderstood and mistreated. In A. Turnbull & R. Turnbull (Eds.), *Parents speak out: View from the other side of a two way mirror.* Columbus, OH: Charles E. Merrill, 1979.

Roos, P. Special trends and issues. In P.T. Cegelka & H.J. Prehm (Eds.), *Mental retardation: From categories to people.* Columbus, OH: Charles E. Merrill, 1982.

Rosen, L. Selected aspects in the development of the mother's understanding of her mentally retarded child. *American Journal of Mental Deficiency,* 1955, *59,* 522.

Roskies, E. *Abnormality and normality: The mothering of thalidomide children.* Ithaca, NY: Cornell University Press, 1972.

Ross, A.O. *The exceptional child in the family.* New York: Grune & Stratton, 1964.

Ross, A.O. *Psychological disorders of children* (2nd ed.). New York: McGraw-Hill, 1980.

Ross, R.T., Boroskin, A., & Giampiccolo, J. *Fairview Behavior Evaluation Battery for the Mentally Retarded (S scales).* Costa Mesa, CA: Fairview State Hospital, Research Department, 1970-1974.

Rutherford, R.B., & Edgar, E. *Teachers and parents: A guide to interaction and cooperation* (Abridged ed.). Boston: Allyn & Bacon, 1979.

Rutter, M. Diagnosis and definition. In M. Rutter & E. Schopler (Eds.), *Autism: A reappraisal of concepts and treatment.* New York: Plenum Press, 1978.

Rutter, M., & Bartak, L. Special education treatment of autistic children: A comparative study. Part II. Follow-up findings and implications for services. *Journal of Child Psychology and Psychiatry,* 1973, *14,* 241-270.

Sabatino, D. Obstacles to educating handicapped adolescents. In D. Cullinan & M. Epstein (Eds.), *Special education for adolescents.* Columbus, OH: Charles E. Merrill, 1979.

Saenger, G. *The adjustment of severely retarded adults in the community.* Albany, NY: Interdepartmental Health Resources Board, 1957.

Safford, P. *Teaching young children with special needs.* Columbus, OH: Charles E. Merrill, 1978.

Safford, P.L., & Rosen, L.A. Mainstreaming: Applications of a philosophical perspective in an integrated kindergarten program. *Topics in Early Childhood Special Education*, 1981, *1*, 1-10.

Salvia, J., & Ysseldyke, J. *Assessment in special and remedial education*. Boston: Houghton Mifflin, 1978.

Santrock, J. The relation of type and onset of father absence to cognitive development. *Child Development*, 1972, *43*, 455-469.

Sarbin, T., & Mancuso, T. Failure of a moral enterprise: Attitudes of the public toward mental illness. *Journal of Consulting and Clinical Psychology*, 1970, *35*, 159-173.

Sattler, J. Analysis of functions of the 1960 Stanford Binet intelligence scale, Form L-M. *Journal of Clinical Psychology*, 1965, *21*, 173-179.

Schaefer, E. Parents as educators: Evidence from cross-sectional, longitudinal, and intervention research. *Young Children*, 1972, *48*, 227-239.

Schaefer, E. Family relationships. In J.J. Gallagher (Ed.), *The application of child development research to exceptional children*. Reston, VA: Council for Exceptional Children, 1975.

Schaffer, H.R. *Studies in mother-infant interaction*. New York: Academic Press, 1977.

Scheerenberger, R.C. Mental retardation: Definition, classification, and prevalence. In J.H. Rothstein (Ed.), *Mental retardation: Readings and resources* (2nd ed.). New York: Holt, Rinehart and Winston, 1971.

Scheinfeld, D. On developing developmental families. Paper presented at Head Start Research Services #5, January 1969, Washington, DC.

Schell, G.C. The young handicapped child: A family perspective. *Topics in Early Childhood Special Education*, 1981, *1*, 21-27.

Schindele, R. The social adjustment of visually handicapped children in different educational settings. *Research Bulletin: American Foundation for the Blind*, 1974, *28*, 125-144.

Schlesinger, H., & Meadow, K. *Sound and sign: Childhood deafness and mental health*. Berkeley: University of California Press, 1972.

Schweinhart, L., & Weikart, D. *Young children grow up: The effects of the Perry preschool program on youths through age 15*. Ypsilanti, MI: The High Scope Press, 1980.

Sears, R., Maccoby, E., & Levin, H. *Patterns of child rearing*. New York: Harper & Row, 1957.

Sellin, D.F. *Mental retardation: Nature, needs, and advocacy*. Boston: Allyn & Bacon, 1979.

Shah, C.P., & Wong, D. Failures in early detection of hearing impairment in preschool children. *Journal of the Division for Early Childhood*, 1979, *1*, 33-40.

Shea, T. *Teaching children and youth with behavior disorders*. St. Louis: C.V. Mosby, 1978.

Shearer, M.S. A home-based parent-training model. In D.L. Lillie & P.L. Trohanis (Eds.), *Teaching parents to teach: A guide for working with the special child*. New York: Walker, 1976.

Shearer, M.S., & Shearer, D.E. Parent involvement. In J.B. Jordan, A.H. Hayden, M.B. Karnes, & M.M. Wood (Eds.). *Early childhood education for the handicapped: A handbook of ideas and exemplary practices*. Reston, VA: Council for Exceptional Children, 1977.

Sheehan, R. Issues in documenting early intervention with infants and parents. *Topics in Early Childhood Special Education*, 1981, *1*, 67-75.

Sheridan, M. *Manual for the Stycar Vision Test.* Windsor, Ontario: JFER Publishing, 1973.

Sirvis, B. The physically disabled. In E.L. Meyen (Ed.), *Exceptional children and youth: An introduction* (2nd. ed.). Denver: Love Publishing Company, 1982.

Sirvis, B., & Carpignano, J. Psychosocial aspects of physical disability. In J. Bigge (Ed.), *Teaching individuals with physical and multiple disabilities.* Columbus, OH: Charles E. Merrill, 1976.

Sisk, D. Unusual gifts and talents. In M.S. Lilly (Ed.), *Children with exceptional needs: A survey of special education.* New York: Holt, Rinehart and Winston, 1979.

Sisk, D. Educational planning for the gifted and talented. In J. Kauffman & D. Hallahan (Eds.), *Handbook of special education.* Englewood Cliffs, NJ: Prentice-Hall, 1981.

Skeels, H.M., & Dye, H.B. A study of the effect of differential stimulation on mentally retarded children. *Proceedings of the American Association on Mental Deficiency*, 1939, *44*, 114-136.

Skolnick, A. The myth of the vulnerable child. *Psychology Today*, February, 1978.

Snell, M. Characteristics of the profoundly mentally retarded. In P. Cegelka & H. Prehm (Eds.), *Mental retardation: From categories to people.* Columbus, OH: Charles E. Merrill, 1982.

Sontag, E., Burke, P., & York, R. Considerations for serving the severely handicapped in the public schools. *Education and Training of the Mentally Retarded*, 1973, *8*, 20-26.

Speers, R., & Lansing, C. Group psychotherapy with preschool children and collateral group therapy of their parents: A preliminary report of the first two years. *American Journal of Orthopsychiatry*, 1964, *34*, 659-666.

Spitz, H.H. The role of input organization in the learning and memory of mental retardates. In N.R. Ellis (Ed.), *International review of research in mental retardation* (Vol. 2). New York: Academic Press, 1966.

Spradlin, J. Language and communication of mental defectives. In N.R. Ellis (Ed.), *Handbook of mental deficiency.* New York: McGraw-Hill, 1963.

Sroufe, L. Drug treatment of children with behavior problems. In F.D. Horowitz, E.M. Hetherington, S. Scarr-Salapatek, & G. Siegel (Eds.), *Review of child development research* (Vol. 4). Chicago: University of Chicago Press, 1975.

Stanley, J. Educated non-acceleration: An international tragedy. Proceedings from the second world conference on gifted, San Francisco, CA, 1976.

Stennet, R. Emotional handicap in the elementary years: Phase or disease? *American Journal of Orthopsychiatry*, 1966, *36*, 444-449.

Stephens, B., & Simpkins, K. *The reasoning, moral judgment, and moral conduct of the congenitally blind.* Final Project Report, H23-3197, Office of Education, Bureau of Education for the Handicapped, 1974.

Stephens, T., & Wolf, J. The gifted child. In N. Haring (Ed.), *Behavior of exceptional children* (2nd ed.). Columbus, OH: Charles E. Merrill, 1978.

Stile, S., Cole, J., & Garner, A. Maximizing parental involvement in programs for exceptional children: Strategies for education and related service personnel. *Journal of the Division for Early Childhood*, 1979, *1*, 68-82.

Stock, J.R., Wnek, L.L., Newborg, J.A., Schenck, E.A., Gabel, J.R., Spurgeon, M.S., & Ray, H.W. *Evaluation of Handicapped Children's Early Education Program (HCEEP): Final report.* Columbus, OH: Battelle Center for Improved Education, 1976 (ERIC Document Reproduction Service, No. ED 125165).

Stott, D. *The social adjustment of children: Manual to the Bristol Social Adjustment Guides.* London: University of London Press, 1963.

Strag, G. Comparative behavioral ratings of parents with severe mentally retarded, learning disability, and normal children. *Journal of Learning Disabilities,* 1972, *5,* 631-635.

Stringer, L., & Glidewell, J. *Early detection of emotional illness in school children: Final report.* Clayton, MO: St. Louis County Health Department, 1967.

Swap, S. The ecological model of emotional disturbance in children: A status report and proposed synthesis. *Behavioral Disorders,* 1978, *3,* 186-196.

Sweitzer, R. Audiological evaluation of the young infant and young child. In B.F. Jaffe (Ed.), *Hearing loss in children.* Baltimore: University Park Press, 1977.

Takanishi, R., & Feshbach, N. Early childhood special education programs, evaluation, and social policies. *Topics in Early Childhood Special Education,* 1982, *1,* 1-9.

Tallman, I. Spousal role differentiation and the socialization of the severely retarded. *Journal of Marriage and the Family,* 1965, *27,* 37-42.

Tannenbaum, A. *Adolescent attitudes toward academic brilliance.* New York: Bureau of Publications, Teachers College, Columbia University, 1962.

Tarjan, G., Wright, S., Eyman, R., & Keeran, C. Natural history of mental retardation: Some aspects of epidemiology. *American Journal of Mental Deficiency,* 1973, *77,* 369-379.

Tarran, E. Parent's views of medical and social work services for families of young cerebral palsied children. *Developmental Medicine and Child Neurology,* 1981, *23,* 173-182.

Tarver, S., & Hallahan, D. Attention deficits in children with learning disabilities: A review. *Journal of Learning Disabilities,* 1974, *7,* 560-569.

Tavormina, J., Ball, N., Dunn, R., Luscomb, B., & Taylor, J. Psychosocial effects of raising a physically handicapped child on the parents. Unpublished manuscript, University of Virginia, 1977.

Terman, L. *Mental and physical traits of a thousand gifted children: Genetic studies of genius* (Vol. 1). Stanford, CA: Stanford University Press, 1925.

Terman, L., & Oden, M. The gifted child grows up. In L. Terman (Ed.), *Genetic studies of genius* (Vol. 4). Stanford, CA: Stanford University Press, 1947.

Terman, L., & Oden, M. *Genetic studies of genius: The gifted at midlife* (Vol. 5). Stanford, CA: Stanford University Press, 1959.

Tew, B., Laurence, K., & Samuel, P. Parental estimates of the intelligence of their physically handicapped child. *Developmental Medicine and Child Neurology,* 1974, *16,* 494-500.

Thomas, A., & Chess, S. *Temperament and development.* New York: Brunner-Mazel, 1977.

Thomas, A., Chess, S., & Birch, H. The origin of personality. *Scientific American,* 1970, *223,* 102-109.

Thompson, R.J., & O'Quinn, A.N. *Developmental disabilities: Etiologies, manifestations, diagnoses, and treatments.* New York: Oxford University Press, 1979.

Thompson, W., & Grusec, J. Studies of early experience. In P.H. Mussen (Ed.), *Carmichael's manual of child psychology* (3rd ed., Vol. 1). New York: John Wiley & Sons, 1970.

Torgesen, J., & Kail, R. Memory processes in exceptional children. In B.K. Keogh (Ed.), *Advances in special education: Basic constructs and theoretical orientations* (Vol. 1). Greenwich, CT: J.A.I. Press, 1980.

Torrance, E.P. Psychology of gifted children and youth. In W.M. Cruickshank (Ed.), *Psychology of exceptional children and youth* (4th ed.). Englewood Cliffs, NJ: Prentice-Hall, 1980.

Tredgold, A.F. *Mental deficiency*. London: Bailliera, Tindall, and Fox, 1908.

Tucker, J.A. Operationalizing the diagnostic-intervention process. In T. Oaklan (Ed.), *Non-biased assessment of minority group children*. Lexington, KY: University of Kentucky, Coordinating Office for Regional Resource Centers, no date.

Turnbull, A., & Blancher-Dixon, J. Preschool mainstreaming: Impact on parents. In J.J. Gallagher (Ed.), *New Directions for Exceptional Children*, 1980.

Turnbull, A., & Turnbull, R. *Parents speak out: Views from the other side of the two way mirror*. Columbus, OH: Charles E. Merrill, 1979.

Turnbull, H.R. & Turnbull, A.P. *Free appropriate public education: Law and implementation*. Denver: Love Publishing Company, 1978.

Turnbull, H.R., Turnbull, A.P., & Wheat, M.J. Assumptions about parental participation: A legislative history. *Exceptional Education Quarterly*, 1982, *3*, 1-8.

Utley, B., Holvoet, J. & Barnes, K. Handling, positioning, and feeding the physically handicapped. In E. Sontag, J. Smith, & N. Certo (Eds.), *Educational programming for the severely and profoundly handicapped*, Reston, VA: Council for Exceptional Children, 1977.

Valett, R. A clinical profile for the Stanford Binet. *Journal of School Psychology*, 1964, *2*, 49-54.

Vincent, L.J., Brown, L., & Getz-Sheftel, M. Integrating handicapped and typical children during the preschool years: The definition of best educational practice. *Topics in Early Childhood Special Education*, 1981, *1*, 17-24.

Walker, H. *The acting-out child*. Boston: Allyn & Bacon, 1979.

Wallace, G., & McLoughlin, J. *Learning disabilities: Concepts and characteristics* (2nd ed.). Columbus, OH: Charles E. Merrill, 1979.

Wambold, C., & Bailey, R. Improving the leisure time behaviors of severely/profoundly mentally retarded children through toy play. *AAESPH Review*, 1979, *4*, 237-250.

Wang, M., & Ellett, C. Program validation: The state of the art. *Topics in Early Childhood Special Education*, 1982, *1*, 35-49.

Ward, M.E. Children with visual impairments. In M.S. Lilly (Ed.), *Children with exceptional needs: A survey of special education*. New York: Houghton Mifflin, 1979.

Welsh, M.M., & Odum, C.H. Parent involvement in the education of the handicapped child: A review of the literature. *Journal of the Division for Early Childhood*, 1981, *3*, 15-25.

Whalen, C., & Henker, B. Psychostimulants and children: A review and analysis. *Psychological Bulletin*, 1976, *83*, 1113-1130.

White, B. *The first three years of life*. Englewood Cliffs, NJ: Prentice-Hall, 1975.

White, B., & Watts, J. *Experience and environment: Major influences on the development of the young child*. Englewood Cliffs, NJ: Prentice-Hall, 1973.

White, R. The concept of competence. *Psychological Review*, 1959, *66*, 297-333.

Whitman, T., & Scibak, J. Behavior modification research with the severely and profoundly retarded. In N.R. Ellis (Ed.), *Handbook of mental deficiency: Psychological theory and research* (2nd ed.). Hillsdale, NJ: Lawrence Erlbaum, 1979.

Wiegerink, R., & Parrish, V. A parent-implemented preschool program. In D.L. Lillie & P.L. Trohanis (Eds.), *Teaching parents to teach: A guide for working with the special child*. New York: Walker and Company, 1976.

Wilcox, P. The Gardner Behavior Chart. *American Journal of Psychiatry*, 1942, *98*, 874-880.

Willerman, L., & Fiedler, M. Infant performance and intellectual precocity. *Child Development*, 1974, *45*, 483-486.

Wolfensberger, W. Counseling the parents of the retarded. In A.A. Baumeister (Ed.), *Mental retardation: Appraisal, education, and rehabilitation*. Chicago: Aldine, 1967.

Wolfensberger, W. *Normalization: The principle of normalization in human services*. Toronto: National Institute on Mental Retardation, 1972.

Wood, M.M. (Ed.). *The developmental therapy objectives*. Baltimore: University Park Press, 1979.

Wood, M.M., Swan, W.W., & Newman, V. Developmental therapy for the severely emotionally disturbed and autistic. In R. McDowell, G. Adamson, & F. Wood (Eds.), *Teaching emotionally disturbed children*. Boston: Little, Brown, 1982.

Ysseldyke, J. Assessment of retardation. In J.T. Neisworth & R.M. Smith (Eds.), *Retardation: Issues, assessment and intervention*. New York: McGraw-Hill, 1978.

Yussen, S., & Santrock, J. *Child development: An introduction* (2nd ed.). Dubuque, IA: Wm. C. Brown, 1982.

Zax, M., & Cowen, E. *Abnormal psychology: Changing conceptions*. New York: Holt, Rinehart and Winston, 1972.

Zeaman, D., & House, B.J. The role of attention in retardate discrimination learning. In N.R. Ellis (Ed.), *Handbook of mental deficiency: Psychological theory and research*. New York: McGraw-Hill, 1963.

Zeaman, D. & House, B.J. A review of attention theory. In N.R. Ellis (Ed.), *Handbook of mental deficiency: Psychological theory and research* (2nd ed.). Hillsdale, NJ: Lawrence Erlbaum, 1979.

Zigler, E. Developmental versus difference theories of mental retardation and the problems of motivation. *American Journal of Mental Deficiency*, 1969, *73*, 536-556.

Zigmond, N., & Brownlee, J. Social skills training for adolescents with learning disabilities. *Exceptional Education Quarterly*, 1980, *1*, 77-83.

Index

A

AAMD. *See* American Association on Mental Deficiency

AAMD Adaptive Behavior Scales, 143

Absence, father, 12

Abstract thinking, 90

Abuse, parental, 108

Academic achievement, 1, 17, 92, 160–161, 183–184, 187

Academic failure, 85

Academic skills, and preacademic skills, 106

Acceleration, gifted, 195–197

Acceptance, 20, 22
in counseling, 215–216

Achievement. *See* Academic achievement

Achievement tests, 166

ACLD. *See* Association for Children and Adults with Learning Disabilities

Action learning, 90

Active listening skills, 46

Adaptation for Profoundly Retarded scale, 143

Adaptive behavior, 139–145
defined, 126–127, 140–141, 142
highest levels for mentally retarded, *150, 151, 152, 153*
mental retardation and, 126
of severely retarded, 133

Adaptive equipment, 119

Adolescents, 12, 48
gifted, 192

Adult(s)
adaptive behavior in, 145
deaf, 92
retarded, 123
severely retarded, 133

Advanced placement, 195

Advocacy, 38, 41, 216

Affective development, infant, *200*

Agency
and due process hearing, 74
professionals and parents, conflict between, 36

Aggression, 6–7, 12, 97, 160, 161, 177

Alcohol syndrome, fetal, 132

Alexander Graham Bell Association for the Deaf, 50

Allergy Foundation of America, 50

Note: Page number in italics indicates entry is to be found in an Exhibit, Figure, or Table.

257

Event recording, 167
Exceptional children, 3, 41, 83, 157.
    See also Child; Children;
    Handicapped children
Expectations, 108, 213
Exploration, 4, 5, 14, 15, 193, 199
Extended families, 1, 3, 33, 46, 47

F

Failures, 85, 193
Fairview Behavior Evaluation Battery
    for the Mentally Retarded, 144
Families, 1, 28–29
    attitude changes in, 210–224
    of children with sensory, physical,
        and learning disorders, 85–121
    communication in, 216
    and community intervention
        services, 34–41
    and disorders, 106–109
    and due process hearing, *74*
    dynamics of, 34, 45
    dysfunctional, 214
    effect of crisis in, 216
    effects on cognitive development,
        13–17
    effects on early language, 13–17
    of emotionally disturbed children,
        157–179
    extended, 3
    foster, 3
    functional, 214
    of gifted and talented children,
        181–202
    gifted training for, 191–192
    in-service programs for gifted, 191
    members of, 29
    of mentally retarded children,
        123–155
    needs assessment for, 219
    relationships with community
        service agencies, 41
    rights and responsibilities of, 55–81
    single parent, 3

skills development for, 210–224
special procedures for 71–75
strengths of, 40
support services for, 39–40
as team members, 38
traditional, 3
of young handicapped children, 1,
    28–29, 211–213, *See also* Family
Family, 1, 3–17, 170
    -child relationships, 214–215
    friends, 216
    impact of handicapped child on, 1,
        19–32
    in intervention programs, 36–39
    social life, 49
    subsystem, 5
    system theory, 214. *See also*
        Families
Family counseling, 215
    drug therapy and, 173
Family education programs
    evaluation of, 203, 224–234
    models for, 203, 205–232
Family practice physician, 34–35
Family therapy, 171, 177
Father(s), 9–12, 22–23, 206
Fears, 7
    of siblings, 31
Federal support, 224
Feminine identity, 11
Fetal alcohol syndrome, 132
Financial problems and assistance,
    33, 35, 41
Flash-Card Vision Test for Children,
    100
Flexibility of gifted, 184, *188*, 202
Follow-up for parent training,
    223–224
Foster family, 3
Frustration, 19, 168, 169
Functional visual efficiency, 86

G

Games, 197, 202
Gardner Behavior Chart, 144

About the Author

ALLEN A. MORI is currently an associate professor holding a joint appointment in the Department of Counseling and Educational Psychology and the Department of Special Education at the University of Nevada, Las Vegas. Dr. Mori received his B.A. from Franklin and Marshall College, his M.Ed. from Bloomsburg State College, and his Ph.D. from the University of Pittsburgh. He has had a great deal of experience working with handicapped children and adults in state institutions and public schools. In addition, he directed a three-year federal model demonstration project for handicapped infants and toddlers at the University of Nevada, Las Vegas. Dr. Mori has published extensively in professional journals and has coauthored three books published by Aspen Systems Corporation.